Photoshop®
Tips, Tricks & Fixes

Imagine Publishing Ltd
Richmond House
33 Richmond Hill
Bournemouth
Dorset BH2 6EZ
☎ +44 (0) 1202 586200
Website: www.imagine-publishing.co.uk

Editor in Chief
Jo Cole

Production Editor
Julie Easton

Design
Danielle Dixon & Sarah Bellman

Printed by
William Gibbons, 26 Planetary Road, Willenhall, West Midlands, WV13 3XT

Distributed in the UK & Eire by
Imagine Publishing Ltd, www.imagineshop.co.uk. Tel 01202 586200

Distributed in Australia by
Gordon & Gotch, Equinox Centre, 18 Rodborough Road, Frenchs Forest,
NSW 2086. Tel + 61 2 9972 8800

Distributed in the Rest of the World by
Marketforce, Blue Fin Building, 110 Southwark Street, London, SE1 0SU.

ISBN 978 1 906078 8 43

IMAGINE
PUBLISHING

CONTENTS

⠿ Tips

006-067
Bitesize advice in the form of over 200 individual tips that cover every aspect of using Photoshop or Photoshop Elements to work with your digital photos. All skills levels are covered, from beginners to improvers, as are all versions of the program. There is sure to be something here for you. Enjoy!

Contents

Tips

08 FEATURE: Top tips
50 of the very best tips for working in Photoshop, introducing you to the power of the program

After

Before

Ultimate **Photoshop** *tips!*

Improve your Photoshop skills today, with this fantastic collection of essential tips, tricks and techniques

On the CD: video tutorials

Load up your free disc and head to the Video Tutorials section where you'll find a host of quick and easy video tips to accompany these pages. Simply click the video you want to watch and select the QuickTime movie from the window.

 et ready for a fast and furious masterclass in all things Photoshop! Over the next ten pages we bring you all the essential information you need to improve your Photoshop skills. From brushes, filters and vector illustrations through to photo restoration, scrapbooking and retouching – we've definitely got it covered!

Brushes

Brushes are indisputably some of the most useful devices in Photoshop. Here we'll present you with some of our favourite tips and tricks, and also show you some of the hidden features and variables that can make your brushwork shine. Go on, grab that Brush tool and get creative!

01 Colour variability

Brushes don't limit you to painting with your foreground colour. In the Brushes palette (F5), click Color Dynamics and adjust the Hue Jitter slider. Now, as you stroke with the brush, the colour used for each brush dab will flip either side of the foreground colour in relation to the colour wheel. The further you drag the slider, the more dramatic this will be.

03 Dual brushes

Dual brushes, such as the Dry brush in the default brush set, combine conventionally shaped brushes with ones that paint with texture to create some surprising results. These can be used in paintings to quickly render specific textures, like foliage on trees. Simply size your brush to the appropriate scale then paint to create foliage!

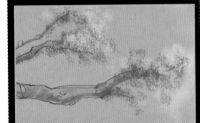

04 Thumbnails

By default, Photoshop displays just the dab footprint of your brushes within the Brush picker. It's far more useful to be able to choose a brush by seeing the stroke it makes, so click in the Brush picker, hit the small palette menu arrow in the top right and choose Stroke Thumbnail.

05 Brush blend modes

Just like layers, brushes have blend modes too! You can choose these from the Mode box in the Options bar when the Brush tool is activated. The Color blend mode is particularly useful for colourising black and white photos. Use the brush at a low opacity for this.

02 Brushed borders

You're not limited to conventional painting with Photoshop brushes – they have some surprising creative uses too, such as creating artistic borders. Brushes from the Dry Media set are especially good for this, as they create nice textures. To create these brushed borders, duplicate your background layer and fill the original with colour. Add a Reveal All layer mask, make sure you have your Brush Opacity Control set to Pen Pressure and brush into the image from the outside edges with black to create your border.

06 Roundness and Angle

A chisel-shaped brush tip, where you can create thick/ thin strokes with the same brush, is far more expressive than a round brush and feels more natural. In Brush Tip Shape there's a small map of the tip: you can change the Angle here by dragging the arrowhead. To change the Roundness, grab one of the dots on the edge and drag inwards. You can also flip the brush on its axis or change the spacing between brush dabs.

07 Scatter for pattern

The Scattering section of the Brushes palette scatters the brush dabs either side of the centre of your brush strokes, and it's great for creating random, natural textures to paint with. You can use any brushes for this, increasing the Scatter value for more random patterns.

08 Brushes and styles

The marks you make aren't limited to being two-dimensional! By applying a style (Window>Styles) to an empty layer then painting onto this layer, you can easily create three-dimensional looking gloopy brush strokes. You can change the look of this style by double-clicking the Effects components attached to the layer. Try using some of the Glass Button styles for this.

09 Create custom brushes

You can create a custom brush from any greyscale design. Simply create your brush design and go to Edit>Define Brush Preset. White areas of the design will be transparent in the final brush, and grey areas will be partially opaque, with full opacity in black areas.

10 Brushes on paths

It can be tricky to trace smoothly and accurately around a shape with a brush. The solution is to stroke a path with the brush itself. First create a path with the Pen, and with the tool still selected, right-click the path and hit Stroke Path. Select the Brush tool from the dialog and check Simulate Pressure. The path will be stroked using your selected brush, so make sure to choose that first and set it to a suitable size.

Vector

Vector art traditionally refers to artwork created by shapes that are defined by points and lines according to mathematical calculations. Because of this, true vector art is scaleable, as opposed to raster art which is made up of coloured pixels. In practice, 'vector art' usually refers to stylised artwork reminiscent of classic Pop art (though it's not limited to this). While vector art is more commonly associated with drawing programs such as Adobe Illustrator and Corel Draw, it's possible to create high-quality vector-style artwork in Photoshop by working with paths and the Pen tools.

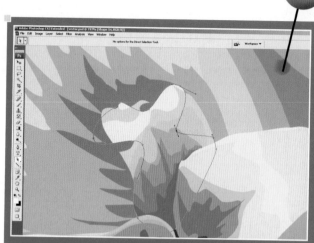

12 Tweaking paths like a Photoshop pro

The Path Selection tool helps you select any path, while the Direct Selection tool enables you to select individual anchor points. Click on any anchor point with the Direct Selection tool to display the point's 'direction line'. You can then click and drag the tiny circles on either end to adjust the point and affect the curvature of the path.

13 Drawing complex shapes

When you select a Drawing tool, notice the right-most symbols in the top menu toolbar. These change the way your paths interact. 'Add To Path' allows you to draw multiple paths on the same path layer, cumulatively forming the final shape. 'Subtract From Path' assumes the shape of the first path and cuts out subsequent paths from that. 'Intersect Path Areas' means the final shape is defined by the overlap of two or more paths. 'Exclude Overlapping Path Areas' means the final shape is everything except the bits where paths overlap.

14 Save time with shortcut keys

The shortcut for the Pen is 'P' – toggle with the Freeform Pen by hitting Shift+P. The shortcut for Path Selection is 'A' – toggle with Shift+A for Direct Selection. The shortcut for the Shape tools is 'U'.

15 Maximise the Path palette

Paths are stored in the Path palette (Window>Paths). New paths are automatically assigned to Work Path and are not saved, by default, in the Paths palette. Save time loading paths by saving them in the Paths palette. Double-click on Work Path, rename the layer and hit Save Path.

11 Know your Pens

Photoshop's Pen tools can be found in the toolbar, represented by a little fountain pen icon. Clicking and holding down this icon expands the menu to show the entire family: Pen, Freeform Pen, Add Anchor Point, Delete Anchor Point, Convert Point. When you click with the Pen tool, you create an anchor point. Creating more than one point draws an invisible line between them – a path. The path is basically an outline of the shape you are drawing. You can use the Pen tool to draw precise shapes by placing anchor points yourself, or use the Freeform Pen tool to draw more naturally (letting Photoshop automatically assign anchor points to your path).

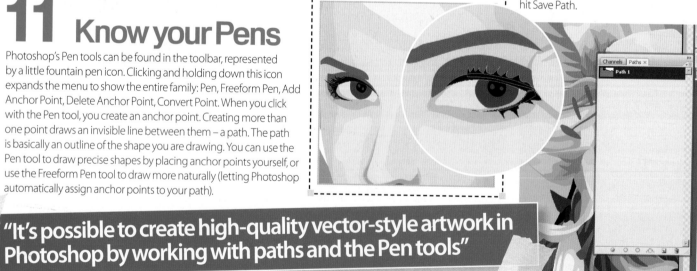

"It's possible to create high-quality vector-style artwork in Photoshop by working with paths and the Pen tools"

Retouching

Everybody is familiar with the glossy magazine look – photos that have been airbrushed to look perfect and, in many cases, painfully artificial. While many magazines take it too far, retouching used in moderation can dramatically improve your images. Here we're looking at some straightforward techniques to boost colour, contrast and remove imperfections; most images come out of the camera slightly soft and undersaturated, and there are always a few spots and blemishes in the real world. The most important lesson to learn when retouching is that less is more. Root your alterations in reality and you'll achieve a far more pleasing image than if you try to create the ideal human being.

16 Boost colour and contrast

Convert your image to the Lab Color mode by choosing Image>Mode>Lab Color. Lab uses a separate Luminance channel to store brightness values, which allows you to boost the colour without making the image muddy. Add a Curves adjustment layer and choose each of the A and B channels in turn. Drag the white and black points in towards the centre symmetrically to create a steeper Curves line. Use identical changes for the A and B channels to boost colour overall, or different values to correct or create a colour cast. Add a slight S curve to the Luminance channel to improve contrast.

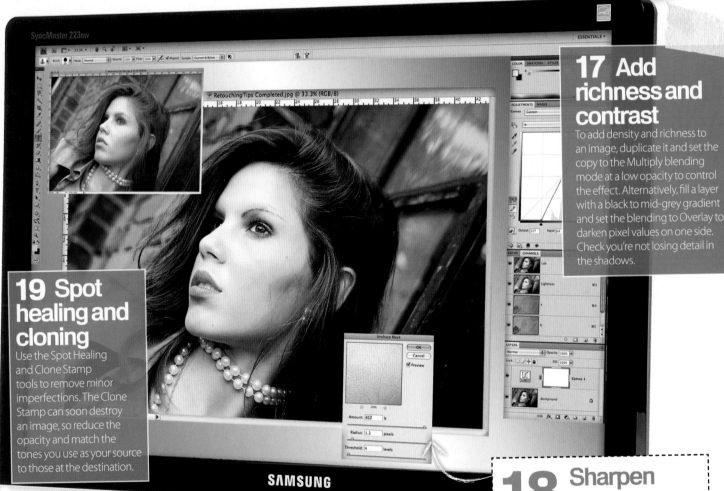

17 Add richness and contrast

To add density and richness to an image, duplicate it and set the copy to the Multiply blending mode at a low opacity to control the effect. Alternatively, fill a layer with a black to mid-grey gradient and set the blending to Overlay to darken pixel values on one side. Check you're not losing detail in the shadows.

19 Spot healing and cloning

Use the Spot Healing and Clone Stamp tools to remove minor imperfections. The Clone Stamp can soon destroy an image, so reduce the opacity and match the tones you use as your source to those at the destination.

20 Liquify

To remove double chins, reshape or accentuate the eyes, use the Liquify filter. Take a copy of your layer then choose Filter>Liquify. Use big brushes to avoid obvious wobbly edges and use the Show Backdrop option to continuously compare where you are with the original image.

18 Sharpen and soften

Modern digital cameras apply sharpening in-camera (unless you use RAW mode), but often there's not enough or too much. To remove over-sharpened edges, copy the layer and add a small amount of Gaussian Blur. Reduce the opacity of the blurred layer to blend with the original. To add sharpness, copy the layer and go to Filter>Sharpen>Unsharp Mask. Blend the sharpened version with the original using the Luminosity blend mode, and adjust the opacity to suit.

Auto Select Layer   Auto Select Groups   Show Transform Controls   Tool Presets   Layer Comps   Brushes

Last Filter   ⌘F

Extract...   ⌥⌘X
Filter Gallery...
Liquify...   ⇧⌘X
Pattern Maker...   ⌥⇧⌘X
Vanishing Point...   ⌥⌘V

Artistic   ▶
Blur   ▶
Brush Strokes   ▶
Distort   ▶
Noise   ▶
Pixelate   ▶
Render   ▶
Sharpen   ▶
Sketch   ▶
Stylize   ▶
Texture   ▶
Video   ▶
Other   ▶

Digimarc   ▶

Tips

Filters

Photoshop's filters are both loved and despised within the Photoshop community. Loved because of their ease of use and amazing versatility; despised due to their frequent abuse at the hands of novices. Filters can accomplish a great many tasks and special effects. There's a real temptation to overuse these features, but our experience has shown that the best work results from the judicious and thoughtful application of these tools. The rule of thumb is that the art shouldn't be a showcase for what filters can do. Rather, the filters should be a supporting element for what the artwork is trying to accomplish.

Polar Coordinates

16%

○ Rectangular to Polar
○ Polar to Rectangular

23 Light burst

The greatest effects can come from unexpected places. One example is to use the often-overlooked Polar Coordinates filter to create an energetic light burst. Begin with a square canvas filled with black. With a large Scatter brush, paint a bright colour along the top third of the image. Go to Filter>Blur>Motion Blur; set Angle to 90, Distance to 150 pixels or more. In Filter>Distort>Polar Coordinates, check Rectangular to Polar.

After
Before

21 Seam killer

If you are trying to create seamlessly repeating textures or patterns, there's no better friend than the Offset filter. Found in the lowly Other sub-menu, Offset can take an image and wrap it around on itself (as long as the Wrap Around option is enabled). This slides the unsightly edge seams of the image towards the centre and allows easy access for attacking them with the Clone Stamp tool.

Offset

Horizontal: 1800 pixels right   OK
                                        Cancel
Vertical: 1000   pixels down
                                   ☑ Preview

Undefined Areas
○ Set to Background
○ Repeat Edge Pixels
● Wrap Around

24 Be smart with filters

Using Smart Filters is as close as you can get to having filters work like adjustment layers. Convert your layer to a Smart Object first (Layer>Smart Objects>Convert to Smart Object), then any filter you employ will be added as a Smart Filter. This means the Filter settings can be edited or even removed long after the effect has been applied.

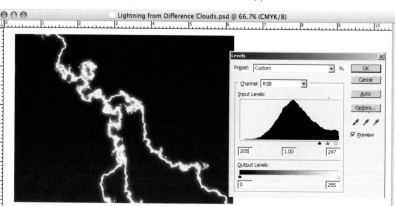

Lightning from Difference Clouds.psd @ 66.7% (CMYK/8)

Levels

Preset: Custom   OK
                                        Cancel
Channel: RGB
Input Levels: Auto
                                        Options...

                                        ☑ Preview
205   1.00   247

Output Levels:
0   255

66.67%   Doc: 5.03M/0 bytes

22 Focal blur depth maps

Create a simple, round, highly feathered selection and save it to a channel (Select>Save Selection). Then in the Lens Blur filter (Filter>Blur>Lens Blur) that selection can be used as a depth map to control the focal blur.

25 Lightning from Difference Clouds

Begin by creating a narrow linear gradient from black to white. Go to Filter>Render>Difference Clouds and you'll see a black electric shape taking form. Hit Cmd/Ctrl+I to invert the colours, and use Levels to isolate the lightning shape. Paint out unwanted areas and set the blending mode to Linear Dodge. Now copy the lightning layer and run a slight Gaussian Blur on the copy. Set the copy's mode to Screen and reduce Opacity to 80%. If desired, use additional copies of the layer to add more lightning bolts.

"The art shouldn't be a showcase for what filters can do. The filters should be a supporting element for what the artwork is trying to accomplish"

26 Mock up your logo on glassware

Create a monochrome logo on a file the same size as the glass image, and save it as a PSD. Then in the Glass Filter settings (Filter>Distort>Glass), load that file as a texture through the fly-out menu next to the Texture drop-down box.

After

Before

28 Flare adjustments

The Lens Flare filter (found in the Render sub-menu) is often difficult to position due to the small preview window. A good workaround is to run the filter on a solid black layer. Then change the blending mode to Screen, and you have a floating lens flare on its own layer!

29 Better bevels with Lighting Effects

Saving a selection as a channel has benefits in the Lighting Effects filter as well. Save a selection in the shape of a line of text, and then identify that channel in the drop-down box for 'Texture Channel' in the Lighting Effects (Filter>Render>Lighting Effects) settings. This allows you to create sophisticated bevels with multiple light sources and highlights.

RIPPED

27 Rough edges

A quick, easy way to turn a straight edge into a random rough edge is to use the Displace filter with the Cloud filter. First create a separate file at the same dimensions as your working file. Fill with black and white clouds (Filter>Render>Clouds), then save and close. Back in your artwork, go to Filter> Distort>Displace and enter the scale values as desired. Hit OK and load the cloud file you've created to use as the displacement map. If the filter missed some edges, run it again with different scale values. Keep in mind that Scale can be a negative value as well as positive.

30 Filter fade

Immediately after running any filter, the Edit menu has a Fade command that allows you to change the opacity and blend mode of how the filter was applied. Think of it as a partial undo. Creative application would include the Torn Edge filter faded to a Color Burn mode at 50% Opacity for a stylised film noir effect.

Restoring your photos

Every old photo we come across tells a story. They originate from a time when the technology to record images was expensive, so every photograph was cherished and carefully posed. Equally, every image that needs restoring will have its own set of problems to address and overcome. In this set of tips we look at some of the common problems you'll encounter and some of the techniques you can use to deal with them. More often than not you'll need to employ a variety of techniques to restore your images. Keep in mind that some of the charm of old photos is the dust, noise and colourisation they have.

31 Restore colour to missing areas

Old photos can have water spots or other areas of damage that have removed painted colour. Restore these areas easily by creating a new layer and painting with sampled colours over the areas of missing colour. Set the blending mode to Color, then use the Burn tool on the original layer to darken the areas where the colour is missing. This helps blend the two layers together nicely and disguise the fix.

32 Sharpen soft details

Old photos can appear to bleed a little, being softer than modern photos. One easy way to appear to increase the detail of the image is to apply a small amount of sharpening to the image. Use the Unsharp Mask filter or Smart Sharpen (both under Filter> Sharpen). If you have too much noise after sharpening, try duplicating the layer, setting the blending mode to Hard Light and applying a medium Gaussian Blur to soften the noise.

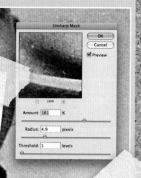

33 Fix tears and scratches

Tears and scratches on the original image can be repaired by using the Clone Stamp tool, and in some cases the Spot Healing tool. To avoid creating obvious lines, select a soft brush and draw a selection around the scratch before starting to clone. Add a small feather to your selection by choosing Select>Modify>Feather. This softens the edges of the selection and helps avoid hard edges when cloning. If the tear goes through facial features or other high detail areas, reduce the size of your brush and zoom in very close to repair small sections at a time.

34 Use Curves to add contrast

Old photos tend to fade, so bring them back to life by adding contrast. Levels and Curves adjustment layers both allow you to increase the apparent detail by pushing or pulling the black and white points. Use the black Eyedropper to select the darkest point and the white Eyedropper for the lightest point, to get an instant contrast boost.

35 Clone out imperfections

Problem areas such as dirt or water damage, or spots and marks from the original scan can be easily corrected with the Clone Stamp tool. Create a new layer and choose Clone Stamp. Make sure you check the Sample All Layers checkbox, and paint onto the new empty layer. Once you've completed your cloning, merge the two layers together.

"Know when to stop and accept the limitations of the image as being part of the charm and attraction of the photograph"

36 Build up smaller adjustments

Some photos are tricky to apply an overall fix to. If we alter the contrast to suit the man in this image, the woman's face loses all detail. Create an adjustment layer to even the tones across the image, then use a further adjustment layer to add the contrast you desire.

37 Colourise for effect

It used to be common for black and white images to be hand-tinted to give the impression of being a colour photo. It's easy to simulate this in Photoshop. You can create a simple two-tone image via Image>Mode>Grayscale, then Image> Mode>Duotone, but this gives no flexibility over where the colour is laid. Instead, starting with a black and white image but in RGB Color mode, add Hue and Saturation adjustment layers. Tick Colorize and set the desired hue. Paint onto the mask, using black to hide the effect and white to reveal it. By building up multiple Hue/Saturation adjustments, each masked, you can quickly add colour to an image.

38 Compare with the original frequently

Keep a copy of the original image at the top of your layer stack so you can switch it on to compare the two images frequently. It's easy to accidentally throw away detail that was present in the original image while trying to restore a specific area, so by flicking between the original and your altered version, you can recognise where this is happening and backtrack if necessary.

39 Accept that you can't fix everything

There are certain characteristics of old photos that make them aesthetically pleasing, and certain problems you simply can't overcome. For example, where there's a face with apparently blown highlights, there's not much you can do to add back that detail. Know when to stop and accept the limitations of the image as being part of the charm and attraction of the photo. If in doubt, step away from the computer and come back to review it later. Finally, sometimes a simple crop can improve an image and cut out big problem areas that would be otherwise impossible to fix.

40 Non-destructive is best

Avoid frustration by using non-destructive effects wherever possible. Changes to hue and saturation can be achieved through Image>Adjustments>Hue/Saturation, but this changes the original pixels. Instead, use adjustment layers wherever possible, as they can be discarded or edited later without reducing the quality of the image.

Mixed media montages

Mixed media art is surely one of the best ways of having fun while creating artwork. Because of its irreverent nature, the artist is very often free to explore artistic possibilities without the constraints of a single medium. Photoshop is a perfect tool for mixed media artwork – its many functions allow you to juxtapose traditional artwork with digital paints, photography with type, scanned textures with generated ones, and so on. With so much choice, it's easy to be overwhelmed. But have in mind an image that you want to create and then find stock imagery to match your imagination!

41 Working with type

Adding typography to a montage can give extra meaning to it. You can manipulate text by clicking the Create Warped Text button in the top menu when you select the Type tool. You can also use the Type Mask tools to make masks with your favourite fonts!

42 All the colours of the rainbow

When creating montages, you'll find yourself working with various images. Usually, they won't look like they belong together – that's where colour correction comes in handy. By using one of the Color Correction tools you can balance out, tweak or even replace colours to bring unity to the final montage. If you're just starting out, a great tool is Variations (Image>Adjustments> Variations), which features multiple previews and allows you to fine-tune adjustments by choosing 'more' or 'less' of your preview.

43 Master your masks

Making a mixed media montage usually involves a lot of careful masking to show only the interesting bits that you want the viewer to see. Photoshop's layer masks are elegantly simple yet extremely efficient at their job. You can use the Marquee or Lasso tools to make basic masks by creating a selection and hitting the Add Layer Mask button in the Layers palette. If you're in a hurry, use the Magic Wand tools to make your selections instead. For more intricate masks, the Pen tool is useful – use the tool to draw out the desired shape. In the Paths palette, click on the path's layer to select it and choose Make Selection, then use that to make your mask.

44 Add originality with hand-drawn artwork

Hand-drawn elements are the easiest way to add a truly unique, personal touch to any mixed media montage. You don't need to be an artist – just scribble out hearts, flowers, whatever with your favourite crayon and scan it in. Once it's in Photoshop, you can manipulate it with the Color Correction tools and change its layer blending mode.

45 Texture

Like hand-drawn art, realistic textures add a lot to your montage. You can scan in various surfaces (paper, cloth, napkins…) yourself, or download a ready-made one off the internet. Sometimes the simplest textures yield the best results!

> "Hand-drawn elements are the easiest way to add a truly unique, personal touch"

Digital scrapbook

Remember film? It was this material that cameras required to capture photos. It had to be developed and resulted in actual physical photographs. Often these photos would be scrapbooked. They would be trimmed, arranged on a page and decorated with assorted embellishments in a layout designed to capture the memory of the event. But in today's world of digital cameras, it makes sense for the pastime of scrapbooking to go digital as well. Photoshop is the perfect tool for this task. Not only can it clean up and adjust the photos to perfection, but it can also be used for the page layout and embellishments.

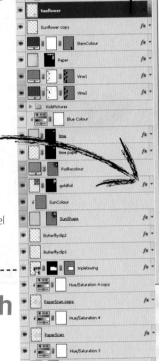

46 Lots of layers

Don't drown in a sea of confusing layers. Photoshop has features to help make sense of things. The most obvious is the oft-neglected ability to give the layer a meaningful name. You can also create groups and assign colours.

47 Layer styles for realism

One goal of digital scrapbooking is to reproduce the same tangible look of traditional scrapbooking. To do so means you need to create elements that appear to have physical depth. Using a small Bevel and Emboss layer style and soft Drop Shadows are essential for this technique.

48 Invest in a scanner

For getting realistic textures, a flatbed scanner is indispensable. Explore the world around you for a treasure of usable textures. Everything from carpet weave to shoe treads to crinkled paper is readily available. Consider creating your own custom grunge and splatter textures by scanning in tea stains and spills. These add tremendous life, warmth and interest to your designs.

49 Weave with masks

You may have a design idea that isn't easily handled by the layer setup. In our example, the vines on the left weave in and out of the photos. The best way to do this is to use layer masks to define visible as well as hidden areas. Hit the Add Layer Mask icon (Layers panel) to create a layer mask, then use a brush with black paint on the layer mask to hide areas that should be behind other layers.

50 Catch the eye

The foundation for any scrapbooking page is the selection of photos made for the layout. One of the greatest benefits of scrapbooking digitally in Photoshop is the opportunity to make the photos as eye-catching as possible. Begin by framing the shot appropriately to capture the action and emotion of the event. Then we recommend cleaning up the photo by removing any unwanted or distracting elements – the Clone Stamp tool is ideal for this. Use adjustment layers to optimise contrast and create more vibrant colours. In our example of the triplets on the swing, a Warming filter was used to give the image a more summery feel

TIP! See video tutorial for more info

"Barrel distortion refers to the effect where a building appears to widen at its middle in a 'barrel' curve"

Correct barrel distortion

Barrel distortion refers to the effect where a building appears to widen at its middle in a 'barrel' curve. It often occurs when photographing a tall building from below due to the distortion created by the camera sensor's angle. Open the image in the Lens Distortion filter and use the Remove Distortion slider until the building shape is right. A play with the Vertical Perspective slider and a final crop might be required for perfect lines.

Before

After

Custom lens settings

Every lens has its own characteristics that might include distortion at the edges in wide-angle optics, or noise in long telephoto lenses. If you're processing a batch of images from the same lens it can be useful to use the default Lens Correction feature, which will remember your settings for distortion, chromatic aberrations and vignetting correction.

Chromatic aberrations

Chromatic aberrations or colour fringing can appear in images where there are high levels of contrast – around the edges of buildings, for instance. It is commonly purple but can be other hues. Use the sliders in the Lens Correction filter, sliding the red/cyan or blue/yellow depending on the colour fringing in your image.

Lens Correction filter
Correct skewed buildings and lens imperfections with ease

When photographing a building at close proximity, the angle of your camera's sensor in relation to the angle of the building can cause distortions. If shooting from front on, the most common of these errors is the appearance that the building is 'falling backwards'.

Fortunately, there is a simple way to right this flaw. Work on a duplicate layer and open up the Lens Correction filter (Filter> Distort>Lens Correction). Next, you have to experiment with the Vertical Perspective slider, pulling it to the left to correct the backward tilt effect. Once you are satisfied that the verticals are looking correct, adjust the Horizontal slider to ensure equally accurate horizontal lines.

If your image still doesn't look right after the Lens Correction adjustments, try using the Straighten tool (which is positioned on the left of the screen). Drag your mouse along a straight line and then let Photoshop work its magic. A final bit of cropping to get rid of any bad edges and your building image should now be back on the straight and narrow. Unless it's the Leaning Tower of Pisa…

Quick tip

Pincushion distortion

This term refers to the effect where horizontal lines in your image rise in the centre and fall at the edges, much the same as barrel distortion on vertical lines.

Sharpen your images with Unsharp

With some subjects, fast-moving sports or wildlife for instance, a little bit of sharpening is often needed to get crisp edges, eyes, etc. If you need to enhance your image, open up the Unsharp Mask and, in the window, make sure that Preview is checked. This means you will be able to check your progress 'live'. If you add too much Unsharp you will blur the detail of the image and it will take on a smudged appearance. Add a little at a time and check over the image at regular intervals for the best results.

When shooting your photographs, try to use RAW file formats whenever possible. RAW files hold more data allowing you more flexibility when editing later. JPEGs, on the other hand, are more fragile and will degrade each time you edit them. Save images as TIFF or PSD files.

Clone Stamp tool

Rid your images of dust spots, unwanted elements and more…

Before

After

To remove any unsightly blemishes, like the dust spot in the photo on the left, try using the Clone Stamp tool. Start by creating a new layer. Ensure you work on this layer for non-destructive editing to your original file; you'll know the layer is active if it is highlighted. The Clone Stamp tool works particularly well when using small brush sizes and selecting source areas multiple times. Make sure you tick the box marked 'Sample all layers', then Opt/Alt-click your source area and start painting. If you want to increase the brush size on the fly, simply hit the square bracket keys for a shortcut – left bracket to decrease, right bracket to increase. Also great for fingerprints or water droplets that may be ruining your shots.

The spot, a dust speck on the camera sensor or on the lens itself, is easy to remove with Photoshop

Crop
A simple crop might be the only step you need to create a better composition. When cropping an image think about the rule of thirds and place your subject on a third intersecting line. Crop out any unwanted elements and make sure your horizon is straight.

Quick tip

Digital darkroom

In the days of film photography, photographers used to dodge and burn, mask or colour in the darkroom. These techniques have been translated into the digital darkroom and can be found in all versions of Photoshop.

Straighten up, ruler out

When taking shots with a handheld camera, it can be easy to misjudge your angles. Skewed horizons can completely ruin an image, so make sure yours are straight by using the Ruler in Photoshop. Hit Cmd/Ctrl+R and drag a ruler down from the top of the screen. Line it up with your horizon to check that it is straight. If it isn't, rotate the canvas to match the ruler and crop the edges for a perfect, poker-straight finish.

Before

After

Tonal adjustments with Curves

Photoshop's Curves adjustments can be the saving grace of a photo, if they're used carefully. The graphical display represents the image with the lower end of the diagonal line representing the darker tones, and the higher end representing lighter tones. Carefully drag the line into a curve shape to see how it affects your image. Be warned, even the smallest adjustments can produce dramatic changes.

Tip

Lens Blur in action

With the Lens Blur filter you can select the amount of the photo that is in focus, and the amount that is out of focus, creating great depth-of-field effects, post shoot.

Correcting a colour cast

If you don't remember to manually adjust your white balance when composing a photo, you can end up with some truly horrific results. This image was left on the wrong setting and, as you can see, this has left a cold blue cast across the whole photograph. If you're not in a position where you can re-take the shot then you can rectify it fairly easily with a little helping hand from Photoshop. As with all these tools, apply the correction a little at a time; you can always add more! Be sure to always have the Preview box selected too so you can see the effects of any adjustment the moment you make it.

01 **Color Balance** Open up your image in Photoshop and navigate to Image>Adjustments>Color Balance. Here a pop-up window will appear; activate the Preview box so you can see your changes as they happen.

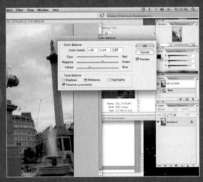

02 **Value added** Play with the sliders, removing the blue tones of the cast. Be careful not to add too much red into the image and try to achieve whites where there should be white.

03 **Crop and straighten** The image is also a little on the wonky side so we have rotated the canvas to make the column straight, and then cropped the image as a final touch.

Keeping your images safe online

In this interactive day and age, we all post images to our online galleries or photo-sharing websites such as Flickr. To guarantee your images stay safe, be sure to embed a digital watermark in them, as well as a visible one. Photoshop offers its users Digimarc which is simple yet effective to use and will ensure your snaps are safe from misuse.

Making the most of Adobe Bridge

Although Photoshop is perfect for editing images, Adobe Bridge is the perfect companion for photographers. It's a powerful media manager where users can organise, browse, locate and view images. EXIF data – which includes details such as the camera and lens used and shot settings – can be viewed in Bridge as well as streamlining workflow systems like batch renaming, creating contact sheets and more.

CMYK vs RGB

RGB (Red, Green, Blue) is the generally preferred working colour space over CMYK (Cyan, Magenta, Yellow, Black) for photo editing. For printing your images Adobe RGB is recommended, whilst images destined for the web will work well with sRGB, this is because the Adobe preset contains more colour information than the latter option.

Non-destructive editing

Perhaps the best thing about editing your photos in Photoshop is that you can non-destructively work on them, keeping your original file safe and whole. Make sure you use these features to their full advantage and use adjustment layers, duplicate copies of images and other non-destructive options wherever you can.

Rescuing shadows and highlights

Don't throw away those badly-exposed photos – take them into Photoshop instead

When shooting in tricky lighting conditions it can be hard to create the right exposure. For instance, if you expose for the sky the shadows can be too harsh, but if you expose for the shadows then the lighter areas can become blown out. Blown-out highlights are impossible to rescue as these areas have lost all image information. Shadow areas, on the other hand, are easier to rescue as there is detail recorded, even if it is unnaturally dark. Load up your photo and head to Image>Adjustments>Shadow/Highlight. Check the box for More Options and start with the top slider. The Shadow slider will lighten up the darker areas (in this case the faces), while the Highlights section deals with the lighter areas (the sky, for example). Experiment to see what amount of exposure compensation is needed for your particular photo. Click the Preview button to flick between the original and edited versions.

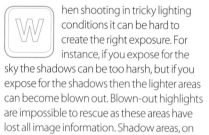
Before

After

Don't be put off from taking photos in tricky lighting situations anymore!

Quick tip

Bokeh effects

Bokeh refers to the quality of the out-of-focus areas in your photo. High-quality lenses produce smooth bokeh effects, but you can easily fake them in Photoshop with layers, the Brush tool and a colour gradient.

Black-and-white conversion

There are numerous ways to convert images to black and white with Photoshop – from simply applying the Grayscale mode to using the Channel Mixer. We prefer to use the Channel Mixer. Simply apply a Channel Mixer layer to your image, select Monochrome and play with the values until you create an effect you are happy with. A final tweak of Contrast will give a great end result.

Working with RAW files in Camera Raw

As we've previously mentioned, shooting in RAW formats produces image files that contain a lot more digital data than other formats, such as JPEG. Like a digital negative, these files can be manipulated further in Photoshop without damaging the original file. Camera Raw is a plug-in that comes with Photoshop and has support for hundreds of cameras and their RAW formats (each manufacturer has its own proprietary RAW format). Camera Raw is an impressive bit of kit and much of the powerful Adobe Photoshop Lightroom program uses the same processing technology.

Small edits, big results!

Sometimes the smallest edits can make the biggest difference. Here a simple straightening to make sure the tower is perfect, some tonal adjustments and a crop to get rid of a distracting element in the foreground has created a much more effective composition.

After

Before

23

Age your photos with real paper

Add a retro twist to your photos by adding paper texture layers

Experiment with Photoshop's various blending modes in the Layers palette to get different effects

R eal paper and other textures can be combined with Photoshop's layer blending modes to give your images an authentic aged look. First you will need a good paper texture. There are plenty of great online resources or, alternatively, you can create your own and scan it in. Once you have your texture, open it in PS and copy and paste it into your artwork, placing it at the top of the layer stack. Various blending modes produce different results depending on your image, so try experimenting. Multiply, Overlay and Soft Light are particularly good for this trick.

Quick tip

Guides without measuring

Add guides to your canvas in percentage increments. This is useful for finding the halfway point; just click View>New Guide and, in Position, enter: 50%.

Add movement with a Motion Blur and a mask

Applying an authentic motion blur to your photos couldn't be simpler. Press Cmd/Ctrl+J to create a duplicate layer of the photo you're working on and then go to Filter>Blur>Motion Blur. In the Motion Blur dialog, adjust the Angle (by dragging the line in the circle) so that it suits your scene and move the Distance slider accordingly. The Motion Blur will now be obscuring your photo so click Layer>Layer Mask>Reveal All and use an airbrush (with a black colour selected) to mask out the areas that you don't want blurred, bringing back the details.

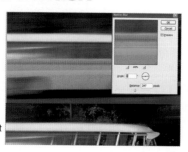

Create dramatic backdrops using the Background Eraser tool

The Background Eraser tool is a surprisingly undervalued tool in Photoshop; with it, you can easily remove background elements a lot more quickly than you could by using the Lasso or Magic Wand tools. You can find it in the Eraser tool flyout menu (or hit Shift+E to cycle through the various erasers). The Background Eraser works best in images that have a high contrast between the foreground and the background.

As an aside, you may notice that a side effect of the Background Eraser is that it may make a few of your foreground elements partially transparent, but this can be fixed by using the History Brush tool to paint them back.

01 Select the colour to protect
Open your file and select the Background Eraser with the following settings: Sampling: Once, Tolerance 50% and tick Protect Foreground Color. Hold Opt/Alt to access the Eyedropper tool and select a foreground colour that you want to protect.

02 Erase the background
Click and drag over the background and start to erase as you would with the standard Eraser tool. If the foreground colour changes, use the Eyedropper to re-sample and then continue.

03 Paste in a new background
With your old background now fully erased, you can copy and paste in a brand new background below the foreground to make your scene more dramatic. Use the History Brush tool to fix any areas that shouldn't have been erased.

Use Color Balance to change the hues of your photos

Color Balance is a more effective way than using Hue/Saturation as it gives you more fine-tuned control. Go to Image>Adjustments>Color Balance and you'll have access to sliders that control the colour levels of the Shadows, Midtones and Highlights. We recommend you start altering the Midtones first as they will have the most dramatic effect before moving on to the Highlights and Shadows.

Save selections as channels

If you've made a selection, especially a fiddly or complicated one, it's a good idea to save it as a channel just in case you want to retrieve it. With your selection active, go to the Channels palette and click on the 'Save selection as channel' icon (the circle within a square). Now, if you want to re-activate your selection, simply hold Ctrl/right-click on your new channel's thumbnail.

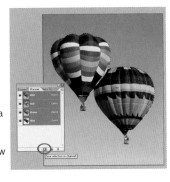

Create a soft focus effect using Gaussian Blur and a layer mask

For a simple soft focusing technique during postproduction, use a combination of Photoshop's blur and masking features. First of all, press Cmd/Ctrl+J to make a duplicate copy of your photo on a new layer, then go to Filter> Blur>Gaussian Blur. You will need to choose a Radius value that works for your specific photo, as each image is unique. Next apply a layer mask to this blurred layer, and use a black airbrush to paint out key areas of detail, such as a subject's face, on the layer mask. You can also adjust the layer's opacity at the end of this process to refine the degree of blur.

⣿ | Let Photoshop edit your photos in perspective with Vanishing Point

Introduced in Photoshop CS2, Vanishing Point takes all of the effort out of Free Transform-ing elements so that they will fit the perspective established in your photo. By simply defining four points of a perspective grid, Photoshop will make sure that everything that you put onto the grid maintains its perspective, allowing you to clone, paint or paste elements to your heart's content. Better still, if you run the filter on a new empty layer, your changes will be non-destructive; they can be hidden to reveal your untouched original below. Plus, you only have to establish a plane once; Photoshop will remember it so you can drop in and out of Vanishing Point as often as you need to.

01 Define the 3D plane Create a new layer above your photo then go to Filter>Vanishing Point. Define your 3D plane by clicking on four corners that match the perspective of your picture. If the grid turns blue it will work – red grids require minor tweaking.

02 Paste your graffiti onto the plane Once your grid is established, click OK to leave the filter. Open a graffiti image file, select and copy the contents then run Filter>Vanishing Point again. Hit Cmd/Ctrl+V to paste in the stock and drag it over the perspective plane.

03 Blend your graffiti Use the handles to Free Transform your graffiti image into its final scale/ position; Photoshop will keep it in perspective for you while you resize it. As a final touch for realism, set your graffiti tag's blending mode to Multiply so that it more seamlessly blends into the wall.

Quick and easy colour changes

Replace one colour for another with a few quick brush strokes

The Color Replacement tool will only replace the colour you first click on

Quickly swap out one colour for another using the Color Replacement tool, which can be found in the Brush flyout menu. Choose Sampling: Once in the top navigation bar and, once you begin painting, the tool will replace only the colour your cursor first clicks on. Experiment with the Tolerance to avoid similar colours being affected. Here we have set Tolerance to 40 and changed the flowers from purple to red by clicking on one area of the purple flowers and sweeping over the rest of the blooms using one continuous brush stroke. After a few strokes, flowers are transformed.

Quick tip

Reducing effects with Fade

If a filter you've applied is a little too strong click Edit>Fade and move the Opacity slider to the left to lessen its potency.

⣿ | Make your photos more vibrant with a Soft Light layer

On some occasions, digital cameras can struggle to capture the tonal range of a shot, which can lead to disappointing, washed-out photographs. However, that's why Photoshop exists and the program offers a number of solutions to remedy this issue. One particularly straightforward trick to restore the vibrancy that you saw when you were taking the photo is using a Soft Light blending mode. Hit Cmd/Ctrl+J to make a layer copy of the photo and change the new layer's blending mode to Soft Light from the drop-down menu in the Layers palette. Move the Opacity slider to the left and reduce it to around 80% to make sure the Soft Light layer isn't too overpowering.

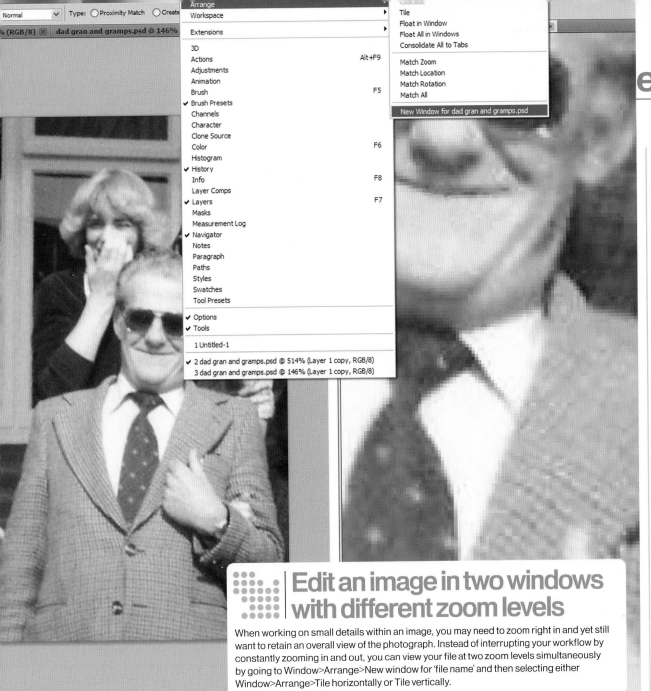

Duplicate layers for non-destructive editing

Avoid permanently altering your photos with no way of getting the originals back; instead of working on your photo directly, simply create a new copy layer by pressing Cmd/Ctrl+J to make an exact duplicate of the photo layer. You can now make any changes you like without worrying about losing your original photo because it's safely on its own layer which you can return to whenever you want for reference.

Don't paste, just drag layers

Often you'll want to bring an existing element from an old file into a new file you're working on. Speed up your workflow by cutting out the need to select, copy and paste; instead, open both documents side by side and simply click and drag the layer from the Layers palette of the first file onto the other document and you've got an instant copy in your new file.

Edit an image in two windows with different zoom levels

When working on small details within an image, you may need to zoom right in and yet still want to retain an overall view of the photograph. Instead of interrupting your workflow by constantly zooming in and out, you can view your file at two zoom levels simultaneously by going to Window>Arrange>New window for 'file name' and then selecting either Window>Arrange>Tile horizontally or Tile vertically.

Content-Aware Fill for unwanted elements

CS5's Content-Aware Fill acts like the Spot Healing Brush tool, but for larger areas; it uses information from the surrounding area to replace unwanted elements. First use the Lasso tool ('L') to draw a fairly close selection around the offending item then go to Edit>Fill and select Use: Content-Aware from the Contents menu. Not happy? Just undo and run it again.

Use the Crop tool to correct a photo's perspective

Sometimes when you're taking a photo of a painting or a sign you won't be physically able to get the image straight on, but you'll be pleased to hear that you can use the Crop tool to fix this problem. Open your image and press 'C' to access the Crop tool. Drag a cropping area around the painting or sign and the contextual menu bar will appear at the top of the screen. Tick the Perspective box and then drag the borders of the crop box to fit the painting/sign and hit Enter. Photoshop will automatically correct the perspective for you, so it's picture perfect.

::: Overlay-neutral blending mode layer

Applying the Dodge and Burn tools can be a great way to heighten the detail and lighting effects within any given image. However, these can be extremely destructive. A better alternative would be to apply an Overlay-neutral layer. Do so by holding down the Opt/Alt key and clicking the New Layer icon at the foot of the Layers palette. Set Mode to Overlay and activate Fill with Overlay-neutral color (50% Gray). Now with a 10% soft black brush you can manually add shadows. A white brush applies highlights.

Before

After

Define Brush Preset: Create texture brushes

Create your own brushes for personal projects

S ometimes you can search and search, and still not find the brush you're looking for. Sometimes you find it but can't afford it. In both instances why not just make your own brush styles? It's simple. Texture brushes especially come in handy for mixed media projects. To create these open your stock, remembering that the largest dimensions brushes can be is 2,500 pixels by 2,500 pixels. This means you must resize or crop your image so that it is 2,500 pixels or less in both width and height. Next you'll need to create a good contrast greyscale image, so with your images set to RGB, we recommend using the Black & White option. Here tweak Reds and Yellows sliders to define highlights and shadows. You can add further effects by applying exaggerated Levels values. Once happy, merge your layer, select Edit> Define Brush Preset and name your brush, it'll then be available from your Brushes palette.

You can soften or sharpen the detail in your brushes applying Blur and Sharpen filters before defining as a brush preset

Quick tip

Smart Sharpen tool

Selected from Filters>Sharpen>Smart Sharpen. Applying this to the final image or high-res photography can really lift exposure and create crisp details. An Amount of 100% and Radius of 1 pixel will get the job done.

Increase creativity productivity with Actions

Actions can be vital in enhancing your workflow. There are operations that you use frequently but pile on extra minutes. Actions can shave these. Programming is simple – start by selecting the Actions palette, then drop down the action menu and click on New Action. Name your action, hit the Record icon, do your thing and press Stop.

Batching with Droplets

Droplets maximise the pre- and post-production phase. These are derivative of Actions you create for file processing. Produce your Action then select File>Automate> Create Droplet. Through the Choose option you can establish a save point, set which Action to batch and from what set. Once complete your droplet will appear. To activate simply drag and drop your image files into it.

Using Channels to make a selection

Some may find the Pen Path time consuming, especially when wanting to make selections with tricky edges. Here Channels can optimise your workflow. To make a Channel-based selection, find the Channel that delivers the most exposure contrast between the object you want to cut and that you want to keep. Duplicate that Channel, and take a black brush, painting to the kept object, and a white brush to the cut object. Make sure you use soft brushes and extreme zooms when applying to hair. Once satisfied you've defined both areas, invert this Copy Channel layer, Cmd/Ctrl-click the Copy Channel thumbnail, select RGB/CMYK Channel, and copy and paste your object.

More radiant skylines

The Brush tool can be a powerful device, even through its most fundamental setting. For example, say you have an awesome landscape photographer, but you really want to make those highlights pop without blowing them out. Simple – just select a large soft pure white brush and apply it, on a new layer, in and around highlighted areas. You can tweak opacity, and the odd lens flare applied can't hurt.

Control the impact of your Filters with the History brush

Use the History brush with the History palette to revert parts of your image to a previous state. Tick a box to the left of a state in the History palette, then continue working on your image. For example you may apply some filters and colour adjustments. Now use the History brush to paint over certain elements of your image; any changes made since the ticked history state will be removed.

Quick and easy magnetic selections

Making selections using the Pen tool or Lasso tool can be a pain-staking job. If the object you are trying to select has a well-defined outline, Photoshop can make this task easier for you with the Magnetic option. Simply tick the Magnetic box when using the Freeform Pen tool, or click and hold the Lasso tool in the toolbar and choose the Magnetic Lasso tool from the fly-out menu; the tools will then automatically snap to the edges when you are drawing your selections.

Paint your selections easily with Quick Mask Mode

Quick Mask Mode is a remarkably easy method of making selections, especially if you have a graphics tablet in your arsenal of artistic tools. By pressing 'Q' (or clicking on the Quick Mask Mode icon that you can find in the toolbar) you can enter and exit Quick Mask Mode, where you can use the Brush tool to paint your selection. The red areas (as shown in the image on the top-right) indicate parts of your image excluded from the selection; painting with white will add to your selection and painting with black will remove areas. When you press Q again your selection will turn into the traditional 'marching ants' appearance.

Create your own Custom Shape

The Shape tool allows you to create a shape with a quick click and drag, and has several useful shapes readily available. Click and hold on the Shape tool and a fly-out menu will reveal the basic common shapes such as Rectangle and Ellipse. Selecting the Custom Shape tool will open you up to a whole host of other more unusual shapes, accessible from the 'Shape' menu in the top navigation bar. You can add to this list by creating and saving your own custom shapes, so that any shapes you may frequently want to add to your work can be dropped in at the click of a button. Here's how…

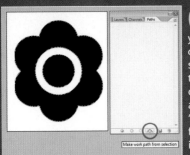

01 Create a path First you will need to create a path of your shape. Use the Pen tool to draw it, or you can make a selection and then click the 'Make work path from selection' icon in the Paths palette.

02 Define the shape Remember, it doesn't matter what size your shape is, as it will be scalable. Once you have a path of your shape, go to Edit>Define Custom Shape, name your shape and click OK.

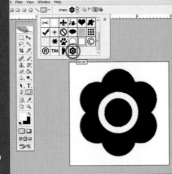

03 Your saved shape You can now access your new shape at any time by clicking and holding the Shape tool, selecting Custom Shape from the fly-out menu, and choosing your shape from the Shape menu in the top navigation bar.

The Crop tool does more than you think

Easily resize your files to become larger and even hide parts of them

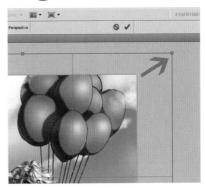

Drag the Crop tool's handles outwards to enlarge an image

The Crop tool isn't limited to just cropping your canvas, it can also be used to quickly increase your canvas size too. You can increase it freehand by dragging the Crop tool over your entire image, then extending the sides or corners of the area beyond the edges of your canvas. Another aspect of the Crop tool is non-destructive cropping. Ticking Hide instead of Delete in the top Options bar will mean that the cropped area will still exist but be hidden from view. Using the previous method to enlarge the canvas will make the hidden cropped areas of your canvas visible again.

Quick tip

Change brush size

When using the Brush tool, you can alter the brush size using the square bracket keys. '[' decreases brush size and ']' increases it.

Step and repeat with Free Transform

The Free Transform tool has a hidden 'step and repeat' ability, which can be used to create some fantastic effects. Here we have created a fleur-de-lys shape (using the Custom Shape tool) pressed Cmd/Ctrl+Opt/Alt+T, placed the pivot point in the centre of the canvas, then rotated the fleur-de-lys shape while holding down Shift. After hitting enter to apply this initial transformation, pressing Cmd/Ctrl+Shift+Opt/Alt+T repeats the transformation, with Photoshop automatically duplicating the shape on a new layer each time. Using this method ensures you get perfect pictures every time, and saves you a whole heap of time and effort.

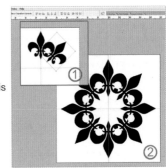

Colour monochrome shading with layers

It's easy to desaturate a colour photo, but many people think that it's much harder to add colour to a black and white one. It's not – in fact it's easy. You can build up colour over layers, using blending modes to integrate the colour you've applied into the contrast in the black and white photo below it. All you need to do is ensure you've got a photo with a good, strong level of contrast and a palette of four-to-six colours which will look natural and complement each other. For this image we've chosen a peachy skin tone, a warm berry red, saturated forest green, dusty violet, blue-black and a soft off-white to add glowing colour.

01 Select your palette Go to Image>Adjustments> Desaturate to ensure there are no colour artefacts in your photo. Select four-to-six colours and place swatches of them on a layer above the photo. You'll use these to add colour.

02 Fill the larger areas Flood-fill the colour that will be most used throughout the image – in this case it's the skin tone. Erase areas which won't be this colour, then set the layer's blending mode to Color and the contrast from the photo will show through. Repeat for other large areas.

03 Paint in details Make a new layer, set it to Color and paint in smaller details such as make-up colours. For hair, Luminosity is a good blending mode to use to keep shine. When it comes to eye colour, use Hue to add bold blues or greens to dark eyes.

Tip

Get a retro look with halftone
Photoshop's Halftone Pattern and Color Halftone filters can produce a fantastic retro look in monochrome (seen here) or a Pop Art look in colour. Go to either Filter> Sketch>Halftone Pattern or Filter> Pixelate>Color Halftone.

Cut out backgrounds with the Background Eraser tool
There's a simple tool for cutting out plain backgrounds. Ctrl/right-click on the Eraser tool (PC) or click the arrow on the tool (Mac) and select Background Eraser from the menu. This will erase all areas of a single colour and tone. The Magic Eraser will erase similar colours and tones, to help remove slightly more varied backgrounds.

Use drop shadows for a 3D collage effect

Scrapbooking is a style of presentation which makes use of the look of traditional photo albums and scrapbooks. To stop scrapbook-style collages looking flat, add a drop shadow to elements to give them a 3D look. Place an element on a new layer and then click on the Layer Effects control (shaped like an italic F) at the bottom of the Layers palette. Choose Drop Shadow from the list and adjust its size and angle. If you're using more than one layer, Photoshop will change the angles and size of all drop shadows you've applied.

Work effectively with fonts
The simple tricks that will make font-based artwork look professional

hotoshop lets you use any font installed on your computer as part of your image, allowing you to create posters and typographic artwork. You can use the Move and Transform tools to place and resize elements of type to create a wide variety of text styles, but there are a few key things to remember when using fonts. The most important is to always rasterise your type. This enables the font you've used to show up on other computers even if the user doesn't have the font installed, and also allows you to use layer effects and blending modes. When a Type layer is rasterised, you can't type on it again. Ctrl/right-click on the layer and select Rasterize Type from the menu. Once you've done this, you can use different blending modes to integrate your type with the image, and experiment with layer effects such as Bevel and Emboss.

Experiment with type placement and layer effects such as Bevel and Emboss

Use Burn sparingly
The Burn brush replicates one of a traditional photographer's dark room tricks: giving parts of an image additional exposure in order to darken them. If overused, this brush can create unwanted pixelation. The Burn brush is best used on very small details. Try using it to subtly darken the line of the eyelashes in a portrait photo or for a quick way to create dark strands of hair.

Soft highlights with Dodge
The Dodge brush should be used almost as sparingly as the Burn tool, but in a different way. Dodge comes from the photographic technique of blocking light to parts of the developing image so that areas become paler. In Photoshop, a large Dodge brush set to a soft-edged variant can add subtle soft highlights to cheekbones in portraits.

Shine with the Smudge tool
The Smudge brush tool is a very useful one – try using it in images with reflections and shine to create a shimmer effect. Stroke sideways with a brush size of around 5px, pulling highlights into darker areas.

Using the Adjustments tools

Using the Adjustments tools under the Image menu is a great way to transform your photographs, improving contrast, colour and tonal balance. Once you have successfully applied an Adjustment this way, unfortunately you can't alter it without undoing the work you have done since. To make Adjustments without editing the original image, go to Layer>New Adjustment layer. Here you will find all the controls from the Image>Adjustments menu. They'll be applied on a separate layer above the Background, allowing you to change their blending modes and individual colour and tonal balance for increased creative control. And they won't permanently affect the original layer, saving you the hassle of having to go back and redo all the work you just did.

Change colours with Hue Shift

It's easy to change the colour of all or part of a photo in Photoshop, especially when you use Adjustment layers so that you have full control of the strength of the effect. One way to dramatically change a photo is to shift its hue using Layers>New Adjustment Layer>Hue and Saturation. Move the Hue slider through the spectrum to adjust the colour scheme – this vivid green 'springtime' shot is actually a bright orange autumn scene in its original state. Reduce the Opacity of the Adjustment layer or change its blending mode for a slightly more subtle effect.

Blending mode and layer mask smoothing
Create perfectly smooth skin

L ook around and magazines are littered with porcelain skin models. You too can obtain such smooth skin texture with this simple technique. Begin by duplicating your photo and pressing Cmd/Ctrl+I, inverting your image. Next, apply a Vivid blending mode. Select Filter>Blur>Gaussian Blur, applying a 1-pixel Radius. Apply a Filter>Other>High Pass with a 2-pixel Radius. Next, select Layer>Layer Mask>Hide All – and your effect has vanished. Don't panic, however, as it's just waiting to be unearthed.

Now all you need to do is select a soft white brush at 70% Opacity and apply to facial skin areas, smoothing skin. To exaggerate the effects, merge all layers – pressing Opt/Alt+Cmd/Ctrl+Shift+E – and repeat this step several times, applying a 90% Opacity brush. You can compliment this process with a little retouching of any visible blemishes, such as spots and wrinkles, using Clone tools before its application.

Quick tip

Soften edges with the Feather option

Select the layer edges, invert and apply Select>Modify> Feather, hitting the backspace key.

Use Liquify Filters to exaggerate facial features

The Liquify Filter (Filters>Liquify) is a great way to apply fun and practical effects alike. This tool is great for tucking in nose sizes, or inflating lips and enlarging, or editing eye shapes. The Forward Warp tool is great for the later, and when applied properly can reshape and sculpt facial regions extremely well. To get exaggerated eyes use this tool to tuck in lips and nose, making them petite. Complement this using the Pucker tool. The Bloat tool does exactly as you'd expect and is great for raising cheekbones and increasing pupil/iris sizes. Just remember whatever you do apply in this filter, its own Tool Options settings all dictate the severity of your effects. You can also apply masks to control your application, through five Mask Option presets.

Create sepia with Hue/ Saturation options

A simple effect once you know how to master several colour adjustment options together. Always duplicate your image first, before desaturating it, or if you have a CS version apply a Black & White layer (create new fill or adjustment option, RGB) to create better contrast. Next, select Image> Adjustments> Hue/Saturation. Activate Colourize, and set Hue at 30, Saturation at 15 and your image will now be sepia.

Controlling temperatures with Photo Filters

At times, especially when photo editing several stock images into a single piece and even in standard photo samples, overall colour tones don't match the theme you're looking to obtain. Here you should use a tool that dictates 'colour temperatures'. So, for example, if your image has a lot of yellow and hot tones, but you want to counteract this, you could activate Photo Filter from the Create new fill or adjustment option, applying a Cooling Filter preset. Vice versa for images that are cooler in tone, which you want warmer in mood.

"You can duplicate your layer to enhance image effects further"

Sharpening images using the High Pass filter

If you want a quick and easy way to bring out the delineation in images, yet not have the hassle of having to guesstimate effects of set slide bars, then why not use the High Pass filter on an image? Simply duplicate your layer, and apply an Overlay Blending mode. Select Filter>High Pass and apply a 1-pixel radius. You can duplicate your layer to enhance image effects further.

Combine photos in black and white

You'll find it easier to combine photos accurately if you desaturate them first. This allows you to adjust their contrast and ensure that dark areas, midtones and highlights are all matched consistently. Once you've got the lighting right, adjust the Saturation to reintroduce colour and then proceed with matching the hues of your image elements.

Invert selections for quick fills

You can change the background colours of images or fill them with gradients without painting over the foreground. Choose the Lasso tool and select the part of the image you want to keep. Go to Select>Inverse and the selection will snap to the rest of the background image, excluding your original selection. While the area is selected you can apply colour and gradient fills.

::: Create reflections with layers and blending modes

Once you've placed an element that will make a reflection and adjusted it, duplicate the layer twice, flip these layers horizontally and place them – remember that you'll need to consider the plane and perspective of the area the image is reflecting in. Then set one layer to Multiply at around 100% Opacity, 85% Fill and the layer above to Normal at around 60% Opacity and 80% Fill. The Distort>Ocean Ripple filter can be useful for water reflections.

::: Sketch on a Multiply layer

If you're drawing and painting an image from scratch in Photoshop then one really useful trick is to draw your sketch on a layer set to Multiply and placed above the background layer. Using Multiply means that the rest of your sketch layer becomes transparent, allowing you to paint in colour underneath it without losing the guidelines you've created. You can move and resize your sketch layer if necessary and also turn the sketch layer on and off to see how your image is building up underneath it.

::: Tweak filters for optimum results

Many people use Photoshop's Filters at their default settings but many – especially those in the Brush Strokes and Artistic categories – can be tweaked to produce a wide range of effects, giving you more control over your image. When you apply a Filter you'll often be taken to the Filter Preview window which will allow you to adjust levels such as the length and angle of brushstrokes. This will be previewed on a section of your image; you can click and drag to look around.

Create and use patterns

Use Photoshop's Pattern Maker to create your own patterns

Select areas from photos or draw your own design to create a pattern with the Pattern Maker

ou can make your own patterns in Photoshop and use them to create imagery like clothing prints. First, select part of a photo or draw a design and select it. Go to Edit>Copy. Next, go to Filter>Pattern Maker. Tick Use Clipboard As Sample, then adjust the width and height settings – these will govern the size of each tile in the pattern. Choose an Offset if you'd like your pattern to be slanted vertically or horizontally; leave the number at zero for a simple, straight pattern. The Use Image Size control will make your pattern the same size in pixels as the original design. Click Generate to create your pattern. Now go to the Pattern Stamp tool, select your new pattern from the menu and apply it to your image.

Quick tip

Use Spatter brushes to blend skintones

Brushes that make splatter marks are better for blending skin – they introduce realistic tonal variation.

Use the Poster Edges filter for bold effects

The Artistic>Poster Edges filter can provide some fantastic effects that look like woodcut illustrations, but first you need to make sure your image is optimised for this treatment. Choose an image with lots of contrast and bright colours, adjusting the Curves, Contrast and Brightness and Hue and Saturation if necessary. Use the sliders in the Poster Edges filter dialog to increase the size of the posterised elements for a really strong, bold look.

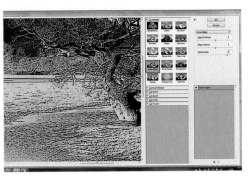

Miniaturise a scene with a tilt-shift effect

Tilt-shift is a style of photography which makes a scene look like a miniature model. You can replicate this effect in Photoshop with a few simple controls and a little bit of trial and error. First, choose a photo appropriate for a tilt shift effect – a cityscape seen from an elevated angle above the streets is ideal. This will give you a good amount of ground area where you can miniaturise people and cars while allowing for tall, blurred buildings in the background to increase the drama of the effect. Next you'll use Quick Mask Mode, a reflective gradient, and the Lens Blur filter to miniaturise it.

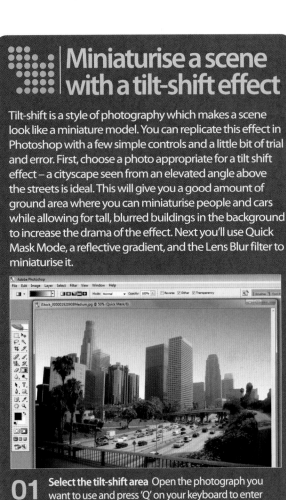

01 Select the tilt-shift area Open the photograph you want to use and press 'Q' on your keyboard to enter Quick Mask Mode. Draw a vertical line through the area that you want to be in focus and miniaturised.

02 Apply a gradient Hit 'G' on your keyboard and choose the Gradient tool. Make sure you choose the Reflective Gradient (fourth from the left in the menu bar). Apply this gradient; it will appear red over the mask.

03 Blur the background Press Q again to exit Quick Mask Mode (the red mask will transform into a selection) and go to Filters>Blur>Lens Blur. Tweak the settings if necessary for an optimised tilt-shift effect.

B0000026.psd @ 33.3% (RGB/8) *

Adding colour to a painting via a Solid Color fill layer

You can easily add more strokes of colour to a painting, and then experiment with the actual colour later by using a solid colour layer. Go to Layer>New Fill Layer>Solid Color. Choose black for the fill initially. Click on the layer mask attached to the fill layer and fill it with black via Edit>Fill. Now paint on this layer with white. To adjust the colour of your strokes, simply double-click the Solid Fill layer thumbnail and choose a new colour from the Color Picker.

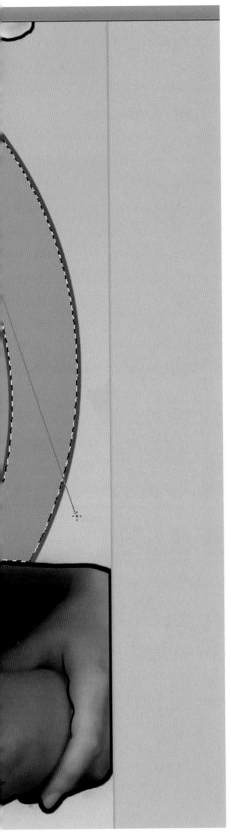

Creating a set of colour swatches

You can easily create a set of colour swatches from an existing image to use in a painting. Open the source image and go to Image> Mode>Indexed Color. Now go to Image>Mode> Color Table. In the Color Table dialog, hit Save, Save this colour set as an .ACT file. Now, open the Swatches panel and via the panel menu arrow, choose Replace Colors. Just navigate to your saved file to load the colour swatches.

Pressure-driven Opacity and Size

In Photoshop CS5, there are shortcuts you can use to set any brush to respond to pressure for Opacity and Size. You'll find these shortcut buttons up in the Options Bar when the Brush tool is active. Activating either of these buttons adds the pressure sensitivity to the brush and overrides any Opacity and Size settings within the Brush Panel.

Organise your favourite brushes via the Preset Manager

When you're serious about painting, you want your brushes in order

ou'll sometimes have a number of favourite brushes within the Brush Picker which are part of a much larger Brush Library, and perhaps you'd like to extract just a few of these brushes and save them to a Brush Library of their own. You can do just that via the Preset Manager. Go to Edit>Preset Manager. From the Preset Type drop-down choose Brushes. Click on the first brush you'd like to separate out from the loaded library and then Cmd/Ctrl-click any others you'd like to save. Now click the Save Set button and give your new Brush Set a name, saving it to a folder. Now, whenever you need this selection of brushes, hit the small panel menu arrow within the Brush Picker, choose Load Brushes and browse to your saved brush set file.

Quick tip

Picking with a click!

When using the Brush tool, you can choose a colour from your image to paint with. Hold Opt/Alt and click to sample the colour.

 | Creating a simple sketch for a painting, without any drawing!

If you need to create a quick outline sketch to paint over, but you're not keen on drawing, you can use a Photoshop filter to save you a lot of time and trouble! Open your start image and go to Filter>Stylize>Glowing Edges. Use a small Edge Width, a high Edge Brightness and use the Smoothness slider to filter out too much detail. Hit OK. Go to Image>Adjustments>Invert. Now, to remove any vestiges of colour, go to Image>Adjustments>Desaturate. Use the Eraser tool to erase any unwanted areas.

Magic Cloning with the Mixer Brush tool

There is a way you can use the Mixer Brush tool and the Bristle Tips to clone a painting over a blank canvas, rather than simply smudging on top of a photograph. You need to start with a photograph, double-clicking the background layer to make it editable. Now reduce the Opacity of this layer to around 3%. Add a new layer and drop it below your photo layer. Use the Mixer Brush tool with one of the standard round Bristle Tips from the Brush presets. Make sure that the Load Brush After Each Stroke button is deactivated that the Sample All Layers option is checked.

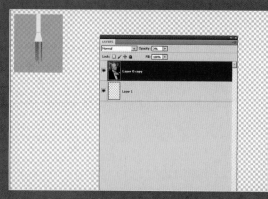

01 **Setting up the layers** Double-click your Background layer. Reduce its Opacity to 3%. Add a new layer, dragging it to the bottom of the layer stack. Now choose the Mixer Brush tool, deactivate the Load Brush After Each Stroke button.

02 **Perform the underpainting** Make sure to check Sample All Layers, set Wet to 1% and Mix to 100%. Choose the Round Blunt Bristle Tip from the Brush presets. Click on the lower layer and start painting with Flow set to around 80%.

03 **Adding detail** When you've finished the first painting stage, reduce the Flow slider to a very low value and start painting again to add back more detail. Use your brush at a small size in small areas to maximise the amount of detail you're cloning with.

Tip

Painting with creative colour using Color Dynamics settings
In the Brushes panel (F5), use Hue Jitter and Saturation Jitter found in the Color Dynamics section to vary the hue and saturation of each brush dab within a stroke, for an impressionistic colour effect.

Starting with a painterly photograph
When you want to paint over a photograph using the Mixer Brush tool, it's a good idea to give yourself a head start by simplifying the tones and detail first. Do this via Filter>Blur>Smart Blur. Use a small Radius value and a slightly higher Threshold value. This will instantly remove any unwanted photographic detail and immediately give your start image a much more painterly appearance.

Using the additional Brush Libraries in Photoshop

Photoshop ships with hundreds of different kinds of brushes in separate libraries you can load. To load these brushes, choose the Brush tool and click in the Brush Picker. Hit the small arrow in the top-right of the Brush Picker and choose the brush library you'd like to try, such as Wet Media or Dry Media. Choose Append to add these brushes to the brushes currently displayed within the Brush Picker or choose Replace to replace the currently displayed brushes.

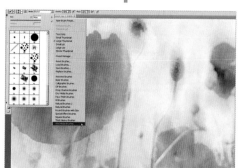

Add glowing colours to a painting

Using an overlay layer can be a wonderful way to paint with light

I t's surprising how the whole mood of a painting can be improved, and the lighting and colour intensified by using just one simple layer and a soft brush. By adding a new layer at the top of the layer stack, with its blending mode set to Overlay, you can add rich, intense, glowing colours in a completely non-destructive way over a finished painting. Once you've added this layer, choose a standard soft round brush and use it at very low opacity to build up these vibrant, glowing colours, choosing the colours to paint with from the foreground colour swatch. The real advantage here is that you can adjust the overall opacity of this layer, within the Layers panel, to tone down the effect, or even make a duplicate copy of the layer to intensify the effect more. Using very light colours on this layer is a great way to add highlights to metal surfaces.

Give your paintings extra shimmer by adding a layer and using a suitable brush

Effective spacing adjustments

Because each brush is made up from multiple dabs strung together to make a stroke, you can use the Spacing slider in the Brush Tip Shape section of the Brushes panel to space these dabs further apart. This means that using just a basic hard round brush, you can increase the Spacing slider to turn your brush into one that paints dotted lines!

Going for greys

If you're looking for simple shades of grey to paint with, display the Color panel (Window>Color), hit the small panel arrow in the top-right and choose HSB rather than RGB. Now, reduce the Saturation slider to 0% and use the B (Brightness) slider to choose whichever grey you need. You can also do this in the Foreground colour picker dragging the sample spot to the right and sliding it up and down the right-hand edge of the picker window.

Quick tip

Protect those textures!

If you're using a brush with Texture active in the Brushes panel (F5), tick the Protect Texture checkbox to make sure that this texture is applied to any other brush you use.

Manipulating tones via a grey layer

The finishing touches can really make or break a digital painting. Even when a painting is almost completed, you can still selectively lighten or darken tones within the painting by using a brush on a Dodge and Burn layer. Here's how you can go about it. Add a new layer from the bottom of the Layers palette and go to Edit>Fill, choosing 50% Gray for Contents. Now change the blending mode for this layer to Overlay in the Layers panel drop-down menu. Finally, you can paint with any brush at low Opacity onto this layer, painting with Black to darken tones and painting with White to lighten. Work with a soft, low-opacity brush if you don't want the effect to take over the image. You can always build up the effect as you go to ensure that you are getting the subtle tones that you want.

Making the most of texture

You don't have to print your finished painting on canvas to get a realistic canvas effect, you can use the Texturiser filter instead. Flatten your finished painting and duplicate the Background Layer. On the duplicate layer, go to Filter>Texture>Texturiser. Within the filter you can choose from a number of textures, including Canvas. Scale the weave of the canvas texture via the Scaling slider, and control the intensity of the pattern via the Relief slider. Choose the light direction for casting shadows from the weave by using the Light drop-down. Click OK and control the strength of the overall effect by reducing the layer Opacity.

::::: Using brushes to create abstract backgrounds

Often, a background in a painting can cause real problems, but Photoshop's wealth of brushes can really come to the rescue here. Often, all that's needed is quite an abstract pattern to draw attention to the subject itself. In this image, the Drippy Water brush – from the Wet Media brush set – was used, with a little Hue Jitter (set in the Brushes panel) to add simple, abstract pools of colour.

::::: Adding lines using a Solid Color layer

To add line work to a painting, and then experiment with colour options, add a Solid Color layer via Layer>New Fill Layer>Solid Color. Choose black from the Color Picker. In the Layers panel, click directly on the mask for the Solid Color layer and go to Edit>Fill choosing Black for Contents. Now simply paint onto this mask with white to add the line work to your illustration. Now you can double-click the solid colour layer in the Layers panel and adjust the colour of the lines in any way you wish!

::::: Use texture in your brushes for natural media realism

You can use texture with any brush, and it's a great way to create natural media effects. Go to the Brush panel (F5) and click Texture. Click in the texture swatch and click the small palette arrow in the top-right. Choose Artist Surfaces, choosing your texture from the loaded swatches. Adjust the size of the texture within the brush via the Scale slider, and use the Depth slider to control how obvious the texture is within the strokes made with the brush.

Building a painting from shadows through to highlights

Whenever you're painting from scratch, always work from dark to light, from shadows up to highlights, and preferably work over a mid-tone filled background layer. The toned background will help you judge your tones more accurately. Starting with the darkest tones in the scene will help you to establish the overall form of the subject and will stop you getting mid-tones and highlights too dark. Also, make sure to use separate layers for the shadows, mid-tones and highlights, and then you can always make a simple levels adjustment to each layer to adjust the tones on that layer.

01 **Blocking in the shadows** After your initial sketch, begin by blocking in the shadows within the subject quite broadly and simply. Make sure to use dark tones and colours here as these shadows will hold the whole painting together.

02 **And now for the mid-tones** Next, block in the mid-tones. These are the tones between the shadows and highlights and will give your painting form and mass. Once again, painting these on separate layers will mean you can adjust the tones later.

03 **And make sure to leave the highlights until last!** Finally, add in the lightest tones in the scene, to give the subject a more three-dimensional appearance. These rules apply equally, whether you're painting in tones of grey or in colour!

Have a try at painting with gradients

Learn a new way to produce images

By drawing lots of individual selections, and filling them with gradients you can create entire images

Start by tracing over a photograph to create an outline sketch on a layer over a photograph. Add another layer beneath this sketch layer. Use the Freehand Lasso tool to 'draw' an area to be filled with a gradient. With your selection active, now choose the Gradient tool. Select one colour for the foreground colour swatch and one for the background. These will be used in your gradient. From the Gradient Picker, choose Foreground to Background for the gradient type, and Linear from the Options bar. Click and drag over the selection to fill with your gradient. Create your entire image by filling with gradients.

Quick tip **Tracing over a photograph** Duplicate your background layer, fill the original background with white. Reduce the opacity of the duplicate layer and trace.

Blending brush strokes using the Mixer Brush tool

Even if you've painted an entire painting using the conventional Brush tool you can use the Mixer Brush tool for some careful blending. Add a new layer to your image, choose the Mixer Brush tool and choose one of the Bristle Tips from the Brush presets. Turn the Mix value of the Mixer Brush tool up to 100% and set the Wet slider to just 1%. Now you have a pure blending brush! Control the strength of the blending effect via the Flow slider. For super-smooth blending try a soft round brush, increasing the Wet value to around 10%.

Tips

Simple wash effects for adding colour to a drawing

The Wet Media brushes are ideal for adding a subtle wash effect to your line drawings. There are a selection of brushes within this set that work ideally on a layer set to Darken blending mode above your black and white drawing. Use these brushes at low Opacity on this layer to create subtle overlays of liquid, wash-like colour.

Keep taking the tablets!

A graphics tablet is vital for painting in Photoshop, but it's also vital that it's set up properly, so that you get natural strokes from your digital brushes. Have a look in your tablet properties (with a Wacom tablet you'll find this via the Control Panel) and make sure that your Tip Feel setting is set to suit your style. Generally, go for a firmer setting for more control over your brushes.

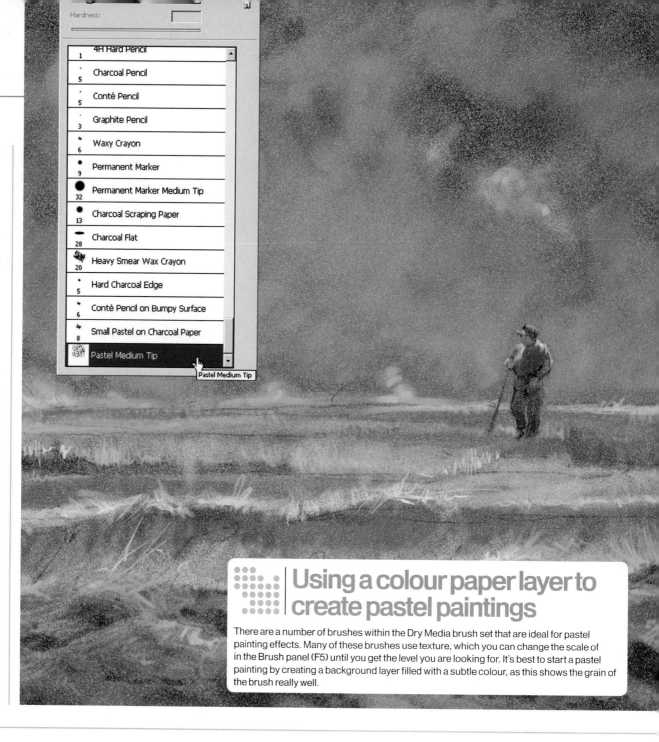

Using a colour paper layer to create pastel paintings

There are a number of brushes within the Dry Media brush set that are ideal for pastel painting effects. Many of these brushes use texture, which you can change the scale of in the Brush panel (F5) until you get the level you are looking for. It's best to start a pastel painting by creating a background layer filled with a subtle colour, as this shows the grain of the brush really well.

Adding colour fills to a line drawing

When you're colouring line drawings, you really don't have to do it all with brushes. Any areas enclosed by lines can be filled with a solid colour or even a gradient. Choose the Magic Wand tool and click inside the area you want to fill to select it. Now, after choosing a colour for Foreground, you can fill the selection via Edit>Fill, choosing Foreground Color for Contents, or even select the Gradient tool, choose a gradient and drag over the selection to fill it.

Simply smudging with the Smudge tool

Via some of the simplest methods in Photoshop you can produce paintings from photographs! Don't underestimate the power of the humble Smudge tool. Add a new layer above a photographic image and choose the Smudge tool. In the Options bar check Sample All Layers and set the Strength to around 50%, Choose one of the brushes from the Thick Heavy Brush Set and simply smudge your way to a painting on the new layer! The Strength value controls how much the tool smudges, so use this at low values for gentle smudging and high values to get really painterly.

Embossing for a painting effect

Give your paint some life!

Give your images a traditional effect and make them jump off the page

In oil paintings, areas of thick paint stand proud off the canvas. The same effect can be achieved in Photoshop. Flatten your painting and duplicate the Background Layer. On the duplicate layer, go to Filter>Stylize>Emboss. The Angle value controls the angle of the highlights and shadows within the Embossing effect, so set this first, making sure that Preview is checked. Use a small Height value for a subtle effect and use the Amount slider to control the intensity. Click OK. Change the layer blending mode to Overlay, and go to Image>Adjustments>Desaturate. Finish via Image>Adjustments>Invert.

Quick tip

Bristle brushes in CS5

Try the new Bristle Tips in CS5 for natural strokes. In the Brush Tip Shape section of the Brush panel you can adjust every aspect.

Adding lighting effects to a painting with a filter

You can drastically change the lighting and drama in a painting via the Lighting Effects filter. Flatten your in-progress painting via Layer>Flatten Image. Now duplicate the Background Layer (Cmd/Ctrl+J). Go to Filter>Render>Lighting Effects. Choose the Omni light from the Light Type setting. Size the light by dragging within the Preview pane and control the brightness via the Intensity slider. Control the depth of tone around the light with the Ambience slider. You can even choose your own light colours via the colour swatches. Adjust the layer opacity to reduce the strength of the effect.

Using realistic paper as a base for your drawings

Although there are ways to simulate paper within Photoshop, there's nothing like the real thing for that added touch of extra authenticity. There are lots of high-resolution paper scans available on the web for free, try **http://www.bittbox.com/freebies/free-high-res-grungy-paper-textures**. You could even create your own scan of some old paper. Once you've got your scanned paper file it's easy to copy and paste it into your drawing, adjusting the size of the paper to suit your drawing via a simple transformation. Remember, because the paper is on its own layer, you can adjust the tone and colour independently of the drawing itself.

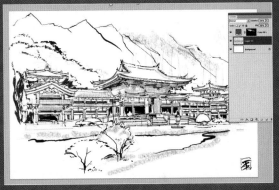

01 **Using layers properly** Create all of your drawing on a layer above a white filled background layer. It's important to work on a layer so that you can add the paper scan beneath it and edit the paper independently.

02 **Copy and paste the paper** Open your paper scan and go to Select>All, followed by Edit>Copy. You paper has now been copied to the clipboard. Return to your main image, click on the Background Layer and go to Edit>Paste.

03 **Size the paper layer to fit** To size the paper layer to fit, go to Edit>Transform>Scale. Hold down the Shift key and drag on one of the corner handles around the Bounding Box to scale the paper. Drag within the Bounding Box to position the paper layer.

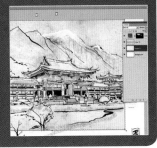

Stroke hose Paths!

You don't have to draw freehand with the Brush tool, you can use the Pen tool. Choose the Pen tool and draw a path. Choose the Brush tool, and select a brush to use from the Brush Picker. Choose your foreground colour and set the brush to a suitable size. Go to the Paths panel, right-click the Work Path, and choose Stroke Path. Choose the Brush as the tool and choose whether or not to use Pressure Sensitivity. A great way to create super-smooth strokes!

One or many?

When you're using the Mixer Brush tool, you can Opt/Alt-click to choose either a solid colour or multiple colours from your painting. To control which of these you choose, click the arrow next to the Mixer Brush Load Color swatch up in the Options bar and check either Load Solid Colors or Load Multiple Colors.

Using a greyscale underpainting
Paint like a pro using shades of grey

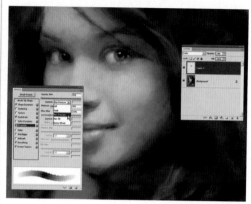

Don't start with colour, get the tones established and then add it!

ver centuries of painting, it's been a common technique for an artist to establish a painting in tones of grey before adding colour to it. This helps to establish the tonality of the painting first, without having to worry about local colour. You can do the same thing in Photoshop. Start by virtually completing your painting just using shades of grey and then add a layer above this painting, setting its blending mode to Color. Reduce the Opacity of the layer to around 30% and then simply paint on this layer with subtle colours. With this technique it's best to set the Opacity control of your brush to Pen Pressure in the Brushes panel, so you can control the intensity of your colours by using more or less pressure on your stylus. Use multiple colour layers to build a complex overlay of colours.

Quick tip

Clever Eraser
Remember, you can use any kind of brush with the Eraser tool. Choose the Eraser, choose Brush Mode and then click in the Brush Picker to select the brush of your choice.

 Saving all your Mixer Brush settings

When you're using the Mixer Brush tool with one of the Bristle Tips (both new to Photoshop CS5) and you've found a combination of Bristle and Mixer Brush settings that you like, make sure to save this combination of both as a Mixer Brush Tool Preset. This will save you loads of time in the future if you have created a cracking brush. Go to Window>Tool Preset. Hit the small panel arrow and choose New Tool Preset. This new Tool Preset will save the Bristle Brush and the Mixer Brush settings as one single preset which you can simply choose from the Tool Presets panel whenever you want to use this brush again. When working on any project in Photoshop, it is usually best to look at how you can save anything that you create, as you never know when it might come in handy for another project further down the line – you'll be super-prepared with a personal library of presets.

Enhance a painting by using glazes

Traditional artists will often add finishing touches to a painting by using thin glazes of translucent colour to add vibrancy and adjust areas of colour. You can do this digitally in Photoshop. Add a new layer and set its blending mode to Overlay. Reduce the Opacity of the layer to around 50%. Now paint onto this layer with your colours. The blending mode of the layer allows the underlying tone and detail to show through the glaze on the layer. Adjust the overall intensity by modifying the Opacity of the glaze layer.

Tip

Using Scattering for more natural brush effects

In the Brushes panel (F5) click on Scattering. Now adjust the slider to control the amount of Scattering used within the brush. This works very well with decorative brushes!

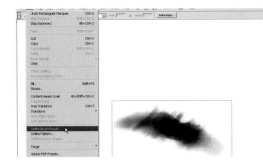

Create your own brush out of an image

You can make a brush out of any greyscale image. Create a new file, choosing Grayscale for Color Mode. Now you can use any brush to paint your own, custom brush and dab in black or shades of grey. Now make a selection around your painted shape and go to Edit>Define Brush Preset. Voila! You have just made a new custom brush!

Adding an Impasto effect with Layer Styles

It's easy to create a great Impasto effect using a Layer Style. Paint some strokes on a layer and go to Layer>Layer Style>Bevel and Emboss. Choose Inner Bevel for Style and Smooth for Technique. Adjust the Depth and Size sliders for the required effect. Choose Up for Direction. In the Angle clock, drag the crosshairs a little closer to the central point in the 11 o'clock position. Click OK to apply the layer style. Paint on this layer as much as you like. To re-edit the layer style, just double-click it in the Layers panel. Try changing the Style to Inner Bevel for a slightly different effect.

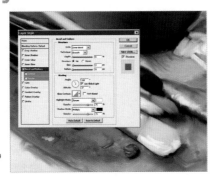

Using layer masks to create stunning illustrations from photographs

Use the power of layer masks to create paintings directly from a photograph. Start by simplifying the photograph via the Smart Blur filter, create a canvas layer and then simply use the power of blending modes, custom brushes and layer masks to reveal the photograph itself in a very creative way. By creating some simple round custom brushes made up of grey and black you can reveal the photo via the masks in a very subtle way, so that multiple, low opacity brush dabs overlap and combine to create a sophisticated, complex image.

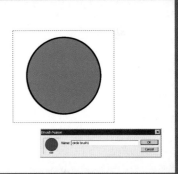

01 Create a custom brush First create your custom brushes. Here the brush dab is a simple grey circle surrounded by a much darker grey stroke. This means that the shades of grey reveal the associated image layer at varying opacities via the layer mask.

02 Hide with a layer mask Duplicate the background layer and fill the original background with a solid colour via Edit>Fill. Now set the blending mode of the duplicated layer to Darken and add a mask via Layer>Layer Mask>Hide All.

03 Paint with white Using white as foreground, use the brush with single clicks on the layer mask itself to reveal the associated image layer. Vary the size and opacity of the brush as you go, to build up a complex patchwork of separate dabs.

Use a path to place your text exactly where you want it

First use either the Pen or a Shape tool to create a Path. Switch to the Type tool and hover your cursor over the path. The cursor will change to the regular text insertion cursor with a small curved line through it. When you click the path, it defines the entry point for the text. Use the Direct Selection tool to move the insertion point or change the text direction.

Set custom keyboard shortcuts

Define your own shortcuts for your own way of working

T he best way to speed up your workflow in Photoshop is to make extensive use of the keyboard shortcuts. It may seem inconsequential at first, but the time it takes to find, point to, and click on a tool or menu item is sometimes entire seconds longer than the time it takes to press a key on the keyboard (especially if you have to mouse across a huge high-definition monitor to get to the toolbar). All those extra seconds can add up over the course of a project. Just learning to use a handful of basic keyboard shortcuts can give you a noticeable speed boost.

You can enhance this speed gain even more by defining your own shortcuts for the tools you use the most. Go to Edit>Keyboard Shortcuts to see a comprehensive list of the functions assigned to different keys. Find the ones you use the most and either memorise the existing shortcut or define one that suits you.

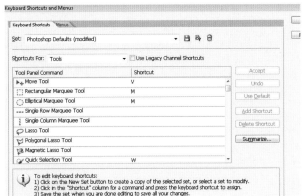

Create your own keyboard shortcuts for the tools you use most often

Quick tip

Quicker file open

Even faster than a keyboard shortcut! Double click on an empty area of the pasteboard (that's the grey interface area surrounding the document window) to get the Open File dialog box.

No nonsense layer copy

You can quickly create a copy of a layer without ever having to touch the Layers panel. Just hold down the Alt key (or Opt key on a Mac) while using the Move tool. The cursor will change to a double arrow and when you click and drag, instead of moving the layer you will produce a copy while the original source layer stays exactly where it was.

Auto Select layers

If your project has a lot of layers it can get frustrating trying to find the layers you need for the element you want to select. With the Move tool active, check the Auto Select box in the options bar. Now clicking on an element will select the layer it resides on. Dragging will produce a bounding box that selects all the layers it touches.

⣿ | Use Match Color to save time

Have you ever had two photos of a similar subject but one has a different colour cast? Trying to composite these together can be maddening. You can try to match them up manually using a Hue/Saturation or Color Balance adjustment layer, but

why not let Photoshop do the hard work for you instead? Open both documents and go to the one you wish to change. Then go to Image>Adjustments>Match Color. In the Source drop-down menu select the alternate photo with the correct colour. Photoshop calculates the differences in hue and corrects it for you.

⣿ | Lock down the transparency for easy editing

If you've ever had a layer that contains gradient transparency you've probably found that attempting to alter this layer with a painting tool introduces numerous headaches because reproducing the exact gradient transparency is nearly impossible. That's where the Transparency Lock comes to the rescue! You can find it near the top of the Layers panel as a small checkerboard icon next to the word Lock – engage that and the transparency values of all the pixels in that layer will be locked down. Paint away with the confidence that your layer's finely tuned transparency will be preserved!

Quick Selection tools take the pain out of some tough selections

Creating good selections has always been a rigorous process in Photoshop. The large assortment of tools designed simply for the task of creating selections speaks to the tremendous challenge involved. Even seasoned retouchers will cringe at the prospect of selecting fur against a similarly coloured background. The new Quick Selection tool makes great headway in the battle for the perfect selection tool. It's smart enough that it learns as you work with it, so it becomes more efficient as you go. Pair this with the Refine Edge dialog and its many available options and you have a workflow that can quickly select almost anything. Almost.

01 **Quick Selection tool** Grab the Quick Selection tool and set the brush Radius to a fairly low value to get the best results. Begin tracing around the inside of the shapes you wish to select. Use short strokes to grow the selection in a more manageable way.

02 **Shape the Selection** When the tool selects an area of the image you don't want, hold down the Opt/Alt key to change the mode to subtract and use it to remove the unwanted areas from the selection.

03 **Refine Edge options** Hit the Refine Edge button to get the dialog box. Each of these settings is useful depending on the subject of your selection. Use the Radius setting for fur or hair, and the Smooth and Contrast settings for crisp edges.

Switch between point and paragraph text
Let Photoshop handle line breaks

Fill any shape you want with auto wrapping text effortlessly

Regular text in Photoshop will continue on a single line until you look up and realise you need multiple lines of text. Instead of trying to do your own line breaking, use Paragraph Text. With the Type tool, drag out a bounding box to serve as your text block. Now the lines of copy will automatically word wrap to fill the block.

If you want to get more sophisticated, create a shape path with the Pen tool or one of the Shape tools. Grab the Type tool and see the cursor changes to indicate the tool recognises the path. Click inside and the shape becomes the text box and the text will refill the shape automatically.

Quick tip

Fill up your layer
Opt/Alt+Delete fills with the foreground colour, and Cmd/Ctrl+Delete fills with the background colour.

Use Mini Bridge to browse your files

If you've used Photoshop's partner program, Bridge, you know just how useful it can be for managing project files. It's easy to use, shows thumbnails for any graphic file, including psd files. It has a slider to adjust thumbnail size, and files can easily be dropped into Photoshop. What's missing? The ability to access it without leaving the Photoshop workspace. Enter CS5's Mini Bridge. It's essentially the Bridge application within a Photoshop panel. Now you can quickly grab the thumbnails of your resources and just deposit them right onto your canvas without the interruption of switching programs.

Spacebar move

If you are zoomed in on your canvas working on detail, you will probably find yourself needing to change the view to a different area. There are multiple ways to accomplish this (zoom out and back in, scroll bars, navigator, etc), but none are as fast and handy as the Hand tool keyboard shortcut. Just hold down the spacebar to get the hand, grab and move your view as needed, then release the spacebar to resume with the previous tool.

Color Picker trick

Photoshop's Color Picker is one of the handiest tools around. But the tool is even more powerful than you may have realised. It can be used to sample the colour of any pixel on your desktop, even the ones outside of Photoshop! Instead of a quick click, hold down the mouse button and drag your cursor over the program's edge. Watch as your foreground colour chip updates as you explore your entire desktop.

On the fly method of resizing brush size and hardness

If you enjoy painting in Photoshop, you realise how disruptive it can be to adjust your brush size with the slider in the Brushes panel. Try this tip instead. Hold down the Opt/Alt key and the right mouse button. You will see an outline of your brush tip. Gesture left and right to adjust the brush size, and up and down to adjust the edge hardness.

Two in one straighten image tool

Fixing crooked horizons has never been that hard to do: pull down a horizontal guide line, rotate the image until the horizon fits the guide, then crop out the empty corners caused by the rotation. But folding that three step process down to a single button is a significant time saver. Strangely, this feature is found with the Ruler tool (it's hiding behind the Eyedropper). Drag out a measurement line that fits the horizon in your photo, then press the Straighten button in the options bar and Photoshop takes care of the rest!

The King of time savers: Content Aware Fill

Learning to master this feature alone can save untold hours of meticulous clone stamping, patching, and layer overlaying. The main purpose is to quickly, easily, and seamlessly fill in a selection based on the area around it. Create a loose selection around the area you wish to edit. Then go to Edit>Fill (or use the shortcut of Shift+F5) and change the use to Content Aware. If you find the algorithm pulling in areas that it shouldn't, temporarily mask out those elements first, so that Content Aware Fill doesn't 'see' them and can't use them.

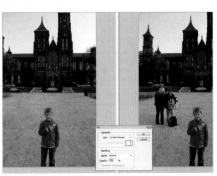

Boost performance with proper preferences

Stave off sluggish responses by letting Photoshop use more memory

I f Photoshop doesn't have all the memory it needs, things can start to drag. Nothing slows your workflow down like staring at a spinning cursor! So go to Edit>Preferences>Performance to begin optimising Photoshop's performance. The most important setting is the Memory Usage. The dialog box will list the available RAM and the ideal range. Allow Photoshop to use as much memory as you can within the suggested range. Next check that the Scratch Disks are enabled and have plenty of available free space. These allow Photoshop to temporarily use empty drive space while working. If your system can support OpenGL, you should use it! OpenGL lets your graphics card carry some of the load instead of your processor. This is especially important if you are using the Extended version of Photoshop and want to do anything with the exciting new 3D tools. It also allows for other features like on-screen view rotation and scrubby zoom.

Quick tip

Easy Screen Capture

Hit the Print Screen button to copy the screen contents to the clipboard. In Photoshop, create a new file and hit Paste.

Make life easy with clipping masks

Clipping masks are an easy way for one layer to 'inherit' another layer's visibility without creating a selection or a layer mask. Place the layer in question directly over a base layer. Hold down the Opt/Alt key and hover your cursor over the line separating the layers in the Layers panel. The cursor will change from an arrow to a pair of overlapping circles. Click and the top layer will indent. This indicates that the layer is clipped to the layer below it, and is inheriting that base layer's visibility. Multiple layers can all be clipped to a single base layer.

Drag and drop layers

To copy a layer from one document to another, simply use the Move tool to drag it over and drop it on. If you are using CS5's new tabbed view, drag the layer to the target tab and hold for a moment. Photoshop switches documents and you can drop the layer onto the inviting canvas. If the two documents are the same pixel sizes, holding down Shift when dropping the layer will place it exactly in the original position.

Tame the sea of layers

If you find yourself drowning in a vast ocean of confusing layers, use groups to get organised. Shift or Cmd/Ctrl-click multiple layers in the Layers panel and then press Cmd/Ctrl+G to fold them all neatly into a group. Not only does this help keep things tidy, but gives you some additional capabilities. When you add a mask or set the blending mode of a group, it effects each layer within that group.

Create quick and easy photo fade outs using a layer mask

To fade one photo into another, begin with each photo on its own layer. Target the top photo and add a layer mask. Make sure the mask is targeted (not the actual layer) and grab the Gradient tool. Select the Black to White gradient preset and make sure the shape mode is linear. Now click and drag in the direction you want the photo to fade.

"If you are drowning in a vast ocean of confusing layers, use groups to get organised"

Copy layer styles

If you want to apply the same layer style to multiple layers, add it to one layer and then in the Layers panel right-click on the little 'fx' style icon to obtain the context menu. Select 'Copy Layer Style'. Then Cmd/Ctrl or Shift-click multiple layers and then select Paste Layer Style from the same context menu.

Learn the blending modes

In the top left of the Layers panel you will find a drop-down menu used to assign the current layer's blending mode. These are extremely useful for quickly creating different effects. The first set of modes include Darken and Multiply and are used to render the white areas of the layer invisible. The second set, which includes Lighten and Screen, render the black pixels invisible. The third set, which includes Overlay, hides the mid-tones of the layer.

Work faster with multiple views

Don't zoom in and out, use two views instead

One document, two views. Keep an eye on the overall image as you work the details

There are times when dealing with the details of a project that you absolutely need to zoom in and work at nearly a pixel by pixel level. The problem with this is that you have to zoom back out to see how your edits impact the overall design. This can lead to a lot of zooming in and out that wastes time and energy. Here's a better approach. Open the Arrange menu (it's located to the right of the regular menus. Look for a icon that resembles the panels of a comic strip) and select New Window. Then select the 2-Up arrangement to display the two windows side by side. These are two views of the same document. Zoom in on one for your detail work and leave the other at a full view. You can see your edits automatically update in both windows as you work.

Quick tip

Auto masks on adjustment layers

There's nothing that saves time like skipping steps and getting the same result. When creating an adjustment layer, make a selection first. That selection automatically gets converted into a mask for the adjustment layer.

Snapshots are your safety net

The History panel holds the last 20 steps you performed in Photoshop. While it's useful, this can be very quickly eaten up if you are using any tool that requires painting or even just browsing the Blending modes. Attempting to reverse your file beyond that can be a very lengthy and frustrating process. So at logical stopping points, hit the camera icon in the footer of the History panel to create a new snapshot. You will see the snapshot thumbnail appear at the top of the History List. Now you can revert your file back to this point at any time simply by clicking that thumbnail.

Create better selections with Color Range

If you are attempting to create a selection based on a particular colour, don't try to do it with the Magic Wand tool. Instead, use the Color Range feature found in the Select menu. This gives you much more control over your selection. The Fuzziness slider controls how strict the selection is compared to the pixel you click on. Enabling the Local Color Clusters option allows you to alter the selection based on colour and proximity, which then is controlled by the Range slider. The drop-down menu even gives easy options for selecting the Highlights, Midtones, and Shadows.

Tip

Keyboard shortcut

The Transform Again command repeats the previous transformation and speeds up the workflow for designs that require specific spacing. Make the initial transformation, then press Ctrl+Alt+Shift+T (Cmd+Opt+Shift+T on a Mac) to repeat the transformation on a copy of the layer.

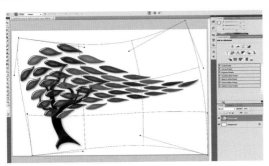

Smart Objects and Warp Transform – a marriage made in heaven

Warp Transform (Edit>Transform> Warp) is great for shaping a layer. After the warp is applied, though, attempting to edit it is infuriating because the warp handles reset. Instead, convert the layer to a Smart Object first, and the shape of the Warp Transformation Handles will be preserved.

Convert a Text layer into a Shape layer

If you are carefully forming letters for an intricate typography effect, this tip is invaluable. Make a copy of a Text layer (to keep the original unedited layer should you need it) and go to Layer>Type>Convert to Shape. This will change the Text layer into a Shape layer just like the layers generated by the Shape tools. This means you are able to alter the shapes of the letters by adjusting the Path Points using the Direct Selection tool. Just be aware that the text is a true shape now, and cannot be edited using the Type tool.

The quickest way to get real 3D text

The 3D text effect is one that seems to always be near the top of any list of cool designer-type treatments. To get the effect before CS5 meant either knowing how to use a 3D modelling and rendering program, or how to cheat it in Photoshop through an elaborate series of selections and manual shading. All that changed with CS5's introduction of the Repoussé feature. Only available in the extended version of Photoshop, this feature tops the list for useful tools that venture into the third dimension. It actually turns a Text layer onto a 3D object. No cheats. No tricks. No illusions. Honest to goodness 3D.

01 **Start with text** Create a regular Text layer using the Type tool. Be selective of your font choice – smooth, bold typefaces work the best. Text with thin lines or many extraneous elements will just end up causing problems later on.

02 **Convert to 3D** Go to 3D>Repousse>Text Layer. Photoshop rasterizes the text and converts it into a 3D object. The Repoussé dialog box invites you to customise the appearance of the object by setting the extrusion depth and behaviour, bevels, and materials.

03 **Render the output** Use the 3D tools to rotate the object into place. Light and adjust your scene as needed using the 3D panel (Window>3D). Now create a final render by selecting Ray Trace Final from the Quality drop-down menu in the render Settings.

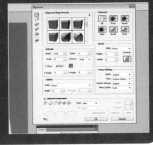

The magical luminosity blending sliders
Remove solid colour backgrounds

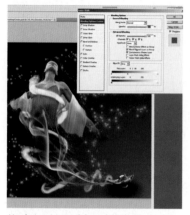

Use the Luminosity sliders to hide the black, white or specified colour channel from a layer

estled in an obscure area of the Layer Style dialog box is a frequently overlooked feature that can shave minutes off your production time. It's the Luminosity slider found under the Blend If section on the Blending Options page. The control is a greyscale gradient with a slider handle at each end. These handles control the visible luminosity range of the pixels on that layer. So if you slide the white handle in towards the centre you will see that the white pixels of the layer disappear. Likewise for hiding the dark pixels by adjusting the handle on the left. This feature really becomes magical when you hold down the Opt/Alt key and split handle to generate a soft edge to the transparent areas.

Quick tip

Create a composite layer
Press Ctrl+Alt+Shift +E (that's Cmd+Opt+Shift+E on a Mac) to generate a new layer that is a composite of all visible layers in the document.

Extend the canvas with the Crop tool

No need to fuss with the Canvas Size dialog box to get more space. It can be done much faster with the Crop tool. While that is entirely unintuitive, it's also quick and effective. Grab the Crop tool and drag it out across the entire canvas. Release the mouse button but don't press enter yet! Grab one of the sides or corners and drag it out beyond the document bounds. Now press enter and enjoy your newly extended canvas!

Photomerge makes creating panoramas very quick, easy and painless

One of the challenges of visiting a breathtaking view is figuring out how to capture the majesty of it within the confines of your viewfinder. One solution is to take several overlapping photos and stitch them into a panorama. That very process can be overwhelming to attempt by hand. Simply trying to match different perspectives and compensate for lighting differences and lens distortion is enough to convince anybody that there has to be a better way. Photomerge is that better way. Instead of the tiresome work being done by hand, it's done by Photoshop. While you do something else. What could be a better time saver than that?

01 **It starts with your camera** To get seamless panoramas you need to have the right photos to support it. Make sure your shots overlap by about 30 per cent when shooting, as this will give Photoshop more information to work with.

02 **Activate Photomerge Magic!** Go to File> Automate>Photomerge. When the dialog box opens, use the browse button to select photos. Tick Blend Images Together but the vignette and geometric distortion should be used as needed.

03 **Take a break** Select the proper Layout option, usually Auto is all you need, and hit OK. Photoshop will start crunching through the files and building your panorama. This might take a few minutes, so go grab a snack while Photoshop does the tough stuff.

Adjustment layers are Photoshop's own 'performance enhancers'

Adjustment layers are created to save you time and effort. They are the original non-destructive editing elements and remain as useful today as when they first came out. Using an Adjustment layer allows you to revisit the Adjustment settings and make changes without having to rework the image from scratch. They also allow you to easily copy an adjustment from one layer (or document) to another.

Non-destructive Dodge and Burn

If you like the ability to use the Dodge and Burn tools to enhance your photos but really wish they came in a non-destructive form, then try the following technique. Go to Layer>New Layer and in the dialog box change the blending mode to Overlay and check the box for fill with neutral colour. (If you are not using CS5 you can use the Edit>Fill dialog box to get a 50% Gray fill.) The new layer will not be visible, but the Dodge and Burn tools will work just fine.

Remove colour casts with a single click

Add a Curves Adjustment Layer and in the dialog box look for a set of three eyedroppers next to the curves window. Grab the grey-filled eyedropper (it should be in the centre) and find a spot on your image that should be a mid-level grey. Look for elements that you know to be reliably void of bright colours like a drab wall, road, or sidewalk. All you need to do is click that spot and Photoshop automatically cancels out the colour cast.

A helping hand when you need it

The Hand tool is an ideal way to pan around your images, particularly when you're working with them highly magnified. A more intuitive way of looking around your photos than using the scroll bars, the Hand tool is simple to use: just select it from the toolbar or press 'H' on your keyboard and click and drag to navigate around your image. There is an option to Scroll All Windows, which is excellent if you have more than one image visible in your workspace, as it lets you pan around them all at the same time.

"A more intuitive way of looking around your photos than using the scroll bars"

Speedy zooming

If you want to speed up the way you work, learning a few keyboard shortcuts will help you. A particularly handy one to know is 'Z' – press it to switch to the zoom tool at any time when editing your shots and you can quickly take a closer look at the image you're working on, without having to go via the toolbar.

Hold down Shift

Holding down the Shift key will unlock further functionality from many of the tools in Elements. For example, pressing Shift with the Move tool selected will restrict whatever object you have selected to move along a straight line – horizontally, vertically or diagonally from its original position. This is useful if you need to be precise about the new position of an object, or if you're replicating something within the frame for example.

Free Transform
Correct proportions and straighten out skewed objects

he Free Transform tool is invaluable for scaling, skewing and rotating either your whole image, or individual objects within your photograph. For example, a shot containing a rectangular object – such as a sign or tall building – may look distorted if you shot it from an odd angle. You can straighten out the edges by clicking Image>Transform>Free Transform or by hitting Cmd/Ctrl+T, with the area you want to alter selected. Grab the handles that are now surrounding your selection while holding down Cmd/Ctrl and manipulate the handles to skew your image and straighten out wonky boundaries.

Quick tip

Use hassle-free Automatic import

Elements offers an easy-to-use automatic importer that searches your hard drive for videos and photos, quickly importing them into the Organizer, ready for you categorise, sort and tag your files.

Organise your multimedia files with ease

Photoshop Elements is split into two parts: the Organizer and the Editor. The Organizer is the perfect place to sort your photos and videos into easy-to-navigate categories, making it simpler to find your files when you need them. Once you've imported some images, you can assign tags to them to make certain subjects or types of photos easier to find (for example, Uncle Joe, black and white, animals, architecture etc) and rate them (0-5 stars). You can also group photos from a particular event into one Album, for example 'Bob's Birthday Party'. Photos within an Album can be re-ordered by simply dragging and dropping them into their new places, making it easy to create slideshows and other projects from them later on.

Stitch several shots together to make a perfect panorama

Sometimes even your widest lens doesn't capture enough of a scene to do it justice. If you're faced with a beautiful sweeping vista that you can't fit into one frame, it's easy to combine a set of consecutive shots to make a panoramic image. Start by mounting your camera on a tripod if you can, to make it easier to line up shots later. Next, in manual mode, use your camera's meter to take a reading from the brightest area in the scene and select an appropriate shutter speed and aperture. With your camera in portrait orientation, take a series of shots, panning round slightly after each one but leaving some overlap to give Elements a point of reference when it stitches them together. About 20-25 per cent overlap is ideal.

01 **Pick your shots** Open up the shots you want to combine in the Editor, then click File>New>Photomerge Panorama to call up the dialog box. Click Add Open Files and your images will appear in the Source File list.

02 **Choose a method** Down the left side you'll find options. Perspective and Cylindrical are useful in really wide panoramas, while Interactive Layout is needed if the software can't align one or more of your shots.

03 **Generate your panorama** Auto takes care of everything for you. Ensuring Blend Images Together is ticked, select Auto and click OK, then Photomerge goes to work. Version 9 offers to fill in edges, otherwise crop off the excess to complete your image!

Tip

Match photo styles in PSE 9

With the photo you want to edit open, click File>New>Photomerge Style Match. Click and drag any of the stylised images open in the Style Bin into the image area to see its qualities imposed upon your original file. Tick Transfer Tones if you want the colours altered too. Use the Style Intensity slider to reduce or intensify the effect and play with the other sliders to create the right look.

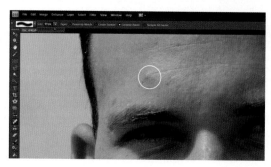

Clean up any blemishes with the Spot Healing Brush

Give the people in your photos clear skin in seconds: with your image open, select the Spot Healing Brush from the toolbar ('J') and resize the brush to roughly the size of the blemish you want to cover. Choose a soft brush to ensure the edges blend seamlessly, then simply click the blemish and watch it disappear!

Add another dimension with 'out-of-bounds' effects

To add a 3D look, open your image in the Editor and click on the Guided tab, then select Out Of Bounds from the Fun Edits section (version 9). To select the area you want to 'protrude' from your shot, click 'Add a frame', then drag and resize the selection over your subject, leaving some of it outside the box. Hold down Cmd/Ctrl+Opt/Alt+Shift and drag one of the corners to add some perspective, clicking the green tick when done. Use the Quick Selection tool to draw around the part of your subject you want to extend outside of the frame, holding down Opt/Alt and clicking on areas you've selected by mistake to remove them from your selection. Once you're happy click Create Out of Bounds.

A RAW deal

Perfect the exposure in RAW files from your camera in Elements

I f your camera offers this functionality, shooting RAW files lets you really make the most of the image quality offered by your sensor. RAW files are the digital equivalent of negatives: they contain all of the raw, unprocessed information captured by the sensor at the time you took the photo: they contain more data than JPEGs and – as such – can take more manipulation in the digital darkroom. Open a RAW file in PSE and it should launch Adobe Camera RAW – downloadable for free from **www.adobe.com/downloads**. Alongside a preview window, a set of sliders let you perfect the exposure in your shot. Start with White Balance – a range of presets similar to those you find in your camera's menu are available, so choose the one that gives the tones you want, or set the colour temperature

Use the free Adobe Camera RAW plug-in to process your digital negatives with ease

using the slider. Use the remaining controls to perfect the exposure, using the Recovery control to reveal detail in slightly overexposed areas and Fill Light to lift the shadows, then Clarity, Vibrance and Saturation to adjust the level of detail and the colours.

Quick tip

Straighten out wonky horizons

Choose the Straighten tool and select Grow or Shrink Canvas to Fit. Use the tool to draw along the edge you want to straighten and the image will rotate. With the Crop tool, trim the edges of the frame, then hit Enter.

Sharpen photos like a pro

Unsharp Mask is one of the best sharpening methods available in Elements. With your image open in the Editor, click Enhance>Unsharp Mask and tick Preview. Amount refers to the degree by which you want the software to increase the contrast between neighbouring pixels. For print, 150-200% is a good starting point. Radius determines the number of pixels surrounding edges in your shot will be sharpened – go for 1-2 to keep results looking natural. Threshold tells the software how far away from an edge sharpened pixels can be – experiment until you have the result you're happy with, keeping this value below 20 where possible.

Improve skin tones with just one click

It's best to attempt this with a properly calibrated monitor for the best results. With your portrait open, duplicate the background layer (Cmd/Ctrl+J). In the Enhance menu, choose Adjust Color>Adjust Color for Skin Tone... and a dialog box will appear with three steps to follow. Start by clicking an area of the person's skin in your photo – try to avoid choosing an area with a lot of obvious make-up applied as this may affect the result – the forehead is usually a good place to start. The sliders will automatically adjust to reflect your selection – move them to fine-tune if necessary. If things start looking odd, hit Reset to start again, or if you're happy, click OK to see the corrected image in its full glory.

The clever brush

The Smart Brush tool – which first appeared in version 7 – lets you perform a range of tasks that would otherwise prove tricky. Pick an effect from the pop-up menu that appears when you select the tool, refine the selection that the tool makes if necessary, and then see the effect applied to your final image in real time.

Go into more detail

If you want to be more precise about where an effect is applied, select the Detail Smart Brush from the toolbox. This tool doesn't make an automatic selection for you, so your chosen effect will only appear where you paint onto your image, giving you more control over tasks like selectively colouring a black and white shot or brightening up a dark sky for example.

Remove unwanted objects

Clean up your shots with an innovative new tool introduced in Elements 9

The excellent new Content Aware Healing feature – new to Elements 9 – allows you to clean up distracting dust spots or remove unwanted objects from your images completely automatically. Take advantage of this technology not just when cleaning up skin in portraits, but also on occasions where you have large objects like lampposts or people to remove. With the shot you want to fix open in the Editor, select the Spot Healing brush. Choose a hard brush but leave the size the same for now – we'll adjust that momentarily. Select Content Aware for the Type to take advantage of this excellent new technology, which will manipulate the pixels surrounding the area you're cleaning up to give a seamless result. Now adjust the brush size to roughly match that of the object you want to clean up ([to make it smaller or] to make it larger). A dark spot will appear initially, before quickly being replaced with your newly cleaned-up pixels. Note how the underlying textures and tones are perfectly reproduced.

Use the new Content Aware Healing functionality in PSE 9 to achieve flawless results when removing objects from images

Quick tip

Take action!

From version 7 onwards, Elements comes with the facility to install and run Actions to help automate tasks. You can install your own Actions created in Photoshop as long as Elements supports the features recorded in those Actions – access them via the Editor's Guided tab.

A High Dynamic Range image

High Dynamic Range (HDR) images comprise at least two photos of the same scene, taken at different exposures to expand the dynamic range captured. The shots making up the final image need to line up as perfectly as possible for the best results, so it's a good idea to mount your camera on a tripod if you have one. Once you have your images, open them in the Editor, then click File>New>Photomerge Exposure, followed by Open All. Use the sliders to fine tune the appearance of your final image, or choose Simple Blending for an automatic fix, clicking Done when you're finished.

Add an atmospheric reflection to images

PSE 9 offers a Guided Edit that lets you add a reflection to any image and manipulate its properties to create a realistic result. Find a shot in the Organizer that you think would suit having a reflection added – landscapes tend to work well. Open it in the Editor and select Guided Edit, choosing Reflection from the Fun Edits. Click the Add Reflection button to extend the canvas automatically, then use the Eyedropper to choose your background colour and Fill Background to apply it. Now choose an effect to make it look more realistic – we chose Water Reflection for this shot – and use the sliders to adjust the intensity and distortion. Finally, use the Crop tool to trim off the excess and click and drag the Gradient tool if you wish to add a gradient to your reflection.

Use Photomerge Exposure in Manual mode for advanced blending

Open your selected images in the Photomerge Exposure editor as before, then click the Manual tab. Drag your background image from the Project Bin and your Source image into the left pane. Use the Selection tool to add areas of your source image to your Background image, removing mistakes with the Eraser. Tick Edge Blending and adjust the transparency for a smoother result, then click Done.

Share albums on the web

Upload your images to the Organizer and click Share. Depending on your version of Elements, you'll have a range of options. The latest version offers the option of sharing directly to sites like Flickr, Facebook and SmugMug, as well as creating an online album, so just follow the steps and get your photos on the web in a flash – perfect for sharing images with family and friends!

Make light work of processing multiple files

Elements offers batch processing. Click File>Process Multiple Files, then choose the file containing the shots you want to develop. Set the destination folder, enter the dimensions you want your shots to be and choose the file type if you want this to change. You can also choose to add a watermark and there's the option of performing some basic edits. Click OK when you're done.

> "Use a black brush to paint over the areas you want to hide – choose unusual ones to create interesting effects"

Use non-destructive edits to create a custom border

With a source image open in the Editor, hit Cmd/Ctrl+A to select your whole image, then Cmd/Ctrl+Shift+J to cut it to a new layer. Select your new layer and click Add Layer Mask. Use a black brush to paint over the areas you want to hide – choose from the selection of unusual shaped ones in the menu to create a range of interesting effects. Simply paint around the edges of the image, correcting mistakes by painting with a white brush instead and adjusting the Opacity if desired.

Master selections for localised adjustments

Elements provides a range of tools to help you make selections. Pick the image you want to alter and open it in the Editor. Shapes with straight lines suit the Polygonal Lasso tool or the Rectangular Marquee tool, however for something more complicated, choose the Magnetic Lasso tool. It will try to detect the edge of your subject,

sticking to those edges as you draw around it. This works best if you have plenty of contrast between your subject and the background. Once you're back at the point you started, a small circle appears – click to close your selection, before applying your localised edits.

Find friends quickly using Automatic People Recognition

This automated feature was introduced in Elements 8 – the software analyses your images, searching for those with people in them, then allowing you to tag them to make them easier to locate later. In the Organizer click the View menu and make sure Show People Recognition is ticked. Click on an image for a closer look and you should find the software has recognised there's a person in the frame, surrounding their face with a white box. Click the text that reads 'Who is this?' and type in the person's name – a tag will be created in the Tag list. Go to your next image and repeat to add a new person and, eventually, Elements should 'learn' what certain people look like, allowing for automatic tagging to take place.

One-step teeth whitening

Use the Smart Brush tool to give any subject sparkling pearly whites

irst introduced in version 7, this feature is accessed via the Smart Brush in the toolbar. Hit 'Z' on your keyboard and zoom in to get a closer look at your subject's teeth, then select the Smart Brush. From the list of options, select Pearly Whites, resize the brush if necessary and then click each of the teeth to create a selection. Use the minus (-) icon to remove any extra areas selected by mistake – the whitening effect is applied/removed automatically. Notice how an adjustment layer is created in the Layers palette – you can edit this layer to fine-tune the results, for example by clicking the colour thumbnail and selecting a custom colour from the palette, to ensure you get the shade you want.

Use the Smart Brush to apply a one-click fix and perfect your portraits

Quick tip

Your best shots

Can't decide which of your photos look the best? In version 8 or 9, the Auto-Analyzer will review your images for you!

Change the colours in an image with ease

The Replace Color command allows you to change the colour of parts of your image. With your photo open, click Enhance>Adjust Color> Replace Color to open the dialog box. Using the eyedropper, click on the colour you'd like to replace, before clicking Add to Sample and clicking any further hues that you want to add. If there's anything selected that you don't want to change, click Subtract from Sample and select those areas. Use the Fuzziness slider to fine-tune the extent to which similar surrounding colours are automatically selected when you click. Use the Hue and Saturation sliders to alter the colour and the Lightness slider to perfect the result.

Advanced technique: learn how to work with layer masks

Previously, the advanced method of working with layer masks was reserved for owners of the full Photoshop software, however the latest Elements release brings this ability to users. Although it is possible to unlock this functionality in earlier versions using plug-ins, Elements 9 offers unprecedented built-in layer functionality that will hugely benefit more advanced photo editors. Adding a layer mask makes it simple to make detailed selections and to produce selective colouring effects, to name just a couple of applications. We have chosen to add a selective colouring effect to a black-and-white image, which is achievable in just three easy steps.

01 **Duplicate and desaturate** To create your own layer mask, with your image open and the Background layer selected in the Layers panel, hit Cmd/Ctrl+J to duplicate it, then select your duplicate layer and touch Cmd/Ctrl+Shift+U to desaturate it.

02 **Make a mask** At the bottom left of the Layers panel, click 'Add layer mask' – note the white rectangle that appears next to your thumbnail. Currently, everything you can see is incorporated into your mask; to choose what's included and what isn't, first ensure your mask is selected.

03 **Reveal hidden detail** Select the Paintbrush, adjust the size, and then paint everything you want to reveal from the layer below. Hit 'Z' to zoom if you need to look more closely at the edges. If you make an error, switch the paintbrush colour to white and just paint over your mistake.

Correct common lens problems

Banish vignetting in a few easy steps

M ost lenses will generate some form of distortion, but Elements provides an easy way to rectify many issues, including vignetting and perspective issues. Click Filter>Correct Camera Distortion>Select Preview then choose one or more of the options to correct. Remove Distortion rectifies pincushion/barrel distortion – enter a figure to straighten out curved lines. Move the Vignette Amount to darken or lighten the edges of the frame and adjust the Vignette midpoint to determine the amount of the frame affected. Use the Vertical Perspective sliders to correct issues caused by tilting the camera up or down to take a shot, often seen in photos of tall buildings when photographed from ground level. Move the slider to the left or right, straightening out converging verticals. Horizontal Perspective helps to enhance detail in an image and combat motion blur or camera shake, while adjusting the Angle rotates the image to perfect the result after correcting the perspective.

Quick tip

Quick red-eye removal

The Red-Eye Removal tool offers a way of correcting this problem: select the tool, click in the centre of each pupil and you're done!

Generate faultless group shots with Photomerge

How many times have you opened up a series of group shots, only to find that someone's looking the wrong way in one, someone else is blinking in another? Combining these two shots solves the problem. To create a flawless image, select the photos you want to merge in the Organizer and open them in the Editor. Click File>New>Photomerge Group Shot, then choose the best image from your set that you want to merge other elements into. Now select the Pencil tool and simply draw around the objects you want to add to your final image, using the eraser to fine-tune your selection if necessary. These selections will automatically be added to your final image – easy!

Go full screen

Elements versions 8 and 9 allow the luxury of editing photos in full screen mode directly from the Organizer rather than having to launch the Editor – perfect if you only have a few small tweaks to make. With the photo you want to edit selected, hit F11 to enter full screen mode. A Quick Fix palette floats on the left side of the screen, revealing the editing options open to you. Work your way through the icons to perform your quick fixes and you're done!

Back-up your photos

PSE 8 and 9's Automatic Online Backup feature helps to safeguard your precious images by providing owners with 2GB of free online storage, to which your files can be automatically backed up – it's a useful feature whether you already back-up to an external storage device or not. Your online storage space is expandable up to 20GB, but you'll need to pay extra to upgrade to Elements Plus.

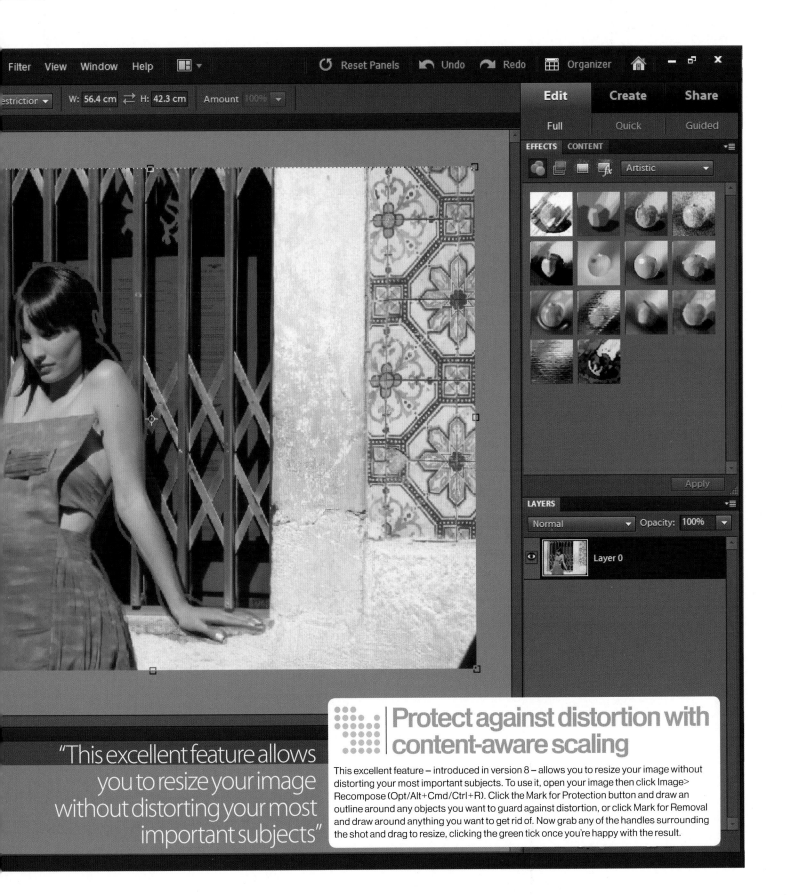

"This excellent feature allows you to resize your image without distorting your most important subjects"

Protect against distortion with content-aware scaling

This excellent feature – introduced in version 8 – allows you to resize your image without distorting your most important subjects. To use it, open your image then click Image> Recompose (Opt/Alt+Cmd/Ctrl+R). Click the Mark for Protection button and draw an outline around any objects you want to guard against distortion, or click Mark for Removal and draw around anything you want to get rid of. Now grab any of the handles surrounding the shot and drag to resize, clicking the green tick once you're happy with the result.

Tricks

070-173

In this section of the book we will be looking at a whole host of quick tricks that you can apply to your photos to take them to the next level. We'll be covering everything from tool tips to how you can add special effects to your images using just the power of Photoshop. Follow along with our features, tutorials and quick tips to enhance and improve your photos.

164 Selections
Learn how to select certain parts of your image easily so that you can make localised adjustments to correct colours in your photos, among other things

Before

After

92 Match Color
Copy colours from one image to another

Before

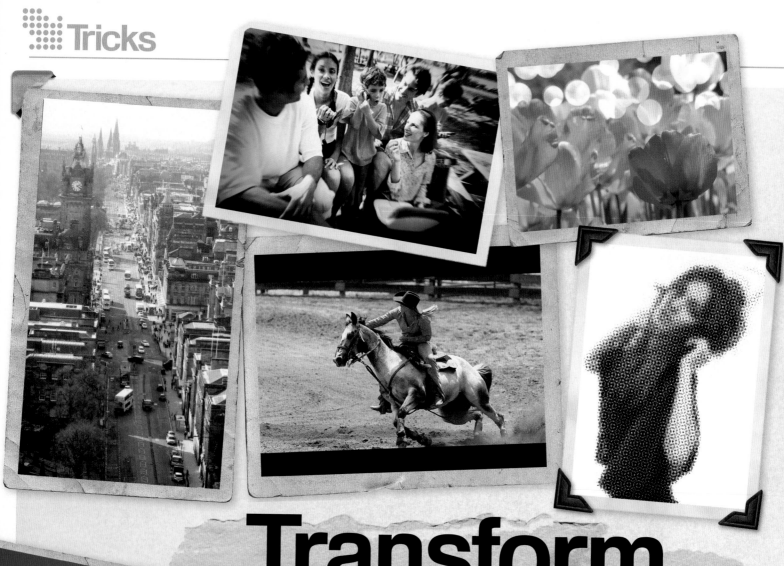

Transform your photos

Discover how to re-create ten traditional photo effects and turn your images into something special

n a time when dangerous chemicals were readily available, imaging had taken a turn for the better. This is when Louis Daguerre had invented his self-titled process, the Daguerreotype, founded nearly 200 years ago and kicking off the ten effects discussed here.

From the moment the world saw images captured on a solid medium, artists and their methods changed permanently. Painters of the past had interpreted the things they saw in their own unique way, and were sometimes found to be untrue to real life. But when the printed photograph exploded on the scene with its candid realism, its popularity quickly grew. From

> "From the moment the world saw images captured on a solid medium, artists and their methods changed"

cyanotype and halftone effects to the lith print and bokeh, we've given you a variety of styles to explore.

A large part of each effect is the texture involved, and it's this that makes each effect unique. Photoshop's Noise filter is a great feature for injecting a speckled texture into your image, or it's worth sourcing real-life materials to re-create the original look. Searching sites like **PhotoshopDaily.co.uk, Tutorial9.net** and **Noupe.com**, makes finding the right texture easy and inexpensive, although each site has its own usage guidelines.

So take hold of your mouse and get comfortable on your seat, and let your creativity wander through these ten defining photo effects in art's history. There are no source files, but each technique works on any image.

Daguerreotype
The one that started it all

When Louis Daguerre discovered the photographic process in the first half of the 19th Century, he must have been ecstatic. His invention for turning what we see in our everyday lives into a solid and fixed medium was an outright revolution, and art undoubtedly took on a whole new meaning.

Re-creating this unique effect in Photoshop requires a lot less patience than Daguerre himself must have endured. His new-found method required extremely long exposure times, and as a result, moving subjects appeared to be blurry and static subjects contained lots of detail.

What's most prominent in a Daguerreotype is its texture, which comes through the surface of a silver-plated sheet of copper used in its original form. Head to resource website **www.tutorial9.net** for a wide choice of metallic and worn surface textures, to download for free and apply to your image.

Daguerreotype effect

BEFORE

AFTER

Sharpening texture

01 Sharpen image Duplicate your image and head to Filter>Sharpen>Unsharp Mask. Set Amount to 180%, set Radius to 6px and hit OK. Go to Image>Adjustments>Brightness/Contrast, and increase both sliders to 40 to give more punch and brightness.

02 Metal texture Download a free metal texture from **www.tutorial9.net**; drag to the image. Resize (Cmd/Ctrl+T) to fit over the image, and change its blend mode to Lighten. Add a layer mask to the texture, and use the Brush, with 0 Hardness, 50% Opacity, to remove heavy texture.

Daguerreotypes were renowned for their fantastic texture that was created by the metal surface it was originally exposed with. To enhance the texture for this effect, once positioned over your image, go to Filter>Sharpen>Smart Sharpen and adjust the Amount and Radius settings for different strengths.

03 Vignette Create a new layer, select the Brush ('B'), and hit F5 to open the Brushes palette. Use the Stipple Dense brush from the Natural brushes set (access via drop-down menu in palette). Set to black at a large size, paint over the corners. Use the Eraser tool with a soft edge to fade the black paint from the centre outwards.

04 Scratch it up Use a mixture of Natural, Assorted and Mix Media brushes to apply marks and scratches to your image. Apply each mark to a new layer, and lower the opacities of each one. Use Edit>Free Transform to bend and stretch each mark as you go.

05 Adjustment layers Add the Gradient Map adjustment layer via the Layers palette, and set to black and white. Change its blend mode to Saturation. Add the Levels adjustment layer, and darken the shadows and brighten the highlights.

71

Cyanotype

Not long after the time Louis Daguerre had revealed his self-titled photographic process to the world, cyanotype entered the scene to present a more abstract method of image making. The cyanotype effect, consisting of muted blue-green tones and areas of bleached white, was commonly explored by artists through the late 19th Century. And not only by artists, but also by engineers who found the effect useful for documenting their plans, resulting in the 'blueprint'. A cyanotype image can be re-created in Photoshop using the Duotone colour mode. With the help of blend modes, the punchy effect can be successfully enhanced for that cyanotype, white and blue trademark look.

Cyanotype effect

AFTER

BEFORE

> "The colour version is created very easily using Photoshop's dedicated filter for the effect"

Halftone Use dots to create the image

The halftone effect was used mainly in the reprographic field through the second half of the 19th Century and into the 20th, using dots of varying sizes and spacing to resemble the true image when viewed from a distance. The effect can be somewhat mesmerising, especially in colour halftone where the individual CMYK colours are carefully positioned and overlapped, creating an out-of-focus illusion from close up.

In and around the Seventies, traditional ways of halftoning, involving screens, were surpassed by computerised methods used to form dots with spacing. We've split the effect into both colour and black and white to give you a taste of both worlds. The colour version is created very easily using Photoshop's dedicated filter for the effect.

Black and white halftone

01 **Convert to Bitmap** With your colour image open, go to Image>Mode> Grayscale, and hit Discard to remove all colour. Go back into Image>Mode and choose Bitmap to open its dialog box.

02 **Select your method** In the Bitmap window, set the Method to Halftone Screen and leave Output as it is. Hit OK to apply this stage of the effect, and the Halftone Screen dialog box should pop up.

03 **Set the frequency** In the Halftone Screen window, set Frequency to 15 lines/inch (the effect of the frequency will depend on your image's resolution), set Angle to 45 degrees and Shape to Round. Hit OK, and zoom to 100% to see the results.

01
Choose a channel Open up the Channels palette and pick the channel with the most contrast. Ctrl/right-click and select Duplicate Channel. In the pop-up box, set Document to New and hit OK. In this new document, set Image>Mode>Grayscale.

02
Cover with blue Go to Image>Mode> Duotone, and set Type to Tritone. For Ink 1, open its colour palette and input '0994ff' into the # field. For the remaining two inks, set one with Pantone 633 EC and the other with Pantone 3115 EC (both of these are in the Color Bridge CMYK set).

03
Apply blend mode Drag the image's layer onto the Create New Layer icon to duplicate. Change the duplicate's blend mode to Hard Light, and lower its Opacity to 50%. This should strengthen the effect. Create a blank layer, Edit>Fill with white, and add a layer mask. Use the Brush tool with a large Chalk tip and erase the centre to form a frame.

Polaroid

The Polaroid camera will always be remembered for its nostalgia inducing emotions. It's also well known for its all-in-one processing, framing a photo in a square window of off-white card. It was a revolution in its own right, taking photography one step closer to instant image making. The trick behind the Polaroid effect is creating the paper that borders your photo, framing your image just above centre. For the more aged Polaroid effect, try increasing the yellow tones by going to Image>Adjustments>Color Balance and shifting the Yellow/Blue slider to the left.

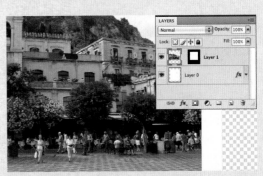

01
Create a background Create a document 18cm wide by 22cm high. Double-click the layer to make it editable, then open Layer Styles. Select Color Overlay and pick a creamy tone. Go to Image>Canvas Size, and expand the dimensions by 5 for Width and Height. Drag an image onto the canvas and resize using Cmd/Ctrl+T. Use the Rectangular Marquee tool to draw a square, leaving a thin border top and sides. Click the Add Layer Mask button and also the small 'chain link' between the layer mask and image's thumbnail. Move your image into place.

Instant colour halftone
Use Photoshop's dedicated filter to get exactly the effect you want

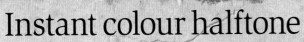

Colour halftone process

Photoshop has a dedicated filter for colour halftoning, making this a very quick effect to apply. Go to Filter>Pixelate>Color Halftone, and in the Max Radius field enter 30 and hit OK. Your image is now split into dots of CMYK colour, but if the dots appear too small or big, increase the Max Radius number. The resolution of your image will affect the number of dots created for the effect, so it's worth experimenting with settings for the right balance – but make sure your image is still recognisable from a distance.

02
Further layer styles
Double-click the image's layer, and in the Layer Style menu select Stroke with a Size of 3px, then hit OK. Double-click on the background layer with the Color Overlay, and apply a Drop Shadow layer style, with Opacity 75%, Distance 23px, Size 35px and Angle set to 120 degrees.

Cross processing

Most likely to have been discovered by mistake, the cross processing effect was originally created by running a roll of colour negative film through the wrong processing chemicals. A waste of chemicals, we hear you say? This surprisingly wasn't the case, as the results showed rather peculiar colour variations and hues, especially noticeable in the shadow tones of the image.

A sense of realism is still present, but with a shift of artistic meaning. This is perhaps why it stuck in the hearts of traditional artists throughout the Seventies and into the Nineties, and now it's been reincarnated using Photoshop. Here's how this effect can be reproduced in all its glory.

BEFORE

"The effect was originally created by running a roll of colour negative film through the wrong chemicals"

Cross processing effect

AFTER

01 **Apply red** Go to Layer>New Adjustment Layer>Curves to apply non-destructive colour editing. Select the Red channel, and create a narrow 'S' shape by dragging the line of the graph. The amount of red variation is down to personal preference.

02 **Adjust green** Select the Green channel from inside the Curves adjustment layer and apply a similar 'S' shape to the Red. The more the curve is moved, the more contrast and colour will be added to your image.

03 **Increase Blue** Select the Blue channel and apply a reverse 'S' shape to the graph from the one done with the Red and Green channels. This gives the shadows in your image a tint of blue distinctive in cross processing.

04 **Apply a blend mode** Change the adjustment layer's blending mode to Color to bring more details back into the shadow areas of your image. If the colours in your image need tweaking, click back on the adjustment layer to edit RGB channels separately.

05 **Boost contrast** Add a Brightness/Contrast adjustment layer and increase the Contrast slider to 30. This gives your image the authenticity needed, with high contrast tones and tinted shadows.

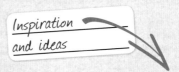

Inspiration and ideas

To see lots of cross processed images, head to photo-sharing website **www.flickr.com**, and simply enter the name of the effect in the search field. This will bring up thousands of thumbnails that have had this effect used by many different artists. This is a great place for inspiration for your own cross processed image.

Lith print

Lith effect
before

AFTER

Lith printing dipped in and out of artistic interest throughout the chemical-based darkroom era of photography. The original processes were very difficult to control and duplicate, but to this day the lith print effect has refused to go out of fashion. This is because of its distinctive artistic appeal, and Photoshop is the saviour of this modest yet powerful style.

A key point to remember when creating your lith print is placing emphasis on the contrast of the highlights and shadows. A unique characteristic of the lith print is its ability to have soft and glowing highlights next to harsh, dark shadows. Another trait of the lith print is its rich texture complementing the warm tones.

01 **The lith tone** Duplicate your image's layer and head to Image> Adjustments>Hue/Saturation. Before making any adjustments, tick the Colorize box. Set the Hue slider to 40 and Saturation to 30. Hit OK to apply the lith tone.

02 **Add texture** Duplicate the top layer and go to Filter>Noise>Add Noise. Select the Uniform box, tick Monochromatic and set the Amount slider to 30%. Hit OK. Reduce this layer's Opacity to 30% to soften the texture. Apply the Gaussian Blur filter, Radius 1.5, to soften further.

03 **Vignette** Hit Create New Layer. Go to Edit>Fill; set to black. With the Elliptical Marquee, draw an oval selection over the image; hit Shift+Cmd/Ctrl+I to invert. Apply a layer mask, set layer blending to Soft Light. With a black soft brush, remove the inner edge to create a vignette.

Lomograph

Founded in the early Nineties, Lomography has risen to much success with artists looking for that alternative effect. The company, which produces the 'Lomo' camera, has a lot to offer in terms of artistic output, as each camera has its own unique arrangement of optics for producing different effects.

Lomography is an inexpensive and friendly way for visual artists to explore a more expressive method of capturing images. Photoshop has that important flexibility needed for re-creating its effects to any heights. We've gone for the blurry and discoloured effect, but your options are wide open when in comes to Lomography.

01 **Blur** Drag the background layer to Create New Layer to copy. Go to Filter>Blur>Radial Blur; enter 15 in Amount, set Method to Zoom, and Quality Best. Apply a layer mask; use a large soft brush to remove blur from the centre.

02 **Channels** Create a layer and use a black, large soft brush to paint a vignette. Lower the layer Opacity to 50%. Go to Layer>New Adjustment Layer> Channel Mixer; adjust Red/Green Output Channels colour

03 **Add noise** Duplicate the background layer and go to Filter> Noise>Add Noise. Enter 10 for Amount, set to Uniform and Monochromatic. Apply the same Noise filter to the layer with the Radial Blur.

Cinematic

There's something special about the big screen that we simply can't stop adoring. It's the capture of a moment with incredible depth and detail, and it's not too dissimilar to that of high dynamic range imaging. What's the secret? Mainly it lies within the framing of the image, whether that's using a 16:9 ratio or a more square format. Here we've gone for the widescreen look with the 16:9 format, and have added the ratio's synonymous black letter box border.

Sharpening and applying noise are two elements not to be forgotten when creating the cinematic effect. An image with a blurred background works best too, and this also works well with a moving subject.

Cinematic effect

01 Cinematic proportions Select the Crop tool, and in the Options bar set Width to 16 inches and Height 9 inches. Crop your image with these dimensions with the best composition. Double-click its layer to make it editable.

02 Insert bars Create a new layer and drag it to the bottom of the layer stack. Go to Image>Canvas Size, and set Height to just over one third of the height of your overall image (see Current Size). Go to Edit>Fill and set Contents to Black, then hit OK.

03 Add film grain Drag the image's layer onto the Create New Layer button to duplicate. Go to Filter>Noise>Add Noise, and set to Uniform, Monochromatic, with Amount set to 7% (the strength of the effects will depend on the resolution of the image). For the final tweak, use Unsharp Mask to add definition.

BEFORE   *AFTER*

Long exposure

The long exposure effect has existed ever since film photography was accessible to artists, revealing its creativity and sometimes abstract effect. Using Photoshop's Blur filters, such as Radial blur, you can create the effect of movement. Combine this with an image of a Ferris wheel and you have

what appears to be an image taken with a long exposure. In most photos of a Ferris wheel, the lights dotted around the edges of its frame and down each spoke will be blurry as it spins. This image of a stationary Ferris wheel is available to download for free from **www.sxc.hu**, with the image number '826566'.

Long exposure effect

01 Set up brush Start by selecting the Brush tool and setting the foreground colour to a light yellow. Set the brush to 0% Hardness with a Size of 21px. Select the Pen tool and carefully draw points around the outer edge of the Ferris wheel.

02 Illuminate lights Create a new layer, and when you've joined the two ends together, Ctrl/right-click and hit Stroke Path. Select Brush in the list and hit OK. Double-click the layer to open the Layer Style menu and select Outer Glow. Set to Opacity 50%, Spread 10 and Size 35px.

Bokeh

Bokeh is used to describe the shapes of the out-of-focus areas of your image. Take, for example, an image with lots depth of field, and in that area circular, blurry shapes appear – although distorted and colourful. This effect can actually take the form of any shape you desire, whether that's matching the blurred shape with an outline of one of your subjects or using a completely different shape.

In Photoshop, this effect is created using the Define Brush Preset command once your bokeh shape is made. Using the Brushes palette, you can scatter the shape and vary its size, as well as use the Gaussian Blur filter and blend modes to really complete the effect.

Bokeh effect

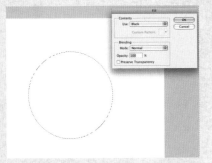

01 Create a circle Create a new white document in Photoshop of 10 x 10cm, at 300ppi. With the Elliptical Marquee tool, hold Shift to draw a perfect circle on your canvas. Create a new layer, go to Edit>Fill and set to black, then hit OK.

02 Add style Hit Cmd/Ctrl+D to remove the selection, and double-click the layer to open the Layer Style menu. Add the Inner Glow style, set to white, Opacity 85%, then set to Screen blend mode and Size 40px. Hit OK.

03 Define preset Delete the white background layer and go to Edit>Define Brush Preset. Give your new brush shape a name and hit OK to save. Open an image and create a new layer. Select the Brush tool, and hit F5 to open the Brushes palette.

04 Set up the brush In the Brushes palette pick your new brush, make sure Spacing is ticked and set to 25%. Tick Scattering and Shape Dynamics, and set Scatter to the maximum. Set Size Jitter to 25%. Apply the brush to your image and set its blend mode to Overlay.

05 Blur and duplicate To finish the effect, select the image's layer and use the Magic Wand tool to select the background. Click on the layer with the bokeh shapes and click Add Layer Mask. Try applying the Gaussian Blur filter to soften the circles.

03 Duplicate lights Duplicate this layer and move to the other side of the Ferris wheel. Use Edit>Transform>Warp to reshape the circle over the lights. For the spokes of the wheel, use the Pen tool to draw over each row.

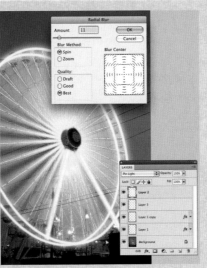

04 Light the spokes Use the same stroke as before for the spokes, but change the layer's blend mode to Pin Light. Go to Filter>Blur>Radial Blur, and set Amount to 11, Method to Spin and hit OK. To enhance the effect, simple duplicate this layer over and over.

"In Photoshop, this effect is created using the Define Brush Preset command once your bokeh shape is made"

Add distortion

To create an out-of-focus look to the bokeh effect, duplicate the layer with the blurry shapes, make sure the Overlay blend mode is set for both, and nudge to one side. Also try going to Edit>Free Transform (Cmd/Ctrl+T) and holding Opt/Alt to enlarge.

The Extract filter

Learn how this filter can be used to remove subjects

Click Preview to see the image with the background removed or OK to extract and exit immediately.

Tools for the job The Extract filter has its own tool set. The Edge Highlighter tool is used to paint around a subject, and when an outline is painted, the Fill tool fills the area with a faint colour. Now you're ready to go back into Photoshop

More tool options The toolbar contains Zoom, Hand, Eyedropper, Edge Touchup and Cleanup tools. When creating an outline to extract, try zooming in close to your image for best results.

After

T he Extract filter has been around in Photoshop since version 5.5, making it a well-established feature. The filter adds to the existing wide choice of selection methods presented in the toolbar (this is found in the Filters menu). It's yet another option, and like all selection methods, suits only certain types of subjects.

However, it's the Refine Edge command (first appearing in CS3) that has pushed the filter out of sight in CS4 and in the latest version, CS5. If you're using an earlier version than CS3, you won't be able to use the Quick Selection tool or the Refine Edge commands. This is where the Extract filter comes into play. The filter requires you to paint around the edges of a subject with what's called the Edge Highlighter tool, and you then fill an area with paint. The filled area is what you end up with.

Extracting large complex subjects isn't one of the filter's stronger points, and neither is extracting around areas where there's little contrast. For large subjects, it's a timely process painting around every edge at a very close magnification. Where we found the filter most helpful was for picking out small parts of an image quickly – and it does this very effectively.

Read on to find out to access the filter in CS4 and CS5, and how to use it for making quick selections.

Why the Extract filter?

The Extract filter is found at the top of the Filter menu, and separates itself from other Selection tools, as it uses its own window. When loaded up, inside the filter you'll notice a number of adjustments and tools specific to the filter. An advantage to using the Extract method is that you paint over the edges of your subject, and the level of precision

is adjusted with the brush size. There are touch-up tools too, and an Eraser tool to smarten up your selection. A disadvantage, however, is that the process of selection is very slow on whatever the subject is. We recommend using the filter for picking out small items in your image for a quick and accurate extraction.

Working non-destructively

The Extract filter works by taking a subject out of one layer and removing the remaining image. This means that when you've created your mask in the filter's window and hit OK, your image is permanently affected by the filter. The way to get around this snag is to create a duplicate of the layer you wish to work on before going into the filter. Drag the layer onto the Create New Layer button at the bottom of the Layers palette, and

then head to Filter>Extract to begin the selection on this duplicate layer. The original image is kept in a perfect state underneath.

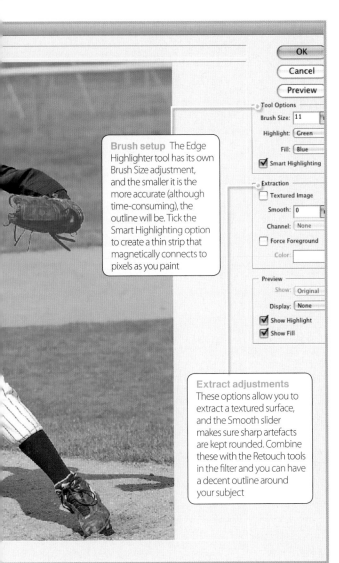

OK

Cancel

Preview

Tool Options

Brush Size: 11

Highlight: Green

Fill: Blue

☑ Smart Highlighting

Extraction

☐ Textured Image

Smooth: 0

Channel: None

☐ Force Foreground

Color:

Preview

Show: Original

Display: None

☑ Show Highlight

☑ Show Fill

Brush setup The Edge Highlighter tool has its own Brush Size adjustment, and the smaller it is the more accurate (although time-consuming), the outline will be. Tick the Smart Highlighting option to create a thin strip that magnetically connects to pixels as you paint

Extract adjustments These options allow you to extract a textured surface, and the Smooth slider makes sure sharp artefacts are kept rounded. Combine these with the Retouch tools in the filter and you can have a decent outline around your subject

Tip

Easy panning

When working up close with an image for an accurate selection, in order to pan around over your image without affecting any of the selection, hold the Spacebar, click and drag your image across the screen.

Select hair with the Extract filter

Selecting hair in Photoshop has never been an easy task, but the Extract filter does a pretty good job. Here's how to mask hair with the filter and its tool.

01 Duplicate and open
Duplicate your layer in the Layers palette to work non-destructively. To open the Extract command, go to Filter> Extract, and you should be presented with a large window with your image in it.

02 Create outline In the Extract menu, zoom into your image a couple of times and use the Edge Highlighter tool to paint over the edges. When you reach the strands of hair, make sure your brush covers the frizzy areas

03 Make the final adjustments
When the outline is complete, hit the Preview button. There may be gaps or rough edges around your subject, so use the Edge Touchup tool to shave layers of pixels from the edges.

In newer versions of PS

If you're a CS3 or earlier user of PS, you can benefit from the Extract filter appearing at the top of the Filter menu. If you're using versions CS4 or CS5, the filter has been removed from the menu and planted online at the Photoshop Updates section on **www.adobe.com/downloads/updates**. Mac users with CS5 will have to go without the Extract filter unfortunately, but we can recommend the Refine Edge command to be a worthy replacement. Once downloaded, install the filter into your Photoshop plug-ins folder and it should appear in the Filter menu after a quick restart.

Precision selections made easy

The Extract filter can be applied to a very accurate degree using the Smart Highlighting command. In the filter's window, under Tool Options, make certain the Smart Highlighting box is ticked before painting around the edges of your subject. This ensures the brush is pixel-sensitive, similar to that of the Magnetic Lasso tool. Zoom in close to your image to make an accurate selection to extract. This process will take much longer though, so it's worth doing on smaller objects.

Visualise effect Before applying depth of field to your image, assess which elements and subjects you want to keep sharp. Usually they fall within the same area for a realistic effect, but there's nothing stopping you mixing in-focus and blurry subjects

Depth of field with Photoshop

Learn how to re-create this classic photographic technique

epth of field has a big role in digital imaging. In fact, the idea of blurring subjects is one of the best ways to draw attention to or away from another subject. Taken from the photographic technique, the Lens Blur filter in Photoshop replicates the effect to near precision in no time at all.

What's more, Photoshop's filters can be manipulated to fit your image. For example, apply one dose of the Lens Blur filter, duplicate its layer and then apply another dose to strengthen the effect. With two layers of different levels of blurring, you can then erase areas of your image to reveal the slightly less blurred image underneath. This creates a more gradual depth of field effect, and is realistic as well.

For an accurate and clean depth of field through your image, make selections around the subjects you wish to control. Adding these selections to individual layer masks allows you to keep these areas sharper than the rest of the image.

The Blur tool is a great aid for 'painting' depth of field. Although not as in-depth as the Lens Blur filter, it works well nonetheless. If you're using Photoshop 7 or earlier, the Lens Blur filter isn't available. For a very similar replacement, try the Gaussian Blur filter.

Editing layer masks To make each layer mask fit with the surroundings in your image, the Brush and Eraser tools are used to edit the black and white layer mask in the Layers palette. You can blend in layers and the effects on them using these tools

Blur filters explored

Depth of field is created using the Blur filters (Filter>Blur), and although there are many within the menu, including Gaussian, Motion and Box Blur, the filter of choice here is Lens Blur. This imitates the real photographic effect made by a camera's lens, and does all the work for you. However, the Gaussian Blur filter is the next best thing, and throws the entire image out of focus in an even manner. Experiment with the Box Blur option too, as this creates a smooth depth of field effect with square-like blurs. If you have Photoshop 7 or earlier, Gaussian Blur is the best available option. For users of versions CS and above, the Lens Blur does just the job.

Shallow and extended effects

Depth of field can be divided into two sub-categories: shallow and extended. The difference is down to how much of the image is left in focus. If your subject is close up, then creating a shallow depth of field is your best bet. This puts most of your image out of focus, keeping the main subject the centre of attention. Using an extended depth of field effect places most of your image in focus. This is more suitable when there's a lot of distance between the foreground and background elements in your image, making for a more gradual blur.

Foreground to background Creating levels of blurriness creates a greater sense of depth in your image. Apply more blurring to the areas of your image that are further in the distance, and also to the subjects that are very close in the foreground

Using Channels The Channels palette is perfect for saving selections into, and the initial selection 'Woman' was used with the Lens Blur filter to make sure she is entirely in focus. The other black and white channel relates to the top layer in the layer stack

A hand-made blur

You can finely adapt depth of field with some help from the Blur tool. The tool does have its limits, but is great for tweaking specific areas. It lets you paint on the blur.

01 Set up the options
Choose the Blur tool and head to the Options bar. Keep the mode on Normal; set Strength to 100% for max effect. Pick a large, soft-edged brush with Hardness: 0%. Duplicate the background layer in the Layers palette.

02 Blur the background
Starting with the background, use the Blur tool to throw it completely out of focus. Keep applying the blur effect in a circular motion, and try to avoid blurring foreground elements.

03 Moving the foreground
Lower the Strength of the Blur tool to 50%, and blur the areas in your image that are closer to the foreground. It's a great way to create a gradual depth of field effect using a tool rather than a filter.

Tip

A time-saver

To apply the Lens Blur filter in small doses, and to save time going in and out of the filter once applied the first time, go to Filter>Lens Blur (at the top of the Filter menu) to quickly apply the effect with the last settings used.

Building layer masks With layer masks on all layers with varying amounts of blur, you can build up the effect of depth of field in a natural, true-to-life way. Here, the trees in the background have been blurred more than the foreground

Choosing the subject

The choice of main subject is important when applying depth of field. Commonly the effect is aimed at the main subject to give it the most attention, though this rule can always be broken. Try mixing it up by blurring the prominent subject in your image and focus on an object further in the background. This works best if your subject has its back to the viewer. Layer masks are really helpful in this scenario, as you can use the Brush and Eraser tools to quickly edit where the blur effect falls.

Utilising selections in Photoshop

Making the most of the Selection tools in Photoshop helps to achieve a more precise depth of field around your main subject. The Magic Wand tool is one of the most effective tools for our main image here, but depending on your subject, try using the Pen or Freeform Pen tools to draw around the subject that you want to keep in focus. The Magnetic Lasso tool is another great option for this purpose, as its slight roughness is great for the effect we're going for.

Tip

Intensify lighting

To aid the depth of field effect, it is useful to apply the Smart Sharpen filter to your main subject that's in focus. Once you reach the final step in the tutorial opposite, select the top layer and go to Filter>Sharpen> Smart Sharpen. Set the Amount slider to 70% and Radius to 6.5px. Hit OK, and the woman in the image should look brighter and sharper, to place more emphasis on the highlights and shadows.

⠿ A MULTI-LAYERED DEPTH OF FIELD EFFECT
Use filters and layer masks to selectively blur your image

01 Making your selection The Quick Selection or Magic Wand tools are useful for making a selection around the woman. Take the Quick Selection tool, set its Diameter to 9, Hardness to 50% and Spacing to 25%. Make the selection around the woman, holding Opt/Alt to correct stray areas.

02 Save As Channel With the Selection tool, Ctrl/right-click inside the selected area and choose Save Selection from the drop-down menu. In the dialog box, enter the name 'Woman' and hit OK. The selection is now saved in the Channels palette (Window>Channels) to load at any time. Hit Cmd/Ctrl+D to remove the selection outlines.

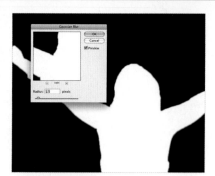

03 Feathering channel To add a soft edge to the selection just made, in the Channels palette click on the Woman channel. The image will turn solid black and white. Go to Filter>Blur>Gaussian Blur and enter a Radius value of 1.5px to blur the channel's edges.

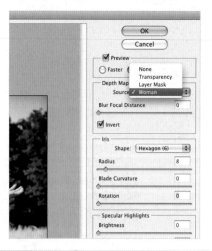

04 Apply Lens Blur In the Layers palette drag the background layer onto the Create New Layer button to duplicate. Go to Filter>Blur>Lens Blur, tick the Preview box and the More Accurate option at the top of the window. Set Source to 'Woman' and tick Invert. Only the background should be blurred.

05 Set Radius In the Lens Blur window, under Iris, set Shape to Hexagon, Radius to 8, and both Blade Curvature and Rotation to 0. Make sure Brightness is set to 0, and that Noise is also reduced all the way to 0. Hit OK, and your image should update.

⠿ Non-destructive blurring

Layer masks are ideal for creating non-destructive selections. They can be deleted to reset an image to its normal state, temporarily hidden or layered on top of each other. In this Technique, apply the Lens Blur filter to one layer then add a layer mask. You can edit the mask using the Gradient tool, or the Brush and Eraser tools make transitions of blurred and non-blurred areas. Copy this layer, apply the Lens Blur filter again, and edit the layer mask to blend in two blurry layers. Shift-click the layer mask to hide and reveal its content. Opt/Alt-click to make the mask visible.

⠿ Hiding the eyesore areas in photos

Depth of field is not only used to add impact and depth to your image – you can also use it to hide certain subjects that are a bit of an eyesore. Whether in the foreground or background, depth of field can blur a subject out of focus to the point where it becomes unrecognisable. This could be something that was too 'busy' compared to the rest of the image, or a subject that shouldn't have been there when the picture was taken. It can also be used as an alternative method of retouching an image – instead of using the Clone tool, for example.

06 **More Lens Blur** Duplicate the layer with the Lens Blur effect at the top of the Layers palette. Go back into Filter>Blur>Lens Blur and keep all settings the same, apart from the Radius. Slide the Radius adjustment up to 50. This is for the most distant trees in our image. Hit OK to apply.

07 **Blend the effect** Apply a layer mask to the top layer in the Layers palette (the one with the most blur). Select the Gradient tool and set the foreground colour swatch to Black. With the white layer mask selected, draw a vertical gradient line over the point where the field meets the trees. Don't worry about rough edges.

08 **Tidying up** We need to blend the join of the field and trees together. Select the Eraser tool and set its Diameter to 800px, Hardness to 0%, and set to Black. Zoom in 50% to your image and apply the Eraser over the tops of the grass and just at the base of the trees to make an even depth of field effect.

09 **More tidying up...** Apply a layer mask to the middle of the three layers in the Layers palette. Change the foreground colour to white from black, and with the Eraser tool set to 500px, zoom out to 33.3%. On the layer mask, erase the foreground part of the field in line with the woman's body to reveal the clearer area.

10 **Crisp results** Duplicate the background layer (bottom in the Layers palette). Drag the copy to the top of the layer stack. In the Channels palette hold Cmd/Ctrl and click on the thumbnail of the Woman channel to activate the selection. Now add a layer mask in the Layers palette.

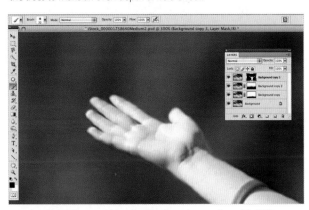

11 **Smarten up** Using the Brush tool set to 8px with 50% Hardness, zoom in to 200% and touch up the areas around the fingers and head to clean up the edges. The Clone tool is also handy for retouching edges, using the blurriest layer to sample from.

Highlighting with Lens Blur

The Lens Blur filter has an option for making extreme highlights stand out, named Specular Highlights. This is an aspect of the depth of field effect that shows overexposed areas of an image. Usually this isn't a great look to have, but in

Photoshop it has its artistic place and is worth experimenting with. Turn the Threshold slider down and increase the Brightness slider to apply the effect. This is best suited to fantasy-based art, where the effect shows extremely bright light sources hitting surfaces.

Warm up your image with Photo Filters

When the depth of field is added to your image, try adding a Photo Filter adjustment layer to the Layers palette. For this image we added a Warming filter to really bring out the warmth in the field and the model's skin. Experiment with different colours and tones, and also apply blend modes such as Overlay or Soft Light to produce different effects.

Content-Aware Scaling

An intelligent method of selectively resizing images

ontent-Aware Scaling came into Photoshop in version CS4. It's grouped with the Transform tools and acts in the same way, but with a bonus.

Found in the Edit menu, Content-Aware Scaling not only resizes your image but also keeps the main subject at its original size. It resizes all the other areas that have no distinct subject. When you use the Free Transform tool in Photoshop to adjust an image's size, the entire contents are affected. Content-Aware Scaling recognises areas of similarity such as sky or grass, and only resizes these.

If an image has more than one main subject, for example a portrait of a group of people, the areas lying between each person are resized. However, this isn't always perfect every time, as Content-Aware Scaling can produce rough patches. This is where some pixels haven't been blended smoothly, so there are limits to the extent of rescaling. It all changes depending on the subject you're dealing with.

Using this technique to resize an image saves possible hours of painstaking cropping, copying and cloning. Combine Content-Aware Scaling with selections saved as Alpha channels, and you can protect areas against any distortion.

Read through this Focus On to discover a solution to distortion caused by Content-Aware Scaling and how best to use this new feature in Photoshop.

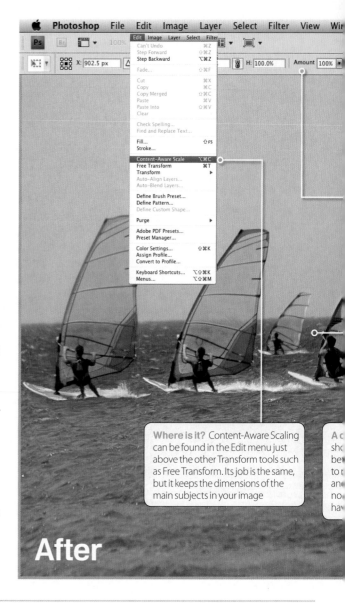

Where is it? Content-Aware Scaling can be found in the Edit menu just above the other Transform tools such as Free Transform. Its job is the same, but it keeps the dimensions of the main subjects in your image

After

Content-Aware Scaling is only available in CS4 onwards, and is an alternative to the Free Transform tool. If you're looking to reshape an image to fit a certain frame without distorting the main subjects, Content-Aware Scaling is made to do just that. It's located under Edit>Content-Aware Scale. Your image is given markers on all four of its corners and sides to show the boundary. By tweaking the settings in the Options bar it can be set to specific dimensions, to protect skin tones, and you can adjust the amount of distortion. By making selections around subjects you can prevent them being distorted.

Using Quick Mask mode

Select the Magic Wand tool and make a selection around your subject. Enter Quick Mask mode by clicking on the thumbnail at the bottom of the toolbar, then using the Brush and Eraser tools you can make your selection more accurate. Experiment with other selection methods – for example try using the Magnetic Lasso tool, which sticks to the edges of your subject as you run it around the edges. Try the Pen tool to create a smoother selection by joining points along an edge. You can then resize these parts or save the selection (Select>Save Selection).

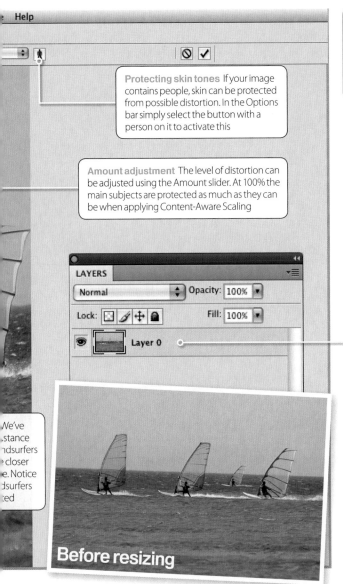

Help

Protecting skin tones If your image contains people, skin can be protected from possible distortion. In the Options bar simply select the button with a person on it to activate this

Amount adjustment The level of distortion can be adjusted using the Amount slider. At 100% the main subjects are protected as much as they can be when applying Content-Aware Scaling

LAYERS

Normal | Opacity: 100%

Lock: | Fill: 100%

Layer 0

We've ...stance ...dsurfers ...closer ...e. Notice ...dsurfers ...ed

Before resizing

Unlock layer To apply the Content-Aware Scale option, you first need to make sure that the layer isn't locked. To unlock a layer, double-click it in the Layers palette and hit OK in the New Layer dialog box

Tip

Combining selections

If Content-Aware Scaling fails to work on all the subjects in your image, when making an Alpha channel use the Magic Wand tool to select multiple subjects and then save the selection as a new channel. This way, you can protect many subjects from distortion.

Making Alpha channels

Content Aware Scaling can work with Alpha channels to protect an area from distortion. They save a selection for repeated use, great for protecting many subjects at once.

01 **Make a selection** Use the Quick Selection tool to select the main subject. Use a small brush for trickier areas, and use the Magic Wand tool to select multiple subjects in your image.

02 **Save your selection** When the selection is complete, head to Select>Save Selection. In the dialog box name your selection and hit OK. Open the Channels palette and you'll see it saved there. Hit Cmd/Ctrl+D.

03 **Locate the selection** Go to Edit>Content-Aware Scale, and in the Options bar, under Protect, select the name of the channel just made. Now when you resize your image the channel won't become distorted.

Protect skin tones in portraits

Content-Aware Scaling has an option to retain quality and shape in skin tones in portrait images. This is ideal if you want to retain the background in a portrait that has a landscape orientation and you need to change it to portrait. Select the option from Edit>Content-Aware Scale, and in the Options bar click on the button shaped as a person. This protects a person's face from distortion and looking blocky from overlapping pixels. It also saves you making a selection around a person each time you want to resize with Content-Aware Scaling.

Minimise distortion when scaling

To minimise any distortion when you use Content-Aware Scaling, simply adjust the Amount slider in the Options bar at the top of the Photoshop interface. With a value of 100% the adjustment is more considerate towards the main subject in your image. However, if you set this to a lower value such as 10%, the main subject and background will both be squashed and moved out of shape. Try to experiment with different values to achieve the correct level of distortion for your particular image.

Resizing techniques

Resizing is easy – deciding the best composition is the hard part

 crucial factor in composing an image is how it has been framed, cropped or resized. Photoshop has a variety of methods for either shrinking or blowing up to bigger dimensions.

It's amazing how the slightest change of framing changes an image's message and how that message is perceived by the viewer. When you come to print your artwork, its size and shape are both important visual clues to its message. The decision of framing an image mostly comes down to the lines of composition, or direction, within it.

Photoshop has a lot on offer for such a simple job as resizing. The Crop tool, found in the toolbar, offers a quick way to trim an image to size, whether it's changing orientation or cropping out distracting subjects from the edge of a frame.

The Content-Aware Scale feature in Photoshop CS4 and beyond and Recompose in Elements 8 and later rescales your image, leaving important subjects intact. Subjects such as people or cars are recognised as one object, and only the areas around those are stretched or squashed.

Use this Focus On as a guide to picking the best resizing method for your image. It'll work equally well whether you want to add more punch with a tightly cropped composition, or enlarge an image and add a Resample method for smooth results.

Options bar In the Options bar the dimensions of the cropping can be set depending on print size, frame size or orientation to suit your composition. You can set these with the Crop tool or Free Transform and Content-Aware Scale features

After

···· Add impact to images with the Crop tool

The Crop tool is invaluable in Photoshop, and a little cropping can make or break your composition. The Crop tool can be set to specific dimensions by entering values in the Options bar. The resolution of the final image can also be chosen here. To freely play with the dimensions of the cropping frame, leave these fields blank. Once the cropping frame is added to your image, you can black out the outer areas with the Shield command. The tool can also be used to straighten an image by ticking the Perspective box. By dragging the corners of the cropping frame to points in your image, it automatically straightens it up.

Before

After

···· Transform menu options

In the Edit menu PS has a range of resizing methods under the Transform option. The Free Transform option is a quick way to shrink an image inside a canvas, whether to throw it out of proportion or keep the resize constrained by holding Shift and dragging. Other Transform options include Skew, Warp and Distort, tweaking an image in multiple ways. You can be specific with the angle, height and skew of the Transform using the Options bar.

For a quick way to access Transform options, hit Cmd/Ctrl+T and then Ctrl/right-click over the image to open the list.

View   Window   onOne   Help

ount 100% ▼   Protect: None ▼

Content-Aware Scaling Under Edit>Content-Aware Scale, an image can be resized while keeping each subject the same shape. We've kept the building in this image in one piece but stretched the sky and river

Edit menu In the Edit menu the group of Transform commands are grouped along with the Free Transform and Content-Aware Scale options

Tip

Editable layers
Before you can use any of the Transform tools, you first have to make sure the layer is an editable one. If the layer is locked then double-click on it and hit OK in the New Layer dialog box.

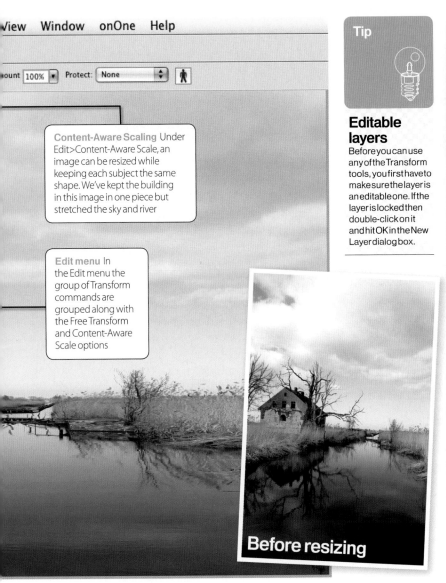

Before resizing

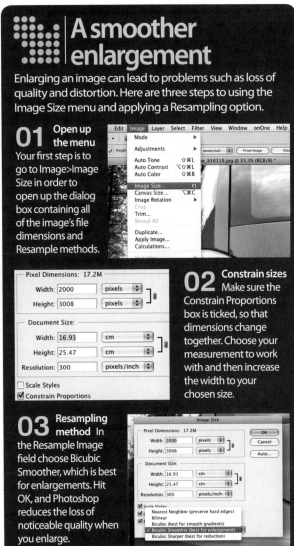

A smoother enlargement
Enlarging an image can lead to problems such as loss of quality and distortion. Here are three steps to using the Image Size menu and applying a Resampling option.

01 Open up the menu Your first step is to go to Image>Image Size in order to open up the dialog box containing all of the image's file dimensions and Resample methods.

02 Constrain sizes Make sure the Constrain Proportions box is ticked, so that dimensions change together. Choose your measurement to work with and then increase the width to your chosen size.

03 Resampling method In the Resample Image field choose Bicubic Smoother, which is best for enlargements. Hit OK, and Photoshop reduces the loss of noticeable quality when you enlarge.

Content-Aware scaling

In PS CS4/CS5 the Content-Aware Scale option is available in the Edit menu. The tool works in a similar way to the Free Transform tool, as it can shrink or enlarge your image, but is very clever. The Content-Aware Scale tool considers the subjects in your image when resizing, and only areas of repetitiveness (for example a blue sky) are affected. Areas of your image such as buildings or people are kept with the same dimension, and skin tones can also be protected. The busier an image is, the less effective the tool is.

Using Image Size dialog box

For precision, use Image>Image Size to resize. Here you can set the exact sizes of the pixel dimensions and the document size too. You choose the measurement, so you know what you're going to get. Essential information is given, such as the file size before and after a change is made. You can set the Resample method when blowing up proportions to make edges of subjects smoother. Methods include Bicubic Smoother or Sharper, and Bilinear.

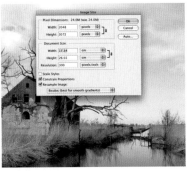

Create the perfect B&W

The best methods for transforming colour photos into punchy monos

removing all signs of colour instantly changes an image's message. The main focus no longer lies on the saturation and contrast of areas of colours, but more on the composition of your image, the posture of your subject and the contrasting greyscale tones.

A successful black and white is all down to the correct balance of lightness and darkness of tones in your image. Photoshop has many ways to turn an image into greyscale, but some are more effective than others. We've experimented with the main options here, and in our tutorial over the page we've taken you through one of the most popular methods for getting great results when converting to black and white.

Photoshop CS3 and above include advanced ways to control the monochrome effect, with the special Black & White adjustment layer. On earlier Photoshop versions, however, the Channel Mixer proves just as useful.

The important point to remember is to make sure, in a black and white, that the viewer's attention is drawn to the right areas of your image. For example, if you're working with a portrait you'll want to keep the subject's eyes bright and defined among the surrounding grey tones, and areas out of focus come second. Choosing the right method of conversion will make sure your entire image looks as good as it can without the added extra of colour.

Channel Mixer adjustment

The Channel Mixer adjustment produces effective results, as you have control over each channel of your image, and the percentage value of how much they affect the image.

01 Open menu
Find the Channel Mixer option under Image>Adjustments, and to remove colour in your image tick the Monochrome box at the base of the dialog. The Output channel will only show Gray, but you can control RGB individually.

02 Adjust channels
Raise the percentage of the Red slider to +60 to increase contrast. If highlights now appear bleach white with little to no detail, lower the Blue slider until detail returns to these areas.

03 Hitting 100%
Making sure the Total value hits 100% isn't always necessary. We lowered the Constant adjustment to make the overall effect darker for our landscape. This part is down to preference and style.

Accurate B&W conversion

Photoshop CS3 and above has a dedicated Black & White adjustment layer. Go to Image> Adjustments>Black & White to open its menu; you'll be given lots of control over specific colour channels, letting you tweak every area of your black-and-white image. This method is one of the most

accurate, although if the effect is overcooked you'll see a slight break-up of tonal quality. This adjustments include a handy Tint option for applying a tonal colour to your entire image, such as a sepia tone or a cool-blue colour overlay. The Color Picker lets you choose any colour for the tone.

The Channel Mixer method

Another great method for converting an image to black and white is the Channel Mixer. With the colour image open, go to Image>Adjustments>Channel Mixer. In the menu, tick Monochrome to remove colours, then adjust each Source Channel (RGB or CMYK) to achieve the black and white effect. If you're using PS CS3 or above, two advantages are the Total Number field that shows how close you are to 100%, and a choice of presets for different monochrome styles, including Black & White Infrared.

Photoshop Snapshot

If, in the process of converting your image to black and white, you capture some great effects along the way, you can save these in a quick Snapshot. In the History palette, after making an adjustment, click on the Create New Snapshot button. Access Snapshots by clicking on their pictures at the top of the palette.

Channel controls When your image has been converted to black and white, the Channels palette changes its appearance. After separating the Red channel in the initial stages of the process, only one channel is left representing the colour information

Apply sharpening To make sure our black and white image looks as punchy as it can, the final stage of conversion is to apply a small dose of sharpening from the Unsharp Mask (Filter>Sharpen>Unsharp Mask). This increases definition of the main subject, and brings out those important details

Layers palette Applying the blend mode Soft Light to a duplicate over the original black and white layer is a great way to quickly add contrast. Lower the opacity to weaken the contrast if it's overpowering

Start photo

Remove the mask With the foreground colour set to black, you can use the Eraser tool to remove the black shield of the layer mask on the top layer in the Layers palette. This layer is the original desaturated version, which is slightly darker than our final version

Painting the effect on accurately

For an alternative method to using adjustment layers, the Sponge tool can be used to convert chosen areas to black and white, simply by painting with its brush. Once selected, set the tool to Desaturate mode in the Options bar. With a large soft brush, paint over the areas of your image that you want to make black and white. This is a great tool for selective black and white conversions, where you only want to convert a small part of your entire image. For greater accuracy, try this method with a selection.

Direct to greyscale image mode

Photoshop offers a very fast method of removing all colour information from your image, although it's not necessarily the most effective. Head to Image>Mode>Grayscale and hit OK in the pop-up warning about the removal of colour. This method offers absolutely no control over the conversion, and results, although monochrome, aren't the best Photoshop can offer. We recommend using this method for comparing results to other methods, with the intention of bettering this effect.

⣿ CONTROL SHADES OF GREY FOR PUNCHY B&W
Create a custom black-and-white conversion using channels and layer masks

Increasing contrast of B&W

For a fast way to convert, and achieve great results, convert your image to greyscale using Image> Adjustments> Desaturate. This converts it to a standard black and white effect with no frills or surprises. To spruce up the effect, go to Image> Adjustments> Levels and move both the White and Black sliders into the centre of the histogram. Tweak the middle slider slightly to the left to boost contrast of the effect for a better black and white conversion.

01 Create a comparison Open your image and go to Layer>Duplicate Layer. In the pop-up box, set Document to New, and give it a name. Hit OK, and a copy of your image will open. Place it next to your original image, side by side in PS.

02 Quickly removing colour On your original image go to Image> Adjustments>Desaturate. This is a quick way to convert to black and white without losing the brightness of your image, but important details can be lost in the main focal point. Keep this version for later.

03 The best channel On the duplicate image, open the Channels palette and click on each RGB channel separately. Choose the best channel of the three, where the main features of your subject (the eyes in our particular image) look their best.

04 Create an Alpha channel Ctrl/right-click your chosen channel and select Duplicate. The same dialog pops up as before; select New under Document, and then hit OK. This is our final version, and only Alpha 1 appears in the Channels palette.

05 Make editable Now go to Image> Mode>Grayscale to make the background layer editable. Go into the Layers palette and drag the background layer onto the Create a New Layer button to create a copy in the palette.

⣿ The Duotone way of doing things

Another way to convert an image to black and white is to change the mode to Grayscale (Image>Mode>Grayscale) then head to Image> Mode>Duotone. This does discard all colour channels in your image and makes just one grey channel, but in the Duotone menu you can apply the effect simply by setting two inks: one black, one white. There are also Levels adjustments in this menu for setting the contrast of these inks for a punchier black and white. There's limited control over the individual channels this way, but you can add more inks with varying colours for different effects/tones.

⣿ Helpful Gradient Maps explored

There are so many ways of converting an image to monochrome, and some are more effective than others. Follow our main tutorial for one of the best ways to do it, or try using Gradient Maps to do the job. Head to Layer>New Adjustment Layer>Gradient Map, and in the menu select the black to white gradient and hit OK. The strength of the effect can be edited using the Curves adjustment with the image's layer selected. To tweak areas of your image to brighten or darken, experiment with Dodge and Burn tools on a duplicated layer of your image.

06 Apply contrast With the duplicated layer selected, change the blend mode to Soft Light. This adds contrast and more punch to the black and white effect. If the effect is too strong, reduce the layer's Opacity to around 60%.

07 Quick comparison The eyes of our subject look perfect, but other areas seem to be bleached white due to the blend mode. Look at the original, desaturated version of your image and compare areas of details that you want to add to the final version.

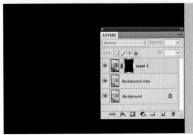

08 Set layer mask With the Move tool ('V') drag and drop the original desaturated version onto your final version while holding Shift to place it exactly over the top. Add a layer mask to its layer, Opt/Alt-click the mask and go to Image>Adjustments>Invert to make it black. Opt/Alt-click again to return to your image.

09 Bring through the detail Select the Eraser tool and set the foreground colour to black. In the Options bar, set the Eraser's Hardness to 0%, choose a large brush size and reduce its Opacity to 20%. Paint over your image to bring the darker parts through, containing the areas of detail.

10 Sharpen up Save your image and go to Layer>Flatten Image. To add further crispness to your black and white, go to Filter>Sharpen>Unsharp Mask. Apply this filter gently to avoid any glowing edges around subjects.

A more traditional look with grain

For that traditionalist in you, why not try adding a bit of film grain to your black and whites? To do this, head to Filter>Noise>Add Noise and in the dialog box tick Monochromatic to remove any colour in the noise effect. Select the Uniform option

under Distribution, and set the Amount slider to around 20% – this depends on how strong you want the level of noise to be. Hit OK, and you have another interesting finishing touch for your black and white image that could fool anyone into thinking it was shot on 35mm film!

Selective black and white technique

To create a selective black and white image, duplicate your image's coloured layer and apply your black and white conversion technique to the duplicate. On the monochromatic layer, add a layer mask. Use the Brush tool at 0% Hardness, with black as the foreground colour, to paint over the areas that you want to see the colour come back through. This is the ideal way to change the focus of your composition from one subject to another.

Match Color

Quickly apply colour information from one photo to another

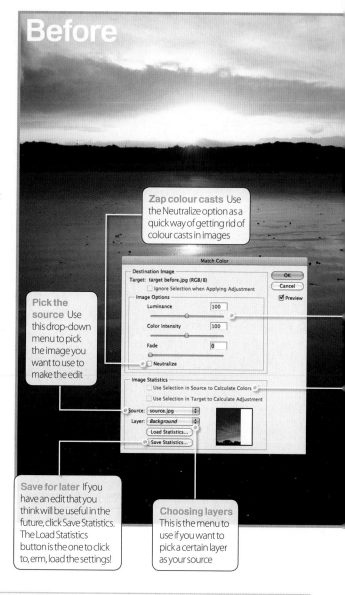

 dobe introduced the Match Color command in Photoshop CS, and it's one of those features that got a bit of coverage at the time but has since faded into the background. Which is a shame, because it can be a powerful editing tool.

As names go, the Match Color command has a perfect one, as its reason for being is to match colours between images (or even the same image), between selections or between layers. There are sliders to control the effect, but we should warn you now – we'd be telling porkies if we said it gives perfect results every time. Sometimes you will need to follow up Match Color with some necessary tweaks, but please don't be put off. When it works, it can be a pure joy.

There are various reasons to try the Match Color command. The most obvious is to apply the colour information from one image to another. This is particularly useful for landscapes, where maybe you'd like to apply the colours of a stunning sunset to an image that's a bit lacking in the stunning skies department. But there are other uses.

If you are creating a photocomposite, you can use Match Color to make the colours consistent in all the different images. You can also use the command to match the colour of one area to another in the same image, so it can be used for quick edits. You can even use it to get rid of colour casts.

Over these two pages we will show you how the tool works and give you an insight into how it can be controlled to get the exact effect you want.

Before

Zap colour casts Use the Neutralize option as a quick way of getting rid of colour casts in images

Pick the source Use this drop-down menu to pick the image you want to use to make the edit

Save for later If you have an edit that you think will be useful in the future, click Save Statistics. The Load Statistics button is the one to click to, erm, load the settings!

Choosing layers This is the menu to use if you want to pick a certain layer as your source

Target a layer to work on

Match Color works on a simple principle – taking colour from one place (the source) and applying it somewhere else (the target). The easiest way is using the whole of one image to apply to the whole of another image (see the walkthrough), but you can be pickier in its application. If you have a certain layer you want to use as the target image, make sure this layer is selected before opening Match Color. If you want to use a certain layer as the source, use the Layer menu

in the Image Statistics area of the Source menu to pick the one you want. The Merged option in this menu will use all layers in a source image.

Adjust photos with selections

Make a selection. This can be the area you want to change or the area to use to make a change. If you made a selection in one image to apply to another, go to Image Statistics, select the source image in the Source menu and pick the Use Selection in Source to Calculate Colors option. If you want to use one area of an image to alter another in the same image, ensure this image is selected in the Source menu of the Image Statistics area, and hit Use Selection in Target to Calculate Adjustment.

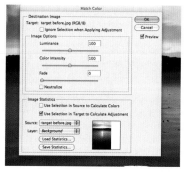

Pick a target This is the start image, which is used by the Match Color command to edit an existing image. This tool gives a quick result and is great for compositing different images into one whole scene

Image options You can make various alterations to the target image before you commit to an edit. The Luminance, Color Intensity and Fade sliders all help the quest for perfection!

Selective edits If you are using selections to make your edit, these two fields will become active for you to choose the one you want

After

Source image

Tip

Fade the effect

If you make edits from the Image Statistics area and find things are a bit too powerful for your taste, use the Fade slider to control the adjustment. Nudge the slider to the right in order to reduce the adjustment.

Use the Match Color command

Here we show how to use Match Color to apply colours of one image to another. This is the meat and potatoes of the command...

01 Pick the image Open the image you want to edit and the image you want to use. Click on the image to edit and then go to Image>Adjustments> Match Color to open up the command.

02 The window When Match Color opens, have a look at the Target area to double-check it's the correct image. Go to the Source drop-down in the Image Statistics area and choose the image you want to use.

03 Commit to the edit Have another check to make sure the correct images have been used for the target and source, and make any adjustments needed. We used the Fade slider to tone the effect slightly. Click OK to make the edit.

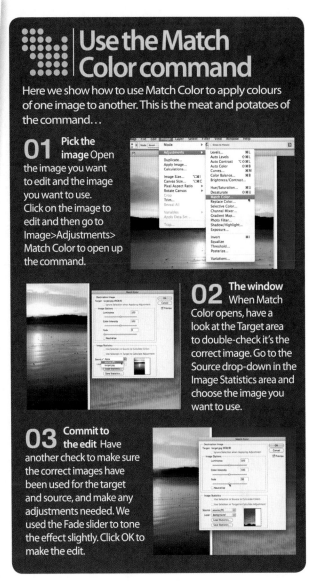

Make some tweaks to the result

There are two options in the Match Color command to alter the target image. You can use these if you feel that your edit isn't going quite according to plan and you need to give the image intended for change a bit of help. The Luminance slider allows you to increase or decrease the brightness. Either use the slider, or if you have a value in mind just enter it in the Luminance text box. If you need to alter the colour saturation of your target image, use the Color Intensity slider. Again, you can enter a specific value by hand if you prefer.

Remove a colour cast from a photo

It is possible to use the Match Color command for editing tasks that have nothing whatsoever to do with matching colour between images. The Neutralize option will automatically remove a colour cast in the target image, which is great for swift photo edits. With an image open, simply select the Neutralize option, click the Preview box to make certain you can see what's going on, and then use the Luminance/Color Intensity options to carry out any tweaks that you think are necessary.

Tip

Vital brush controls

Once you create your brushes and want to use them, your first port of call should be the Brushes palette. From here you can access Brush Dynamics, and the most vital of these are the Jitter options in each category. By raising the Jitter amount for Size and Angle, you can introduce randomness into each flower. Also, play with the Spacing and Scattering values to introduce even more interest and randomness.

Create Japanese flower brushes
Create effective flower brushes from simple stock

 lowers can be tricky and very time-consuming to paint from scratch, especially if you need a lot of them across a single image. At times like these it would be really useful to have a magic 'flower brush' that you could simple paint multiple flowers with in a single stroke.

We'll start by using some source photos for the brushes themselves, and you'll find plenty of these in stock libraries online. Essentially, any brush can be made from a simple black and white image, so first we'll isolate a flower or two and then desaturate it. We don't want these brushes to look too photographic, so we'll next simplify the tones and detail by using the Smart Blur filter.

Next, to give the flowers a more hand-drawn feel, we'll sketch the outline quite loosely with a simple Wet Media brush. Finally, define the drawn flower as a brush You can source your stock from any stock site, or take some pictures of your own for a more personal touch.

READY, SET, CREATE!
Create your own artistic brushes in a few simple steps

01 Source image Regardless of the kind of flowers you use to make brushes, the procedure is exactly the same, and to save you having to paint the footprint for each brush, it starts with copying and pasting a source photo onto a layer above a white background.

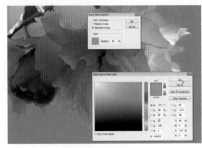

02 Quick Mask With the source image pasted (Edit>Copy on image, Edit> Paste on blank file), pick the Brush tool then a small hard brush in the Brush picker. Hit 'Q' for Quick Mask mode. Double-click the Quick Mask icon and pick a contrasting colour for the mask overlay.

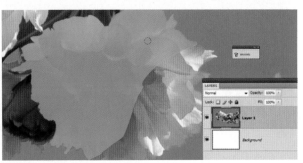

03 Paint to mask For the Color Indicates option, choose Selected Areas and then click OK. Ensure that you're using black on your brush (check the foreground colour swatch), and using the brush at 100% Opacity start to carefully paint over the flower that you want to copy.

04 Correcting the mask Take your time with this, carefully painting over the flower and keeping within its outline. If you make a mistake and paint outside the flower's outline, simply change your foreground colour to white and paint back into the image to hide that part of the mask.

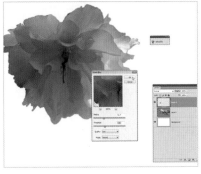

05 Simplify Once the mask is done, hit 'Q' to exit. With the selection active, go to Edit>Copy, Edit>Paste. You can now hide the original image layer. Go to Image>Adjustments> Desaturate. Simplify detail in Filter>Blur>Smart Blur. Set Radius and Threshold to 30 and hit OK.

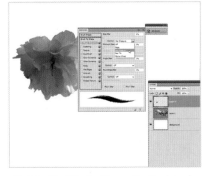

06 Wet Media Choose the Brush tool, load the Wet Media brushes from the Brush picker and select the Rough Ink brush. In the Brushes palette hit Shape Dynamics and set Control for Size to Pen Pressure. Ensure the foreground colour is black and add a new layer.

Tip

Brushes and colour
Brushes can only apply one colour at a time (your current foreground colour). However, if you'd like to apply more colours to your individual flowers, then in your finished composition simply add a new layer and set its blending mode to Color. Now simply paint patches of low opacity colour (with a normal brush) to this layer. You can control the intensity of this colour by adjusting the opacity of the colour layer.

07 Adding line and detail Use this brush at a very small size to loosely trace around the flower, using lots of pressure variation. It's also useful to add a few touches of line within the flowers to give a little detail. When you're happy, make a rectangular selection around the flower and go to Edit>Define Brush Preset. Now give your brush a meaningful name.

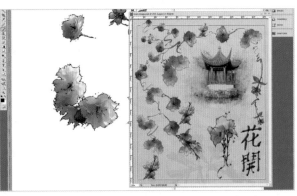

08 The possibilities are endless! To create more brushes, simply use the same procedure over other start images. Now you can use your completed brushes on any image. Either use them in single clicks or use the Jitter values within the Brushes palette to apply many flowers with single strokes.

The Curves adjustment tool

The Curves tool is a powerful Photoshop feature that transforms contrast, colour and tone

he Curves tool in Photoshop is deceptive. To the Photoshop beginner its graph-like appearance can be intimidating, bringing back memories of early maths lessons.

However, it's a powerful tool that can be used to adjust tonal ranges, change colour levels, alter exposure, boost contrast and even create some less conventional photo effects. Although the Curves tool is not as intuitive as some of the other features in Photoshop, the basic functions are simple and dramatic results can be easily achieved.

Here we will demystify the Curves graph, and in doing so show how you can make practical improvements. We'll look at understanding the graph and at what happens as the line changes shape. We'll reveal tips and tricks to make editing your image quick and easy. We will also look at editing the colour channels to recover lost colour. The Curves tool has many more facets than might at first be obvious, and we'll introduce you to as many as we can.

The S-curve explained

With the Curves tool you may notice that to get the best effects you often use a similar shaped curve. It's called the S-curve for obvious reasons.

01 Anchor points Open the Curves dialog. Create three anchor points and use the grid to help place them at equal distances. Opt/Alt-click on the grid to change to a smaller grid for greater accuracy.

02 The dark side Using the bottom anchor point, representing areas of dark pixels, pull it towards the base. This makes the dark pixels darker. The middle anchor point (midtone) remains stationary.

03 Let there be light Now make the light pixels lighter by moving the uppermost anchor point up. By making this S-shaped curve, we've boosted the contrast and have a more dramatic image. This curve is also useful when editing separate colour channels.

Use the Curves adjustment layer

Curves can be accessed via Image> Adjustments>Curves, but can also be activated as an adjustment layer. In the Layers palette, hit Create New Fill Or Adjustment Layer and select Curves. Adjustment layers let you make changes without degrading the original. It also means you can continue to edit a Curves adjustments by double-clicking the adjustment layer. If the changes aren't wanted, you can revert to the original by deleting the layer.

Black and white images to learn

If you're new to Curves, you'll find it useful to practise with greyscale images. The tool reads the tonal depth of pixels, meaning it deals with shadows, midtones and highlights. It's easier to understand the principle when using black-and-white images, as the final image corresponds to the info that

the Curves tool uses: shadows (black), midtones (grey) and highlights (white). To change an image to greyscale, go to Image>Mode>Grayscale.

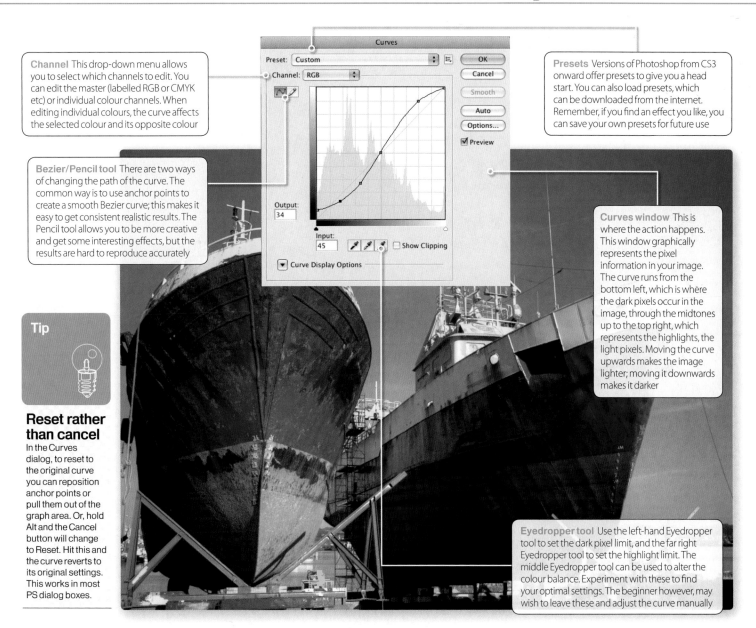

Channel This drop-down menu allows you to select which channels to edit. You can edit the master (labelled RGB or CMYK etc) or individual colour channels. When editing individual colours, the curve affects the selected colour and its opposite colour

Bezier/Pencil tool There are two ways of changing the path of the curve. The common way is to use anchor points to create a smooth Bezier curve; this makes it easy to get consistent realistic results. The Pencil tool allows you to be more creative and get some interesting effects, but the results are hard to reproduce accurately

Presets Versions of Photoshop from CS3 onward offer presets to give you a head start. You can also load presets, which can be downloaded from the internet. Remember, if you find an effect you like, you can save your own presets for future use

Curves window This is where the action happens. This window graphically represents the pixel information in your image. The curve runs from the bottom left, which is where the dark pixels occur in the image, through the midtones up to the top right, which represents the highlights, the light pixels. Moving the curve upwards makes the image lighter; moving it downwards makes it darker

Tip

Reset rather than cancel
In the Curves dialog, to reset to the original curve you can reposition anchor points or pull them out of the graph area. Or, hold Alt and the Cancel button will change to Reset. Hit this and the curve reverts to its original settings. This works in most PS dialog boxes.

Eyedropper tool Use the left-hand Eyedropper tool to set the dark pixel limit, and the far right Eyedropper tool to set the highlight limit. The middle Eyedropper tool can be used to alter the colour balance. Experiment with these to find your optimal settings. The beginner however, may wish to leave these and adjust the curve manually

Edit Curves of colour channels

Curves allow you to edit separate colour channels. When a colour channel is selected, the curve affects the density of the colour, eg red and its opposite, cyan. If the Red channel is selected, moving the curve upwards increases the red in the image; moving it down increases the cyan. It's important therefore to know the colours and their opposites to get the most from this function. In Image>Adjustments>Color Balance, the sliders illustrate which colours are opposites. Think about how the image will be reproduced before making changes. If it's to be printed, make sure it's in CMYK.

Flat spots and down curves

If you are unfamiliar with the Curves tool and are in the process of experimenting, it is easy to get carried away – which can result in wild unrecognisable images. There can be occasions when a bizarrely distorted image is required, but more often than not this is not the case. To avoid the worst of these effects, there are two rules to follow. The first is to avoid flat spots. These occur when the curve follows a horizontal line across the graph. The second is to make sure that the curve doesn't go beyond the horizontal to create a downward curve.

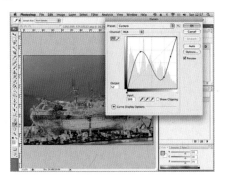

┉ CURVES IN ACTION
See how they can be used for creative effects

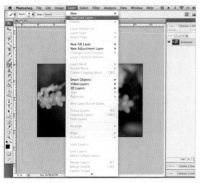

Take it easy
It's easy to get carried away when experimenting with curves, as there are so many aspects that can be edited. Pushing the curves too far can introduce a lot of noise into your image. Less is most definitely more when dealing with curves!

01 Getting started First open up your start image. It's a good idea to begin by creating a duplicate layer. This way you can always revert to your original image, either for reference or to start a new edit. Go to Layer>Duplicate Layer.

02 Strengthen detail To increase the impact of the foreground flowers, we used the Sharpen tool to paint in some detail around the petals of the flower. Be careful not to set the Strength too high as you may end up adding noise. Alternatively, go to Filter>Sharpen>Unsharp Mask and alter the settings to strengthen detail, again being careful not to add too much noise.

03 Curves adjustment layer Create a Curves adjustment layer by going to the bottom of the Layers palette, clicking the middle button and selecting Curves. This opens the Curves dialog. Position two anchor points along the curve – one towards the top and one near the bottom of the curve.

04 S-curve The next step is to create a simple S-curve. Begin by selecting the lower anchor point and pulling it directly down so it sits halfway down the grid section as shown in the screengrab. Push the higher anchor point upwards by the same amount. You will notice this has effectively boosted the contrast. Don't click OK just yet.

05 Fine-tuning In the last step we created an S-curve, but in doing so burnt out some of the highlight areas. To remedy this, pull the top anchor point a little to the right to reduce the curve's angle and return some detail to the highlight areas.

┉ Adding warmth and cooling down

It's easy to change the 'temperature' of an image using Curves. To add warmth, select just the Red channel and pull the curve upwards; this adds red to the image

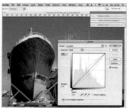

at the same time as removing cyan. Then go to the Blue channel and pull the curve downwards; this adds yellow (the opposite of blue). For a cooler image do exactly the opposite – add more blue by lifting the curve in the Blue channel, and remove red by pulling the curve downward in the Red channel. Simple.

┉ A colourful solution with Hue/Saturation

When using Curves to affect tonal range and contrast, the saturation will often increase. This can help improve the look of a pic, but it's not always a desired effect. To counter it, instead of the Desaturation tool, try using a Hue/Saturation adjustment layer. This keeps the original image intact and lets you toggle the effect on/off later. Go to the Layers palette, create a new fill/adjustment layer, select Hue/Saturation

and reduce the saturation with the slider. Setting the Hue/Saturation layer with a Luminosity blend mode allows more detail to be preserved.

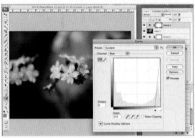

06 Intensify the shadows We're going to create a new shadows limit. Grab the anchor point at the very bottom left of the curve and drag it along the bottom of the graph until the Input window reads 25. You'll notice this darkens the shadow areas and in doing so helps frame the main subject. Hit OK to save.

07 Merged layer Create a new merged layer by pressing Shift+Alt+Cmd/Ctrl+E. This gives you an editable layer but preserves your earlier layers and adjustments in case you need to revert to an earlier version. Create a new Curves adjustment layer as you did in step 3.

08 Rebuilding colour In the Curves dialog box select the Channel drop-down menu and open the Blue channel. On this adjustment layer we are going to remove a lot of the blue from the image by sliding the corner anchor point from left to right along the bottom of the graph until the Input window reads 225.

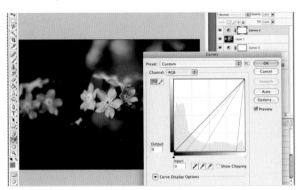

09 More colour To continue to recover colour in the image, use the same technique as in step 8 in the Red and Green channels. Slide the bottom anchor point to the right until the Input reads 100 for green and 40 for red. The screengrab shows how your RGB channel curves should look. Click OK to save the changes.

10 Stepping back Although we've introduced some interesting colour detail to the image, it's beginning to look a little forced. We can remedy this by simply selecting a soft black brush on a relatively low Opacity and Flow setting (30%) and painting out some of the more extreme areas of colour on the adjustment layer.

A quick fix with the Eyedropper tool

You can set white/black points manually. To set a black point, create an anchor point at the base of the curve and pull the base to the right along the bottom of the graph. Amend the white point in a similar way at the top of the graph. This expands the tonal range of

the image. You can also get this effect with the Eyedropper. Click the full Eyedropper on the left and select the darkest pixels in the image. With the empty Eyedropper, select the lightest pixels. The Curves tool will remap the channels to give you a wider tonal range. Experiment also with the middle Eyedropper, which alters the colour balance.

Pencil tool to alter Curves

There are two ways of altering the path of the curve. The first and most common method is to use the Bezier tool. Setting the shape of the curve using anchor points, this ensures a smooth curve and consequently a realistic transition in the tonal range of the image. The alternative method is to use the Pencil tool. With this you can create a broken and erratic curve which, with some experimentation, can create nice poster effects. If you find a good effect but want to fine-tune the curve using anchor points, just click Smooth, and Curves will reintroduce the Bezier curve.

Feathering

Soften selections and remove hard edges by feathering, making layers blend with their surroundings

eathering is an easy way to blend the edges of a layer smoothly with its background. It's a popular method that has evolved over the past couple of versions of Photoshop.

Whenever you make a selection on a layer, you have the option to feather its edges. This means that when it comes to cutting an area out, you aren't left with a hard edge. Instead, the result will be a soft, gradual blur.

It has many uses for all kinds of Photoshop users. Feathering selections will form vignettes, as covered in our three-stepper, and can also help you make collages involving cutout images to piece together.

In Photoshop versions CS3 onwards, feathering has been included with other selection adjustments in one dialog box. This is called Refine Edge, and it can be found in the Options bar as a separate button. Otherwise, you can head to Select>Modify to make the necessary adjustments to a selection.

When feathering, you will find it helpful to take advantage of layer masks. The masks will show you how much feathering is going to be applied, and will also make customising a selection easier.

The three methods for feathering are discussed below. You can apply a feather either before or after making a selection – simply choose your method.

::::: Add a vignette using feathering

A small amount of feathering goes a long way, but a vignette needs a good helping for lots of blurring. Feathering will draw attention to the main subject.

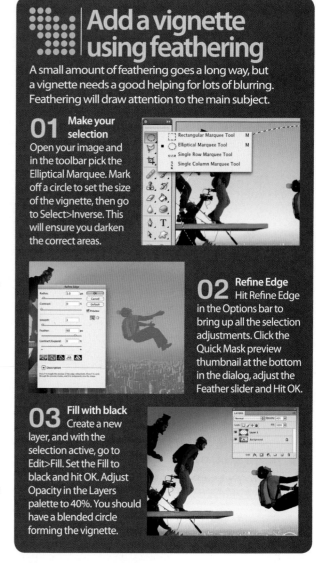

01 Make your selection
Open your image and in the toolbar pick the Elliptical Marquee. Mark off a circle to set the size of the vignette, then go to Select>Inverse. This will ensure you darken the correct areas.

02 Refine Edge
Hit Refine Edge in the Options bar to bring up all the selection adjustments. Click the Quick Mask preview thumbnail at the bottom in the dialog, adjust the Feather slider and Hit OK.

03 Fill with black
Create a new layer, and with the selection active, go to Edit>Fill. Set the Fill to black and hit OK. Adjust Opacity in the Layers palette to 40%. You should have a blended circle forming the vignette.

::::: How feathering works in Photoshop

Every time you draw a selection with the Marquee tool, the Magic Wand or the Lasso, you have the option to feather the edges. Feathering works by blurring or softening the border of a selection, making the edges blend in with the layer underneath. The Feather command takes a chosen number of pixels and blurs them either side of the selection line, half on one side and half on the other. The finished result is a gradual blur into 0% Opacity of the edges of a selection. This technique is perfect for composing collages, as you can blend the images together without any harsh joins. It's also great for softening edges of layers so they're easier on the eye.

::::: Modify selection for accuracy

There are three main ways to apply feathering to the edges of a selection. One of these is via Select>Modify>Feather. This will only work after you've made your selection. Once in Feather, decide on the Feather Radius by entering the number of pixels you want to blur. You don't get a preview when using this method, so any mistakes will involve going back through the menus to make the re-adjustments. Hit OK in the Feather menu, and your selection will now be feathered. To complete this effect, hit the Delete key and watch the edges blur.

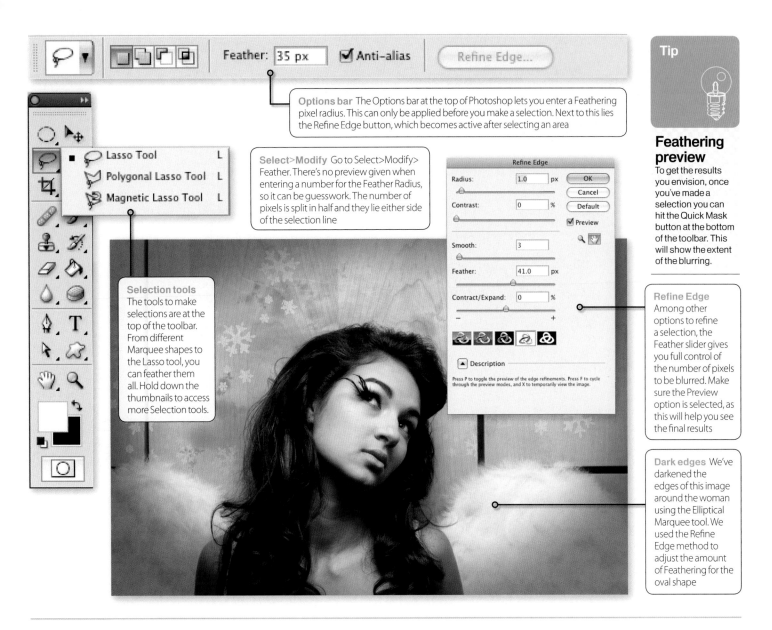

Tip

Options bar The Options bar at the top of Photoshop lets you enter a Feathering pixel radius. This can only be applied before you make a selection. Next to this lies the Refine Edge button, which becomes active after selecting an area

Select>Modify Go to Select>Modify> Feather. There's no preview given when entering a number for the Feather Radius, so it can be guesswork. The number of pixels is split in half and they lie either side of the selection line

Selection tools The tools to make selections are at the top of the toolbar. From different Marquee shapes to the Lasso tool, you can feather them all. Hold down the thumbnails to access more Selection tools.

Feathering preview To get the results you envision, once you've made a selection you can hit the Quick Mask button at the bottom of the toolbar. This will show the extent of the blurring.

Refine Edge Among other options to refine a selection, the Feather slider gives you full control of the number of pixels to be blurred. Make sure the Preview option is selected, as this will help you see the final results

Dark edges We've darkened the edges of this image around the woman using the Elliptical Marquee tool. We used the Refine Edge method to adjust the amount of Feathering for the oval shape

Refine selection for effective feathering

Another way to apply feathering is via the Refine Edge button in the Options bar. This is available in Photoshop versions CS3 onwards, and contains many other selection adjustments alongside Feathering. Once a selection is made, hit the Refine Edge button and use the Feather slider to adjust the amount of blurring you need. With this method you have a number of ways to preview the feather before hitting OK. You can see the effects with a black, white or transparent red mask, and you can also zoom in and out.

Feather before making a selection

Feathering can also be applied to an image before a selection is made. This is the quickest method, but you have to know the exact number of pixels you're going to need. When you've chosen a Selection tool from the toolbar, head to the Options bar and enter a number into the Feather box. You can choose any number up to 250 pixels. You can then go ahead with making a selection and the feathering will be applied straight away.

Start images

Tip

Selection methods

There's more than one way to make a selection around a subject in Photoshop. Here we've used both the Magnetic Lasso and Quick Selection tools to separate the subject from the sky. But if this method doesn't suit your image, try using the Pen tool for the trickier areas of the subject. This tool takes more time than the ones used here, but you can bend and control each point with the Pen tool.

Master Photomerge Exposure

Learn how to use the Photomerge feature in Photoshop Elements 8 and 9

T he latest Photoshop Elements, versions 8 and 9, have a number of Photomerge options and Exposure is just one of these.

Its name aptly describes what it can do, which is cleverly combine two or more shots of the same scene to create one correctly lit image. The Exposure option can save you many hours of painstaking work, and like most of the features in Elements 8, it's very straightforward.

You may be wondering why this is needed, because every camera shoots using the correct exposure, right? But there are some situations when a scene has difficult and somewhat awkward lighting. For example, the sky in our image was too bright for the camera to correctly expose the statues in

one shot as well. To compensate for this, take a couple of shots at different exposure settings so that all areas are correctly lit in at least one of the images. We recommend using a tripod to make sure the images line up perfectly in each capture, as Exposure automatically aligns each image before correcting lighting.

Exposure takes an image at different settings, along with the camera's normal exposure, and uses two or more to combine and recreate the shot at a perfect exposure. It enables you to pick out areas and subjects of perfect lighting using a brush-like tool, and the whole process is simple and fast. It's great for bringing out details in otherwise pitch-black shadows and bleach-white highlights.

A COMPLICATED PROCESS MADE EASY
Take multiple exposures to create perfect results

01 Load and auto-align Open the two statue images of different exposures from your disc. In Elements, select both by holding Shift and clicking on them in the Project Bin. Go to File>New>Photomerge Exposure, and the two images should load up and automatically align.

02 Create the background Now click on the Manual tab in the right-hand side of Exposure. There are two windows in the centre. Drag the darkest image from the Project Bin to the square on the right, which is the background layer in the finished composition.

03 Set the foreground image From the Project Bin, click on the lighter image to load it to the Foreground box. Choose the Selection tool and tick the Show Strokes box. Leave the Transparency slider set to 0 to see the full effect.

04 Paint selections Next, choose the Selection tool and begin to draw lines over the foreground image. The tool only requires a single straight line in order to work on an area, and you should then be able to see the effect change in the Background box.

05 Zoom for details Draw lines over the statues and trees in the Foreground box, but leave the sky, as this is what we want to keep in the Background box. Zoom in to select smaller areas, and use the Eraser to remove any unwanted lines.

06 Correct exposure Once your image is complete, your next step is to use the Transparency slider in order to tweak the strength of the foreground layer over the background. This makes certain that the balance is just right between the two images.

Tip

Automatic alternative
Photomerge Exposure offers multiple ways to merge more than one exposure of an image. In Exposure, there is the Automatic tab with two options inside: Simple Blending and Smart Blending. These are quick alternatives to manually selecting areas of the image, and the Smart Blending option comes with a set of adjustment sliders to tweak the effect even more. The method used is dependent on the subjects in your image, but it's worth trying these automatic functions because the results can be just as accurate as using Exposure manually.

07 Layer composition When you're satisfied with the composition, hit the Done button and the image will appear as a new layer in Photoshop. The background layer should now be under the new layer.

08 Final tweaks The areas around the trees have a harsh line where the background meets the foreground. Use the Eraser tool, set to Brush mode with a soft, large brush to remove these hard edges. Your final step is to select the Crop tool to frame the image and remove any overlap.

VIDEO TUTORIAL
To shed even more light on the subject, there is a video on the disc giving you further tips and techniques on the Lighting Effects filter.

Fantasy
lighting effects

A touch of creative light can spice up any image. We demonstrate how you can be a master of light in Photoshop

mages are all about light. It's the one visual element that's absolutely vital – images simply don't exist without it.

In the real world, light doesn't necessarily behave the way we'd like it to, but within the world of Photoshop we can control light or even completely reinvent it! So, in this feature we're going to create all kinds of light magic, thanks to the power of Adobe Photoshop.

Whether it's turning day into night, switching the lights on, adding a magical fairyland atmosphere or even completely changing the light and atmosphere of an entire image, we'll give you all the tools you need over the next few pages to create each effect convincingly.

To a great extent, light in images is pretty much an illusion, consisting of little else than the tonal contrast between one area and another, and most kinds of lighting effects can be created using some quite simple techniques in terms of digital imaging.

We'll primarily use gradients, layer styles, brushes and masks, and call on the power of the Lighting Effects filter as well. Layer blending modes also play quite a big part in making light look convincing, and give the effects the required degree of intensity and glow.

So think of this feature as your own 'lighting toolbox'. Although many of the lighting effects you'll see may look very advanced and complicated, the vast majority of the techniques used are really quite simple, and the final effects themselves rely ultimately on how you combine and layer a number of them together.

The basics

Although our example image looks very advanced and complicated, it really relies on a few basic techniques to create the dramatic lighting effects.

First, it's essential to separate the subject from the background with a super-accurate layer mask. You can easily generate this from one of the greyscale RGB channels in the Channels palette. With the main subject isolated, we can then apply brightly coloured lighting to a duplicate layer via the Lighting Effects filter, and then carefully reveal this lit layer by simply painting on a Hide All layer mask with a variety of brushes.

Again, the vibrantly lit background is deceptively easy to achieve. All we need here is a filled layer beneath the isolated figure, over which we can apply some simple gradients on layers above set to Screen and Lighten blending modes to create the effect of the large soft light and even the rays of light themselves. Adding a touch of glow to well-placed brush marks is easy via a layer style, as shown in the walkthrough on the right.

> "Although our example image looks very advanced and complicated, it really relies on a few basic techniques to create the dramatic lighting effects"

Glow layer styles Intensely bright, glowing particles and streaks are easy to create by painting on a layer that uses one of the Glow layer styles. See the walkthrough on the right for details

Blending modes Layer blending modes are important for making light look right. All the blend modes from the Lighten group in the Layers palette work well for giving your light layers more punch

Light rays By making simple wedge-shaped selections and filling the selection with a pale blue-to-transparent gradient, you can easily create effective rays of light

Hair light By tweaking the curves on a duplicate layer and using a bright, coloured Omni light via the Lighting Effects filter, you'll be able to create the base for brightly lit hair strands

Light layer Another simple, brightly lit layer hidden with a mask allows you to paint with a soft brush with white to reveal the bright blue light over the figure

Reveal via mask The brightly lit layers are hidden with a black mask, and then it's just a case of painting with white to reveal the bright hair strands surrounding the figure

01 Layer style light Starting with a new blank layer, make a single dot with the Brush tool with white. Go to Layer>Layer Style>Outer Glow.

02 Glow colour You can choose the actual colour of the glow by clicking in the small colour swatch within the main Layer Style dialog.

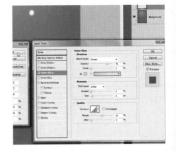

03 Size and Spread To get a soft, subtle glow, use a small Spread value and a higher Size value. Think of Size as intensity and Spread as blur.

04 Auto-glow This layer will automatically apply a glow to anything painted on it. To create a glow trail, use the Pen tool to draw a curved path.

05 Stroke Choose a brush and adjust its size. Now right-click the path and choose Stroke Path. Check Simulate Pressure and click OK.

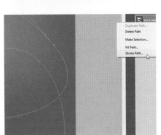

06 Hey presto! Your brushstroke will have the layer style automatically applied. You can adjust the glow's colour/size/spread by double-clicking the layer's FX icon.

Light bulb

As we said earlier, creating lighting effects in Photoshop is quite a subtle art if you want to achieve the most believable effects. Here we're going to light a light bulb – without a single watt of electricity involved. We depend instead, within Photoshop, on the alternative power of the Lighting Effects filter combined with a couple of simple gradients, a layer style and a bit of careful masking. There are many lighting situations such as this where you can't just rely on a single filter or effect, but instead need to approach the whole image in quite an artistic way, relying as much on observation as on flashy Photoshop filters.

Lighting Effects filter

The Lighting Effects filter needs some careful adjustment to make it work the way you want. One of the most important considerations is the positioning and size of your light. You position the light by dragging on the central spot within the light pool displayed in the Preview. To change the size and spread of the light pool, drag on the handles around the outer edge of the pool. You can rotate the light by grabbing the point on the end of the axis line and dragging in a clockwise or anti-clockwise direction. With the Spotlight selected, the brightest point of the light is positioned at the outer end of this axis line.

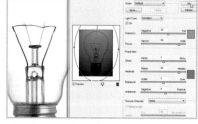

01 **Ambient light** Duplicate the background layer and go to Filter>Render>Lighting Effects. Use a single spotlight with the colour and settings shown in the screenshot to light the layer. Place the light quite high in the image, towards the top of the bulb.

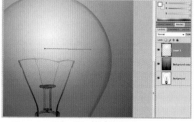

02 **First glow** Add a new layer, and using white as the foreground, pick the Gradient tool with a Foreground to Transparent radial gradient. Drag a gradient from the upper centre of the bulb to the outer edge. Set the layer blending mode to Screen.

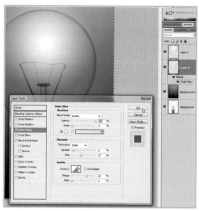

03 **Filament glow** Add a new layer and go to Layer>Layer Style>Outer Glow. Choose a very pale yellow for the glow colour and set the blend mode to Screen. Set Spread to 6, Size to 85 and Range to 65. Choose Softer for Technique and set Opacity to 100%. Click OK to apply the layer style.

04 **Power up!** Zoom into the image and use a small soft brush with a very pale yellow to paint along the filament itself and a little way down its supports. As you paint, the glow will be revealed around your brushstrokes. You can always double-click the layer style and adjust its settings.

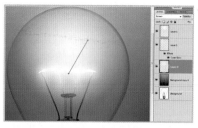

05 **Another glow** Use the Gradient tool on another layer to add an extra small, radial gradient over the filament, this time using a very light blue as the foreground. Again, set this layer to Screen blending mode and adjust its opacity.

06 **Revealing light** Return to the Lighting Effects layer and add a layer mask. Now use a small soft brush with black at a low opacity to paint over the central area of the bulb to gradually reveal light travelling through the glass parts.

Drag the central spot in the light pool to reposition your light

Drag the handle at the end of the axis to resize and rotate

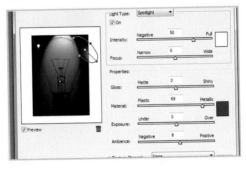

Add more lights by dragging the small bulb into the image area

Add colour

Some of the most effective lighting techniques rely mostly on simply applying colour to layers. Their success depends on using the right blending mode for the layer you're working on.

In this image we've taken a fairly unexciting shot in terms of lighting, and transformed it into a very atmospheric low-key scene with lots of subtle coloured light and stark contrast between the warm interior light and cool moonlight outside. The majority of the light has been 'painted on', using the Brush tool on a single layer. The crucial point about this layer is that its blending mode is set to Color Dodge, so that as well as the colour we add being visible, the actual tones we apply 'dodge' the dark tones on the darker layer below, much as the traditional Dodge tool would, making those areas lighter. By using this method you can literally paint with light!

As with all the images here, we need to set the scene first, and again we'll use the Lighting Effects filter to establish the overall low tone shade in the image. By using the Lighting Effects filter as a Smart Filter, we can readjust the settings at any time during the image-editing process and even mask away the filter in areas such as the window panes.

No night sky would be complete without a few stars, and we can add those with a little help from a Scatter brush and a layer style.

Use simple layer-based lighting effects to transform bland images into masterpieces of subtle lighting and colour. The key to this effect is a basic layer blending mode and the subtle use of brushes

Understand gradients

When creating lighting effects you'll often rely quite heavily on the power of gradients, and different gradient types are suited to different kinds of light. Linear gradients are great for filling selections for light rays, while radial gradients are best suited to effects where a light is brightest in the centre and reduces intensity towards the outer edges of the light pool. It's worth experimenting with gradients so you know exactly how they work.

Tricks

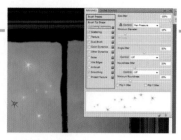

Stars and fairy dust

You can easily create all kinds of stars, sparkles and magical glowing fairy dust, simply by modifying a pretty standard brush. Any round brush will work, or you can use one of Photoshop Starburst brushes. In the Brushes palette (F5), increase the Size Jitter and make sure to use the Scattering Dynamics category to create a brush that will 'spray' these stars randomly with a single stroke.

Light via masks

You can add light to an image simply by using a layer mask. Use the Lighting Effects filter to lighten the whole layer and then paint on a Hide All mask with a soft white brush to reveal the light! By using the soft brush with its Opacity Control (Other Dynamics in the Brushes palette) set to Pen Pressure, you can reveal the lighter layer at various intensities to 'paint with light'.

Smart lighting effects

You can use the Lighting Effects filter as a Smart Filter in CS3, CS4 and CS5, so you can go back to it at any time during the image creation process to change the light colour, size or position. To do this, right-click the target layer and hit Convert to Smart Object. When you apply the filter in the usual way, it'll be listed as a Smart Filter below the target layer. To re-edit it, double-click it in the Layers palette.

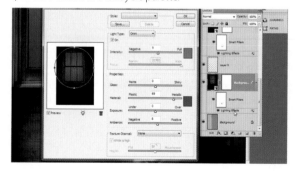

Northern Lights

Although the effect of the Northern Lights is quite easy to create in Photoshop with a little brushed colour, some motion blur and blend modes, to make it convincing we need to prepare the start image carefully. This is another instance where we'll first use the Lighting Effects filter, not to add light but to reduce the light levels in the original image to contrast with the bright, colourful sky and also give us the chance to reveal some light on the landscape via layer masks.

01 Sky gradient Duplicate the background layer; fill the original with a Foreground to Background linear gradient using two shades of mid blue/black. Click the upper layer; go Filter>Render>Lighting Effects.

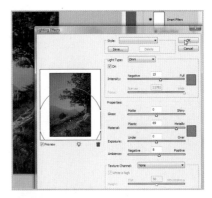

02 Lighting Effects filter Use two Omni lights, utilising two shades of petrol blue for the light and material colours. Experiment with the size and settings for the lights to create an atmospheric twilight lighting effect.

03 Layer mask Generate a layer mask from a copy of the Blue channel in the Channels palette and apply this layer mask to the Lighting Effects layer, to reveal the gradient layer beneath within the sky area.

04 Northern Lights Click the gradient-filled background and add a new layer. Now use a soft brush with a bright colour of your choice to start adding the Northern Lights to the sky. Use quite random strokes, and a photo for reference.

05 Blurring the lights Blur each layer of the Northern Lights via Filter>Blur>Motion Blur, using quite high values and a suitable angle. Create more Northern Lights layers with different colours using these same techniques.

06 Layer blend modes Each Northern Lights layer can be set to a Lighten, Overlay or Color Dodge blending mode, and you can adjust the opacity for the best effect. The effect works better if the streaks of colour are quite random.

Lighting Effects Smart Filter mask

As we've demonstrated, there are many advantages to using this particular filter as a Smart Filter, but there's yet another one, which really helps with this project. When you're using Lighting Effects as a Smart Filter, you automatically get a layer mask attached, which you can use to hide the effect by painting onto the filter mask with black. That's how we've added the light to various parts of the finished image. Just target the filter mask and use a soft brush with black at partial opacity to hide the effect and consequently reveal the lighter, original unfiltered layer. If you reveal too much light, simply paint into the mask again with white to reveal the filter effect once more.

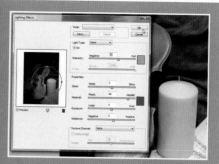

01 Setting the scene
Set the scene by using the Lighting Effects filter on a duplicate background layer using the two shades or orange/brown and an Omni light. Take care to adjust the size/position of the light.

02 Light through the candle
On a new layer, using a very light yellow as the foreground, use a Foreground to Transparent gradient over the top of the candle. Set the blending mode to Screen and clean up around the candle with a layer mask.

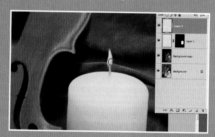

03 Flaming good!
The flame itself is easily established by using a small soft brush. Use bright yellows and oranges here at medium opacity on a new layer. Apply a little motion blur at 90 degrees by going to Filter>Blur>Motion Blur.

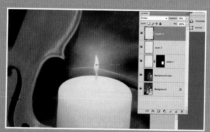

04 Final glow
Using a bright yellow/orange, drag a radial Foreground to Transparent gradient out from the centre of the flame. Set the layer blending mode for this to Screen and adjust the layer opacity to suit.

Heavenly rays
Here comes the sun! A wedge-shaped selection on an empty layer filled with a White to Transparent linear gradient. Blur it a bit and set the layer blend to Overlay. Another elliptical selection filled with a gradient on the ground completes the effect.

Light a candle

Not all lighting effects need to be so dramatic, and it's often the most subtle, seemingly ordinary ones that work best. Naked flames are notoriously tricky to photograph, so here we'll throw away those matches and light a candle in Photoshop. Once again, we're just going to be dealing with gradients, glows and layer masks in order to achieve the ultimate in lighting believability.

More inspiration

Now you're incandescent with enthusiasm for all things light-related, dive into Photoshop and use your new 'lighting toolkit' to spread light around your Photoshop world. To whet your appetite just a little more, here's a potpourri of lighting goodness! All these examples use a combination of the essential techniques we've covered and carefully blended together.

Electronic digits

If you've only got 24 hours, do it in digits! Create your type and set the Fill slider to Zero in the Layers palette. Inner Glow and Outer Glow layer styles will give you both a vibrant fill for the digits and a powerful glow outside.

Lightning

Lightning can strike twice! Make a narrow Black to White gradient on a layer, and go to Filter>Render>Difference Clouds. Tweak the levels and go to Image>Adjustments> Invert. Set the layer blending mode to Screen and colourise via Image>Adjustments/Hue and Saturation.

Torch beam

Find your way with a torch! Just light the sign with a spotlight in the Lighting Effects filter so it rakes across the surface. The beam comes from filling a selection with a White to Transparent linear gradient and adding blur on a layer set to Screen.

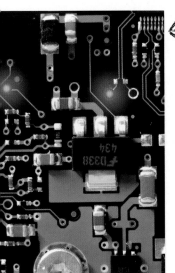

Bright LEDs

Make your own LEDs! Create a circular selection on a new layer and fill with your chosen colour. Light up the LED by using Outer Glow and Inner Glow layer styles. Take your time to tweak the settings in the Layer Style dialog.

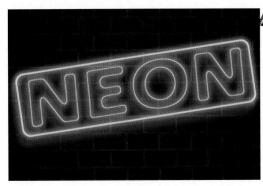

Neon

A sign of the times, proving how useful layer styles are! A simple stroke around letters created with the Type Mask, combined with Outer/Inner Glow styles. Make a copy layer and set it to Color Dodge for the reflections.

Composing with Smart Objects

Intelligent editing with non-destructive results

mart Objects first came with Photoshop CS2, and they made the editing process of a composition much easier. Smart Objects are controlled from inside the Layers palette, and are used to edit certain objects separately from the rest of the composition.

Sounds complicated, but Photoshop has made the process of editing Smart Objects simple. By double-clicking on a Smart Object's layer thumbnail, the object opens in a separate document for you to edit. This also applies to RAW files imported from a DSLR. Using Smart Objects, RAW images can be edited separately at any point in your workflow.

There are other advantages to using Smart Objects for editing photos and objects, vector- or raster-based files. When a layer in your composition is converted to a Smart Object, it can be made smaller and then enlarged back to its original size without any loss of image definition – a major bonus if you're experimenting with the arrangement of your layers.

One of the main jobs of Smart Objects is to preserve the original quality of a layer, so that you can work in a non-destructive fashion. They can play a major role by connecting multiple layers together, and when one is edited, the other Smart Object layers are automatically updated with the changes.

⠿ Repetitive editing made easy

If you're creating a composition consisting of multiple objects and need to apply the same edits to each one, you can convert one of these objects to a Smart Object (Layer>Smart Objects>Convert to Smart Object). Then simply duplicate the Smart Object's layer by dragging it onto the Create New Layer button as many times as you need. To edit one of the objects, double-click the layer's thumbnail and your image object will open as a new document. Perform the necessary edits, go to File>Save, go

back to your original composition and notice how all other objects have been updated automatically without the need to edit each one separately. You can also select all the original layers and create one Smart Object layer.

⠿ Scaling definition retained

Smart Objects have many advantages for artists transforming and resizing images. Converting an image to a Smart Object (Ctrl/right-click on its layer and select Convert To Smart Object) allows you to resize your image without losing image quality. For example, making a non-Smart Object very small using Photoshop's Free Transform, and then resizing the image

back to its original size, the image becomes distorted and pixelated. But if you resize an image to small dimensions and back to its original with it set as a Smart Object, no distortion will occur.

Smart Objects Convert a layer to a Smart Object by Ctrl/right-clicking and selecting Convert to Smart Object. A converted layer indicates that it's a Smart Object by showing a small symbol on its thumbnail

Smarter editing
With our main images converted to Smart Objects, we have used Transform commands to shape them to the billboards without the risk of losing detail. By double-clicking on a Smart Object's layer thumbnail, each image can be edited separately in its original form

Tip

Smart Objects and layer masks

If you're creating a composite image and need to apply a selection with a layer mask, make sure you convert your image to a Smart Object before applying the layer mask.

Clipping masks/ Smart Objects

When converting a layer to a Smart Object you're restricted to the adjustments in Image>Adjustments. With clipping masks you can use adjustment layers.

01 Unavailable options
When you've created a Smart Object, most of the adjustments in Image>Adjustments aren't available. Instead, head to the Layers palette with the Smart Object in and hit Create New Adjustment Layer.

02 Apply mask Select an adjustment layer; we chose Levels to darken our ball object to bring it closer to the ambient lighting. Before making adjustments, Ctrl/right-click the adjustment layer and select Create Clipping Mask.

03 Set adjustments
The clipping mask makes sure that only the layer below is affected by any adjustments, and not the whole image. Making the necessary adjustments to an object can be changed at any time.

Replace contents with ease

Among the many advantages to editing compositions using Smart Object layers is the ability to replace an object with a new one at any stage. With a Smart Object selected, head to Layer>Smart Objects>Replace and then pick an image that you want to put in its place. Once imported into your composition, because it's now a Smart Object it can shrink or enlarge back to the original without the fear of losing image definition. Such dramatic resizing with normal layers can destroy pixel definition and is only undo-able by stepping back in History states.

RAW file editing in ACR

If you take pictures using the RAW file format with a DSLR, you can edit these using Adobe Camera Raw software, which pops up as you open Photoshop. You can convert RAW images into a Smart Object with Adobe Camera Raw by ticking the Open In Photoshop As Smart Objects option in the Workflow dialog box (via the underlined text at the base of the interface). This allows you to go back into Camera Raw by double-clicking the Smart Object's layer thumbnail in Photoshop.

Master toning adjustments

Photoshop's multiple methods of toning images

A lItering the tones and colours of an image changes its mood and message. In this guide we give you a rundown on the top toning tools.

Whether you're making corrections to the colours of a specific subject or experimenting with the overall tones for an abstract feel, the popular toning adjustments include Color Balance, the Duotone colour mode and using the Channel Mixer adjustment layer for controlling specific colour channels.

Different tones can convey different messages. There's a quick method in Photoshop for creating a sepia image, and you can see how this was done in our main artwork on the right.

The Channel Mixer is the trickiest of the three options, because you're given delicate control over all the channels and each of their values. This method is great for converting to black and white. Making a selection before jumping into the Channel Mixer, you can alter one subject at a time.

Applying the Duotone mode replaces all the coloured channels with one grey channel. When inside this menu, the variety of colours you can apply to create your duotone is vast. However, options are also available for applying up to four inks to create a Quadtone effect. This is a quick method, but remember to save an original of your image before you apply any of these effects. Try it for yourself on your images.

Before

::::: ## Use the Channel Mixer to change tone

When we talk about toning, we're really talking about adjusting channels. If your image is set to RGB mode (Image>Mode), only the Red, Green and Blue options show in your Channels palette. With your image separated into these three channels, you can carefully tweak each one for a different tone. Open up the Channels palette and click on any of the available channels to see where their colours are distributed through your image. Head to Image>Adjustments>Channel

Mixer, and you'll see all these channels listed, with percentage values. This method of toning is popular for creating powerful black and whites, but slide the RGB percentages to create a colourful overlay. Bear in mind – a little goes a long way.

::::: ## Apply set inks to your image

Applying a duotone requires you to change the mode of your image to Grayscale. The option Image>Mode>Duotone then becomes available, and inside its menu you can choose how many tones you want to apply, whether that's Mono, Duo, Tri or Quad. For each tone you can choose the specific colour from a huge list of Pantone swatches to build up layers of tones. Keeping black as the top ink in the menu

ensures the shadows look natural. This method of toning is fast, and makes creating sepia toning easy. Try boosting contrast after applying the duotone effect to make your image look more dramatic.

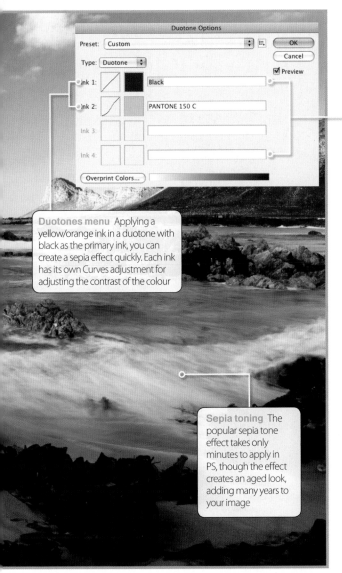

Duotones menu Applying a yellow/orange ink in a duotone with black as the primary ink, you can create a sepia effect quickly. Each ink has its own Curves adjustment for adjusting the contrast of the colour

Quadtone effects In the Duotones menu you have options for applying up to four inks in one go. This can soon become overwhelmed with colour, and for the sepia effect, using a duotone (two inks) does the job just nicely

Sepia toning The popular sepia tone effect takes only minutes to apply in PS, though the effect creates an aged look, adding many years to your image

Tip

Repeating actions
If you plan to use a specific tone for a set of images, you can set up an action (Window>Actions). Recording the steps of a particular tone you like, you can hit Play each time it comes to apply it to another image.

Add warmth to animal portraits

Gradient maps provide quick methods of applying a new tone to your image, and can give animal portraits a sense of warmth and power. Here's how's it done.

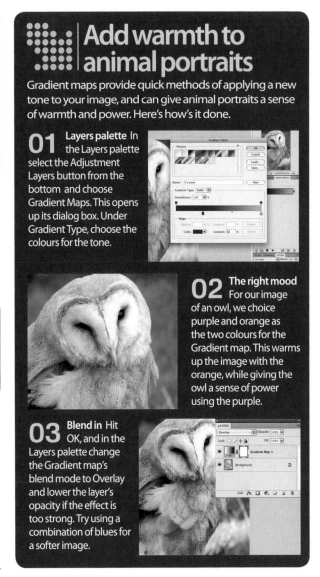

01 Layers palette In the Layers palette select the Adjustment Layers button from the bottom and choose Gradient Maps. This opens up its dialog box. Under Gradient Type, choose the colours for the tone.

02 The right mood For our image of an owl, we choice purple and orange as the two colours for the Gradient map. This warms up the image with the orange, while giving the owl a sense of power using the purple.

03 Blend in Hit OK, and in the Layers palette change the Gradient map's blend mode to Overlay and lower the layer's opacity if the effect is too strong. Try using a combination of blues for a softer image.

Apply a map for non-destructive editing

A Gradient map is a great way to choose variations of colour in the toning process. In the Gradient Maps dialog box, you can set any number of colours to apply to the mix, as well as where they appear through the Gradient map. After arranging the colours in the map, apply a blending mode, for example Soft Light, in the Layers palette to mix in the effect with the lighting in your image. This method is well worth experimenting with – being an adjustment layer, it doesn't harm your original image underneath.

The quick option for toning your image

Photoshop's Image>Adjustments> Color Balance option is a quick method for adjusting colour tones. Each slider in its dialog box represents two opposing colours, and by increasing the amount of one colour, the opposing side reduces in strength. This is ideal for subtle tweaks to an image. If, for example, your image has too much red, this can be reduced. Adjustments can also be made separately to shadows, midtones and highlights for greater precision.

Improve your brush skills in Photoshop

The Wet Media brush set holds some of PS's most effective brushes

T here are many additional brush libraries that ship with Photoshop out of the box. One of the best of these extra brush sets is the Wet Media brushes.

This is a large selection of preset brushes which, as the title suggests, are ideal for replicating traditional wet media effects, especially watercolour techniques, and here we're going to look at exactly how best to use a selection of these.

All these brushes are great for creating images with flowing, calligraphic lines and washes of subtle colour, complete with sophisticated textures and stroke edges.

You can use any of these Wet Media presets straight out of the box with no adjustments at all, but you'll find out here that there's a lot about them you can modify via the Brushes panel, and they therefore make great candidates for brush experimentation too!

So, if you're looking for lovely wet inky lines, subtle washes of colour with just a hint of texture, smooth sinuous calligraphic strokes or loose, quite random puddles of colour, you'll find everything you need tucked away in this incredibly useful but often overlooked Photoshop brush library. Here we've gone with a Japanese theme for our artwork – but feel free to apply these techniques to other genres such as portraits and still lifes.

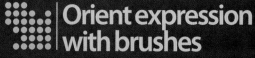

Orient expression with brushes

The Wet Media brushes are ideal for creating oriental characters. The way you set up your brushes and do the strokes makes all the difference.

01 Set up In the Choose any of the round Wet Media brushes from the set, and set Brush Opacity to 50% to allow for a transparency within the stroke. In the Brushes panel (Window>Brushes) in Shape Dynamics set Size Control to Pen Pressure.

02 Feel the pressure Start the stroke at the thickest end with lots of pressure. As you release the pressure, your stroke will get thinner. Make each stroke using this pressure technique and with a quick flick of the wrist.

03 Stroke direction Each stroke needs to be made in a particular direction, from thick to thin, so take care to work out the direction for each individual stroke within the character. This can take a little practice, but practice makes perfect.

Wet Media brushes and texture

Many of the Wet Media brushes use texture, and it's always worth exploiting this option even further. When one of these preset brushes features texture within its stroke, you'll see the Texture category checked within the Brushes panel (Window>Brushes). If you click on the Texture category itself, you find the options for choosing a new texture for the brush (by clicking in the small patter swatch), or modifying the scale and the depth of the current texture via the sliders. From the Mode drop-down option you can also choose the particular blending mode that's used to overlay the texture onto the default brush stroke itself. Experimenting with these options really amplifies the creative potential of these brushes.

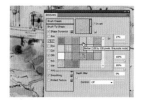

Feeling the pressure with a tablet

Using a pressure sensitive graphics tablet and stylus is really vital when it comes to using Wet Media brushes, especially if you want to create nice sinuous, calligraphic strokes. With the Size Jitter control set to Pen Pressure in the Brushes palette, you'll find that a tiny amount of pressure produces very fine lines, and by increasing your drawing pressure the stroke will thicken accordingly. Remember that the Minimum Size slider determines how small the brush is when minimum pressure is applied to the stylus. Make sure to adjust the pressure sensitivity of your graphics tablet.

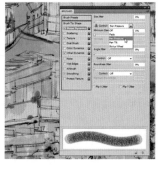

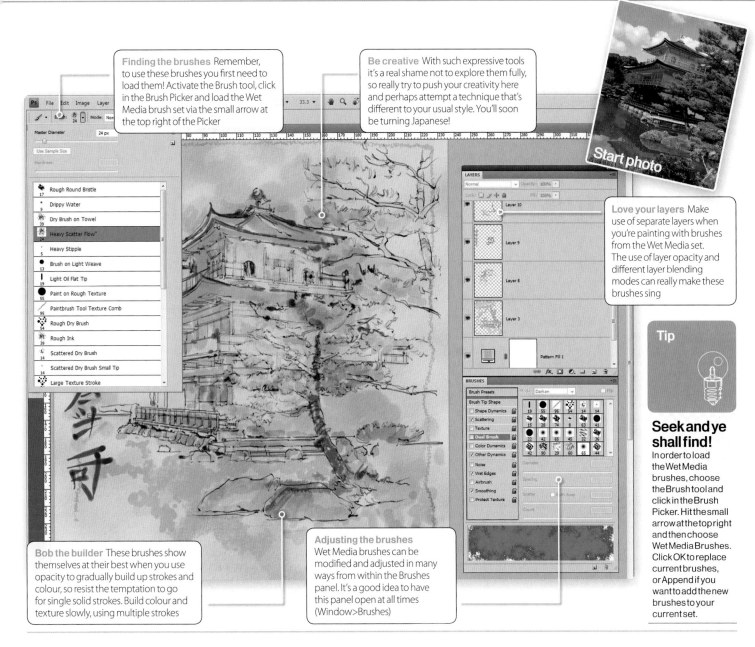

Finding the brushes Remember, to use these brushes you first need to load them! Activate the Brush tool, click in the Brush Picker and load the Wet Media brush set via the small arrow at the top right of the Picker

Be creative With such expressive tools it's a real shame not to explore them fully, so really try to push your creativity here and perhaps attempt a technique that's different to your usual style. You'll soon be turning Japanese!

Start photo

Love your layers Make use of separate layers when you're painting with brushes from the Wet Media set. The use of layer opacity and different layer blending modes can really make these brushes sing

Tip

Seek and ye shall find!
In order to load the Wet Media brushes, choose the Brush tool and click in the Brush Picker. Hit the small arrow at the top right and then choose Wet Media Brushes. Click OK to replace current brushes, or Append if you want to add the new brushes to your current set.

Bob the builder These brushes show themselves at their best when you use opacity to gradually build up strokes and colour, so resist the temptation to go for single solid strokes. Build colour and texture slowly, using multiple strokes

Adjusting the brushes Wet Media brushes can be modified and adjusted in many ways from within the Brushes panel. It's a good idea to have this panel open at all times (Window>Brushes)

Mix one brush with another

Some of the Wet Media brushes are 'Dual brushes', as you'll see from this category of the Brushes palette. A Dual brush overlays the footprint of one brush on top of another, and this is really useful for creating brushes based on simple brush types but which have an interesting outer edge to the stroke. From the Mode drop-down in the Dual Brush category, you can control which blending mode is used when overlaying the brush footprints within the stroke.

What you see is what you get

As with other brush sets in PS, it can be tricky to remember exactly what each brush looks like in use. With this in mind, it's worth taking a little time to make a menu for yourself showing each of the brushes in a visual way. Just create an A4 Photoshop file at 300dpi and make a few strokes with each brush, labelling each as you go. A quick trick to save you time in the long run.

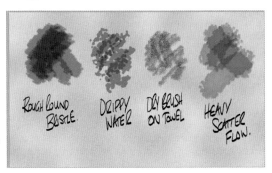

Tip

Add some authenticity

To make your images look even more convincing, it's a good idea to add in elements such as Japanese calligraphy or decorative objects. Check out these Japanese floral brushes here: **http://designfruit.com/blog/2007/01/17/japanese-foliage/.** They are free to download and offer a wonderful decorative feel to your images. Another great option is adding a paper texture such as rice paper or even bamboo to give it a really tactile feel.

::: TURN PHOTOS INTO A WASHY MASTERPIECE
It's all about building your strokes

01 Gestural sketch Start by pasting the supplied start image on top of a simple clouds-filled background. Reduce its opacity and add a new layer. Using a very dark grey for the foreground, use the Light Oil Flat Tip brush to carefully trace over the main outlines in the scene.

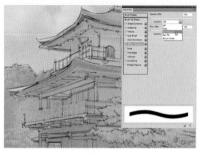

02 Pressure options Used at a very small size, this brush is perfect for creating nice sharp spontaneous strokes, which are ideal for a simple line drawing such as this. You can choose whether or not to use opacity driven by pressure for this brush via the Brushes panel, giving your strokes more tonal variation.

03 Drippy Water The Drippy Water brush is great when used at a large size and low opacity for adding quite broad, random patches of colour to the entire canvas. Use this on a layer with its blending mode set to Color Burn.

04 Adjusting spacing This brush also reacts very well to changes in the Spacing value in the Brush Tip Shape section of the Brushes panel. Increasing this value allows you to add spots of colour to the painting that are spaced further apart and even more random in their placement.

05 Inky accents The Brush Light Texture Medium Tip is great for adding watery, inky accents to certain areas of the initial line drawing. Use the brush at around 60% Opacity on a Normal layer. Use swift movements here to create dynamic strokes that run from thick to thin.

::: Wet Media via layer masks

All the Wet Media brushes are wonderful to use on layers masks, and this is a great way to produce convincing natural media style paintings. The best way to do it is to choose a reference photo and duplicate the background layer. Run the Smart Blur filter (Filters>Blur>Smart Blur) on the duplicated layer, experimenting to find a nice blend for the Smart Blur filter sliders. Having applied

Smart Blur, add a layer mask to this layer (Layer>Layer Mask>Hide All). Now paint onto this layer mask with a selection of the Wet Media brushes using white as the foreground, at a medium opacity. As you build up your strokes, the image layer will appear in a very painterly way.

::: Drawing with brushes in Photoshop

Often it's all too easy to think of these kind of brushes in terms of using them to 'paint' solid areas of colour, but the brushes in this set are so responsive and expressive that it's much better to think of them as drawing tools. The marks you make with these brushes are equally as important as the actual quality and specific look of the brush. When you're painting, make a determined effort to think about the individual marks you're creating. It's even worth spending a few minutes before you start painting just doing small sketches to get used to the kind of marks you can make.

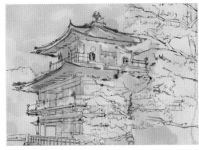

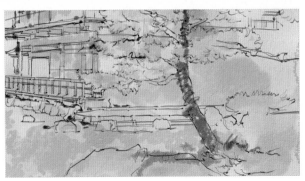

06 **Fluid colour** Use this same brush at a much bigger size to add touches of subtle colour here and there throughout the painting. Once again, the brush's opacity level is important here, creating fluid patches of colour that overlay one another.

07 **Heavy Scatter Flow** The Heavy Scatter Flow brush is great for creating areas of colour that are very soft and have the appearance of wet-in-wet watercolour. Once again, make sure to use this at a low opacity on a Color Burn layer. This is a great way to add in the impression of soft foliage.

08 **More paint, more texture** For very wet colour that appears to migrate through the paper grain, use the Paint On Rough Texture brush. Used at low opacity, with attention paid to brush pressure, this brush really adds to the Wet Media feel. Remember, you can change the texture used with this brush (see the boxes below).

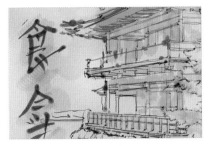

09 **Texture Comb** Another very realistic brush here is the Paintbrush tool Texture Comb. This rake-like brush is ideal for adding areas of colour that have lots of movement and textural interest. Once again, use this brush quickly and expressively. It's ideal for the abstract areas of colour beneath the written characters.

10 **Dry brush** More definite areas of rough, dry colour with lots of texture can be added using the Dry Brush On Towel brush. Use this on a Normal layer, with the brush opacity set fairly high in order to add touches of more opaque colour here and there.

11 **Classic strokes** The Watercolor Heavy Loaded brush works very well for more defined strokes of traditional hard-edged watercolour. Short dabs with this brush can bring focus and definition to more important areas of your painting. Once again, use this on a Color Burn layer at medium opacity.

Adding realism with paper textures

To make Wet Media brushes look even more convincing, it's useful to add a paper texture to your entire canvas. Directly above your filled background layer, add a Pattern Fill layer (Layer>New Fill Layer>Pattern). Click in the Pattern swatch in the Pattern Fill Layer dialog, hit the small right pointing arrow and choose Artist Surfaces. Now choose one of the paper patterns and adjust the scale. Set the blending mode for this layer to Color Burn.

Make the most of beautiful blending modes

Wet Media brushes work best when individual strokes overlay and blend together in a subtle way. With this in mind, it's best if you make good use of layer blending modes rather than working on Normal layers. It's worth experimenting here, especially with Overlay and Color Burn modes. As well as using these blending modes via layers, you can use them directly with the brush by choosing your desired mode from the Mode drop-down in the Options bar while the Brush tool is active.

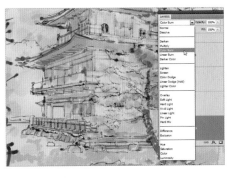

Sharpen your images with the High Pass filter

The High Pass filter offers an easy way to sharpen up blurred shots

igital photography has changed the way we think about taking photos. While film and processing is slow and expensive, digital is fast and free – well, except for the initial cost of the camera.

When we look at the way cameras have evolved in the last few years, we can understand why there are a lot more people taking snapshots. In the past we would only take photos of the things we really wanted to keep. Let's face it, a 36-exposure film will go pretty fast if you're snapping away at every interesting thing you see while out for the day – but with a digital camera and a good memory card you can snap hundreds if not thousands, depending on the quality.

Most people will have a form of digital camera, be it on a phone or a traditional point-and-click camera. When we look at the technology of a digital camera, we see that the sensor picks up the picture a bit like a mosaic, then pushes it together. Sometimes this means images aren't as sharp as we'd like. Normally we'd use the Unsharp Mask to correct sharpening issues, but there's an equally interesting and easy way to sharpen – using the High Pass filter.

Soft detail In our before image, the detail is pretty soft. The feathers around the face look smooth, and the wet areas on the top merge in with the rest of the feathers. It is in need of some sharpening!

Weak colours One side-effect of a slightly blurred image is that colours tend to lose definition. In our duck, the beak isn't as vibrant as it could be and the tones are a bit flat

Before

::::: What is the High Pass filter?

The High Pass filter is located in the Others sub-menu within the Filter menu. This filter has many useful applications and is normally used to create image sharpening, softening and high contrast images. It can also be used to create line art. The filter keeps the edge details, where any sharp colour transitions are, and ignores the rest of the image relative to a specified radius. The effect also removes small details from the image and can be seen as having the opposite effect of the Gaussian Blur filter. While this may sound very technical and confusing, it's actually very simple and the effects can be created on as little as two layers.

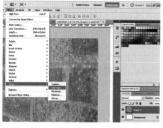

::::: High Pass softening techniques

The main use of the High Pass filter is in advanced sharpening techniques, but it can also be used to soften an image. Usually when we want to soften an image we use the Blur tool or filters, but this can mean we lose details. With a High Pass soften we don't actually lose these details. To do this, follow the same techniques that were used in the tutorial but invert the High Pass results. A good tutorial for this can be found at **www.photoshopessentials.com/photo-editing/smooth-skin/**.

More detail After a blast of the High Pass filter, definition springs out from areas such as the duck's head. The feathers are more defined, especially the wet ones

All in moderation It's tempting to whack the slider up to maximum, but you will end up with a horrible result. Here we have pushed the detail as much as possible without ending up with a fake effect

Stronger colour After the filter has been run, the colours are generally brighter in the areas that are more defined. This is very apparent in the beak. We have also achieved a stronger tonal range on the neck and chest area

After

Tip

Less is more

When using the High Pass filter always keep in mind that a lower Radius value will bring in better results. Most techniques use a Radius of 0.5 pixels to 6 pixels.

High Pass sharpening

In this walkthrough we'll look at a way of sharpening an image using the High Pass filter. This is often called 'an advanced form of sharpening', but it's very easy…

01 First steps We begin by opening our start image in Photoshop; the filter will enhance the edges and make the image appear sharper. Next, we need to duplicate the background layer by pressing Cmd/Ctrl+J.

02 High Pass filter We now want to run this new layer through the High Pass filter. This can be found by going to Filter>Others>High Pass. Slide the slider so that Radius reads around 2.5 pixels (see the 'Less is more' tip).

03 Blending modes Now we have an image that looks a bit like an embossed version of our original photo. Set the blending mode to Overlay – if the effect looks too sharp then reduce the opacity a little.

High contrast images

The High Pass filter can be used to create high contrast pictures when used alongside adjustment layers. When we think about adding contrast to photos we usually head for the Levels or Curves dialogs, but we can use the High Pass filter. Start by reducing the saturation in a Hue/Saturation adjustment layer and the contrast in a Brightness/Contrast adjustment layer. Now create a merged layer and run the High Pass filter. A good example can be found at **http://photo.tutsplus.com/tutorials/post-processing/3-fantastic-uses-of-the-photoshop-high-pass-filter/**.

Reduce a photo to its lines using High Pass

We can also use this filter to be creative; by using the High Pass filter on a photograph we can extract its lines and create line art. This is useful if you want to give the effect of something being drawn by hand. We start by running the High Pass filter, followed by the Note Paper filter. Finally, we reduce it further still by using the Threshold tool. A great tutorial for this technique can be found at **www.lunacore.com/photoshop/tutorials/tut011.htm**.

Resolution

Understanding the nature of every pixel in your image

The foundation of everything we do digitally is dictated by pixels. When we talk about quality, pixels are more often than not part of the equation, and this is where resolution comes into play.

Resolution is the number of pixels per inch in your image, and for short this is known as ppi. There are two resolution values which are commonly used: 72 and 300ppi. The larger the ppi, the bigger an image can be printed – and for on-screen purposes 72ppi is used, and 300ppi is best suited for printing.

But the factor that decides the final quality of an image is its pixel dimensions. The lower the pixel dimensions, the smaller the image size. When you increase the resolution (ppi) of an image that already has small pixel dimensions, you effectively make its print size even smaller.

In this guide you'll learn how to control resolution, whether for print or for on-screen purposes. Discover what happens to your image when you resample pixels – and we also uncover what the tick boxes in the Image Size menu really mean.

Resolution is the difference between an image with lots of definition and an image with a blocky, pixelated appearance. Always look out for high-resolution stock images to use in your artwork. This enables you to print bigger, zoom in closer and still have good definition.

Crop tool Using the Crop tool removes important pixels from your image, and as a result lowers an image's resolution (ppi) and ultimately reduces print size

Crop Tool   C
Slice Tool   C
Slice Select Tool C

⋮⋮⋮⋮| The right resolution for printing

Depending on the use, images ideally should be set at specific resolutions. When you prepare an image for print, the best resolution is 300ppi. However, this can be made smaller for printing draft-quality inkjet prints for example, and in this case 150ppi is acceptable. When printing with inkjet printers with photographic paper, 200-300ppi would suffice. The difference is in the definition and clarity of the result. More definition can be seen in an image printed at 300ppi than at 200ppi using the same size paper and dimensions. When an image is printed, the term dpi (dots per inch) is then used to describe its resolution.

⋮⋮⋮⋮| Setting the right ppi for your monitor

If you aim to use artwork purely for a website or for other on-screen purposes, image resolution should be set at 72ppi. The extra pixels in 300ppi become redundant for displaying on-screen, as clarity is still maintained at 72ppi. A monitor only considers the pixel dimensions of your image, which changes how big or small it's going to be displayed on-screen. If you know the output of your artwork, for on-screen or for print, before creating it make sure the image's dimensions and resolution are set in the New dialog box in Photoshop.

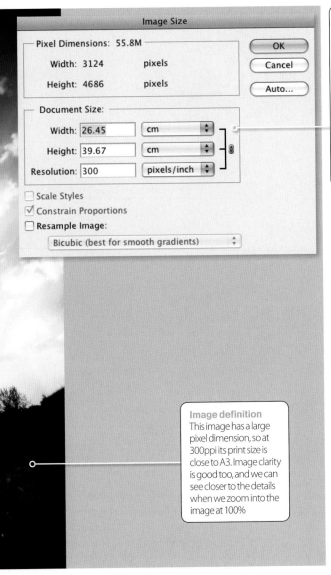

Image Size menu Under Image>Image Size, the image's pixel dimensions are given, as well as document size and resolution. The resolution is in pixels per inch (ppi for short). The resolution of 300ppi is used for print

Tip

File size and resolution

In the Image Size menu, if the Resample Image box is ticked the file size of the image changes as well. If you need to increase the pixel dimension of your image, keep an eye on the before and after values of the file size at the top of the menu.

Image definition This image has a large pixel dimension, so at 300ppi its print size is close to A3. Image clarity is good too, and we can see closer to the details when we zoom into the image at 100%

Changing image resolution

Image resolution is altered using Photoshop's Image Size menu (Image>Image Size). Here we show you the ins and outs of adjusting the dimensions of your image.

01 Constrain sizes Open the dialog box and make sure the Constrain Proportions box is ticked. Keep the Scale Styles box ticked and uncheck the Resample Image box. The pixel dimensions section should grey out.

02 Adjust resolution Using the Resolution field, enter a value suited to your purpose. For printing enter 300, and for on-screen use enter 72. You'll notice the Width and Height values change to show the document's size.

03 Adjusting pixels Tick Resample Image to change the pixel dimensions of your image. PS adds/removes pixels to cater for the change in size. Pick the Resample method for best results, depending on your image.

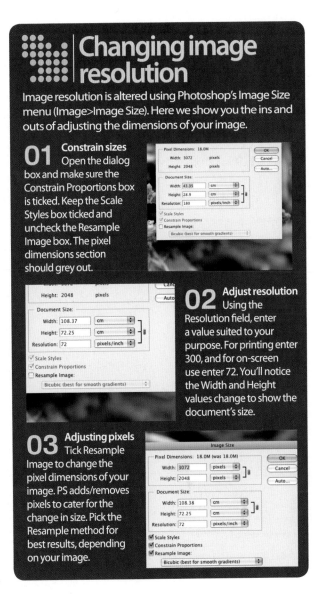

Resample dimensions

The option to resample your image is located at the bottom of the Image Size dialog box. This option enables you to adjust the actual number of pixels in your image, resulting in pixels being either added in or taken out by Photoshop. If you choose to resample your image, a list of options becomes available for methods of interpolation – the way PS blends each pixel. The option to resample an image should usually be avoided, as it affects quality and definition, and is best kept to small amounts.

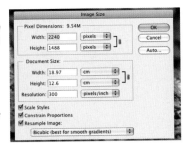

Use the Crop tool to alter resolution

Using the Crop tool lowers an image's pixel dimensions, and as a result affects its print size. The Crop tool can be set to a certain resolution for the cropped image. This feature is ideal for setting to either 300ppi or 72ppi to suit the use of the image, whether for print or a web-based purpose. Drastically cropping an image will result in a small print size, so we recommend that you use the Crop tool for trimming the edges of your image.

Understand how histograms work

Histograms may look scary, but they offer a very simple way of transforming your images into stunning scenes with just a few tweaks

essentials

SKILL LEVEL
::::: Beginner
Intermediate
Expert

TIME TAKEN
::::: 30 minutes

ON THE DISC
::::: All tutorial files

VIDEO TUTORIAL
::::: Understand
Histograms.mov

t first glance, a histogram in Photoshop or on the back of a digital camera looks like a bunch of lines on a bar chart.

To the casual happy snapper that's pretty much all they need to know, but for the avid photographer and for the Photoshopper, this provides a wealth of information about our digital images. We can utilise this information to when making changes in post-production.

We will start by defining what the histogram represents and how it works. Then we can take a look at the RGB colour space and how this fits into an RGB histogram. We'll then start looking at an example image and how the histogram displays that information. Later we will work with an image that has a red colour cast and use the Curves adjustments to remap the histogram and improve overall colour and tones.

An RGB histogram is a graphical measure of pixel tonality shown as a bar chart. The horizontal axis is a measure of tonal range. For a 24-bit RGB image, tones are defined by a number between 0 and 255. 0 is total black and 255 is entirely white. Mid grey has a value around 127. Black (0) sits on the far left of the graph, grey is in the middle and white (255) is on the far right. The vertical axis represents the number of pixels for a specific tonal value.

THE TONAL STRUCTURE OF AN RGB HISTOGRAM
How histograms relate to various shades and colour combinations

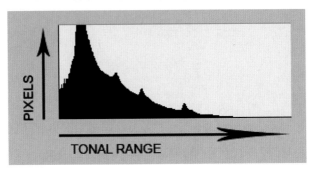

01 **Reading the histogram** Looking at the histogram image, we can see tonal range running along the X axis from left to right (0 black up to 255 white) and the number of pixels for any given tone running up the Y axis. All the tones are derived from various combinations of red, green and blue (RGB), which make up our digital image. Every image has a corresponding histogram reading.

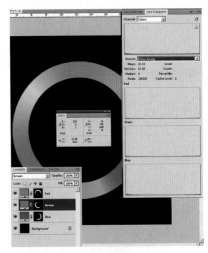

02 **The RGB colour space** So how do we visualise these colour combinations? Open up 'RGB_rings.psd' from the CD and go to Window> Show Layers. You'll notice the three layers representing RGB with varying amounts of red, green and blue. Wherever they overlap produces more colours of various shades.

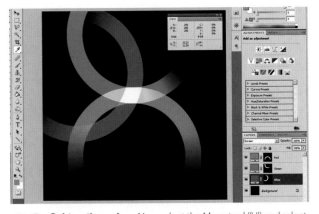

03 **Subtractive colour** Now select the Move tool ('V') and select each layer in turn and drag it towards the centre so that the pure red, green and blue areas overlap. You should achieve white in the middle, which highlights the fact that RGB is subtractive colour, as opposed to CMYK, which is additive colour.

04 **The Histograms palette** Now we know how RGB colour works, let's look at this in relation to a histogram. Open up 'wheel_barrow.jpeg' from the CD and go to Window>Histograms. In the Histograms palette, select the All Channels view from the menu on the right, and also check the Show Channels in Color option.

Tip

Working in 16-bit colour
It's also worth experimenting with 16-bit (48-bit) colour if possible. More colour information means that images are less likely to suffer from image banding effects and a 'combing' effect in the histogram. This is where blank gaps appear in the histogram where there are no pixels for that particular tone. You can work in a higher bit mode by shooting in Raw format or scanning slides and artwork at the higher bit depth.

HISTOGRAM ADJUSTMENTS

There are many ways to improve images with the histogram. Many tools adjust the histogram indirectly. The more direct way to change the histogram and adjust images is via the Levels and Curves palettes.

Adjust white and black points in Levels By creating a Levels adjustment layer then moving the Highlight and Shadow sliders inwards, you can improve contrast.

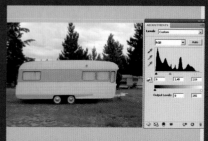

Create an 'S' curve Create a Curves adjustment layer and then try creating an 'S' curve . This will improve contrast and saturation.

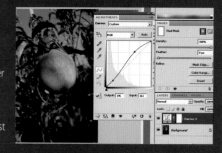

Eyedroppers in Curves You can use the Eyedropper tools in Curves to quickly adjust your white and black points.

Clipping warnings Hold down the Alt/Opt key when dragging sliders in Levels in order to show areas that are clipped (one tone).

Try working in 16-bit colour Working in 16-bit colour will give you a wider tonal range with which to make adjustments.

05 Palettes The composite RGB channel is a black histogram. Separate red, green and blue ones sit underneath. This image was photographed at night, so there's a dominance of darker colours and therefore a larger peak on the left-hand side of the histogram where it represents the darker tones.

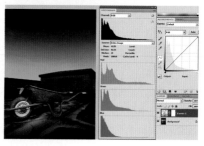
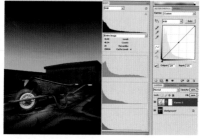

06 Curves Turn on the Info palette (Windows>Info). Add a Curves adjustment layer by clicking on the black and white circle at the bottom of the Layers palette. If you're in CS4/CS5, the adjustments have their own Adjustments palette. Older versions show a pop-up window. With the Curves adjustment active, pick the Eyedropper (I).

07 Measuring colour – Eyedropper tool Move the Eyedropper tool over to the orange sky and hold down Cmd/Ctrl and then click. It will add a point on the curve to represent where that sample sits along the histogram. It's roughly in the middle, which is about right, as this orange is a fairly average tone.

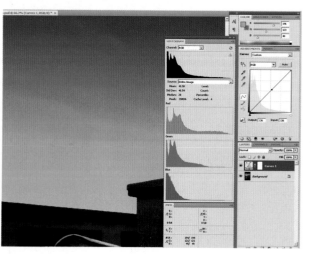

08 Measuring colour – Color Sampler tool Now hold down the Shift key and click. The tool switches to the Color Sampler and should add a sample marker point to the image. In the Info palette, values for RGB should be visible. In this case R:194 G:121 B:49 . This is the red/green colour combination that makes up the orange hue.

ADJUST THE HISTOGRAM TO IMPROVE TONAL RANGE
Use Curves to correct colour and improve contrast

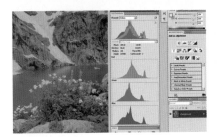

09 Examine the image Open 'mountain_lake_before.jpeg'. This has a noticeable red colour cast. Roll over what should be a neutral grey area on the rocks with the Eyedropper tool. If you look at the R value in the Info palette, it's higher than the G and B values. Grey should have near equal amounts of red, green and blue.

10 Add a Curves adjustment Add a Curves adjustment layer as before and double-click on the white Eyedropper tool in the Curves palette. Select the R value to 253, the G value to 253 and the B value to 253, and click OK. This is just off pure white. We have now set our default white point.

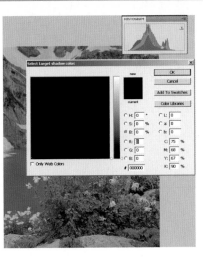

11 Setting the black point Now let's set our black point. Double-click on the black Eyedropper tool and set the R G B values to 0,0,0. This is complete black. We'll leave the Midtone dropper values set to the default RGB of 128, 128, 128.

12 Remapping the black and white point Select the white Eyedropper tool in the Curves palette. Examine your image and look for the brightest area. In this case, the petals of the flowers look the brightest. Click on the petals with the Eyedropper. You should see improvement in the highlight areas.

13 Setting the black point This time, let's repeat the process using the black Eyedropper and clicking on the darkest point of the image. The rocky crag at the back looks suitable. Now the image should not only have the cast removed, but the white and black points have shifted to give improved contrast.

14 Adjusting the midpoint Now adjust the midpoint. This only works effectively if you know an area of the image should be neutral grey. In this case the rocks in the foreground should be grey, so click with the midtone Eyedropper. You could also use this dropper on a grey card if you took an extra shot under the same lighting conditions.

15 The adjusted histogram While we've been making all these dropper selections, Photoshop has been updating the histogram behind the scenes. Double-click on the Curves Adjustment Layer icon in the Layers palette to bring up the changes. Select each colour channel and you'll see how the histogram has been updated.

Further reading
Take your understanding further

If you want to use histograms to help compose and expose your photographs accurately, check out some of these useful websites. Look in the Tutorials section of **www.luminous-landscape.com** and read the fantastic lesson in using histograms to achieve well exposed images. Another favourite tutorial of ours can be found at **www.photoxels.com**. This is a really simple guide to the basics of histograms, and perfect for those who are new to photography. For further reading about the use of histograms within Photoshop, check out **www.tutorialhero.com**. This site has some great diagrams and annotations to help you visualise how histograms relate to real-life images. Of course, the best way to improve your knowledge is by practising – open up the Histograms function in Photoshop and experiment!

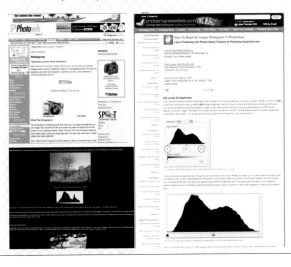

Magic Wand tool

Become a selection wizard with the Magic Wand tool

 ost people associate magic wands with magicians and their showmanship, but Photoshop has its own Magic Wand tool, and it's not used for pulling rabbits out of hats.

The Magic Wand tool is one of Photoshop's main Selection tools, and it's a handy way to customise your selections. It works by sectioning off particular colours inside your image. The selection process is affected by a collection of adjustment options. In this guide, we give you a rundown of the most important adjustments to remember.

The most effective way to use the Magic Wand tool is to zoom in to your image close enough to see each pixel. Then the four Selection adjustments – New, Add, Subtract and Intersect – can be used with more precision.

The Select menu at the top of Photoshop contains all its hidden adjustments, which affect the way the tool behaves. These options range from a collection of Modify adjustments, a Transform Selection option, and among many others, both Grow and Similar adjustments are found under the Select menu.

This comprehensive Selection tool can be used for separating two or more subjects, or singling out specific colours. With all these adjustments and modifications, you can't put a foot wrong making selections with Photoshop's Magic Wand tool, as we show you over these two pages.

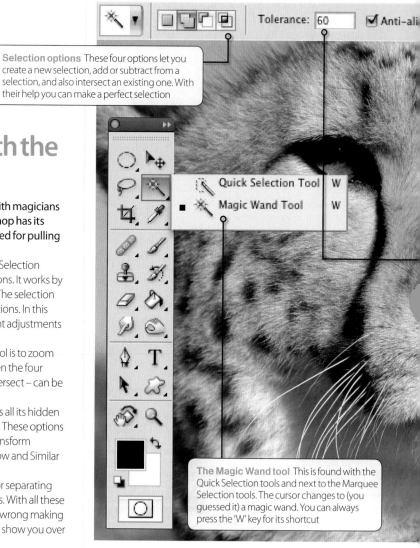

Selection options These four options let you create a new selection, add or subtract from a selection, and also intersect an existing one. With their help you can make a perfect selection

The Magic Wand tool This is found with the Quick Selection tools and next to the Marquee Selection tools. The cursor changes to (you guessed it) a magic wand. You can always press the 'W' key for its shortcut

---

Quick Mask mode explained

A selection is represented by a black and white dotted line, also known as 'marching ants'. Another way to view the marching ants is in Quick Mask mode. Select the Edit In Quick Mask Mode button at the bottom of the toolbar, and watch the selection change into a light-red colour cast. This colour cast allows you to see the selection in more detail, and you can add or subtract pixels easily in this mode. With the Brush and Eraser tools, you can paint or erase the colour cast to alter the selection. Click on the Quick Mask Mode icon inside the toolbar to return to Standard editing mode, and to see the marching ants.

Increase the spread of a selection

The Magic Wand tool works by selecting pixels of a similar colour, and it comes equipped with a Tolerance adjustment. The Tolerance of the Magic Wand tool decides how much of your image a selection will cover. The Tolerance is preset to 32, but you can easily change this to suit the size of the area you want to pick out. Just enter an amount into the Tolerance adjustment box to change it. The bigger the number, the larger the area it covers. With the Tolerance set to 32, a selection spreads across only a small area of a certain colour.

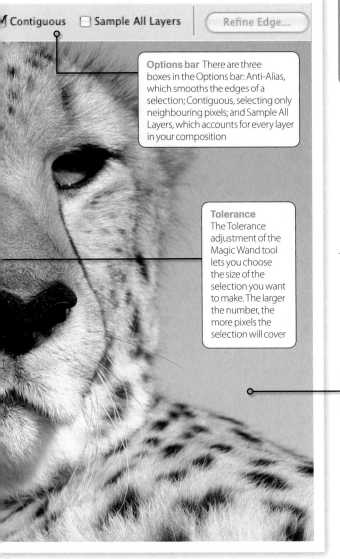

Contiguous   Sample All Layers   Refine Edge...

Options bar There are three boxes in the Options bar: Anti-Alias, which smooths the edges of a selection; Contiguous, selecting only neighbouring pixels; and Sample All Layers, which accounts for every layer in your composition

Tolerance The Tolerance adjustment of the Magic Wand tool lets you choose the size of the selection you want to make. The larger the number, the more pixels the selection will cover

Boosting colour We increased the saturation of the fur in this image. We selected the blue sky first, then went to Select>Inverse to select the cat. We used a Tolerance value of 60 for the sky to select a large area

Tip

Using Refine Edge
When a selection is made, the Refine Edge option (CS3 and above) becomes available in the Options bar. Using this, you can do multiple selection adjustments such as feathering and smoothing.

Making a selection with Magic Wand

The Magic Wand is highly versatile and is used to separate areas of colour. In this three-stepper we make sure you tick every box when selecting with this tool.

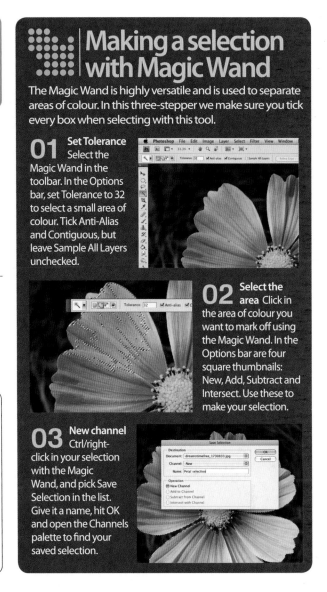

01 **Set Tolerance** Select the Magic Wand in the toolbar. In the Options bar, set Tolerance to 32 to select a small area of colour. Tick Anti-Alias and Contiguous, but leave Sample All Layers unchecked.

02 **Select the area** Click in the area of colour you want to mark off using the Magic Wand. In the Options bar are four square thumbnails: New, Add, Subtract and Intersect. Use these to make your selection.

03 **New channel** Ctrl/right-click in your selection with the Magic Wand, and pick Save Selection in the list. Give it a name, hit OK and open the Channels palette to find your saved selection.

Magic Wand adjustments

Once a selection is made you can change it in two ways. Grow and Similar are both found under the Select menu, or you can Ctrl/right-click anywhere inside a selected area to find them in a drop-down menu. Grow makes the selection gradually bigger and will select the same colours. The Similar adjustment picks out all the colours that are similar to the ones already inside your initial selection, but it jumps to any part of your image that is similar. Similar is ideal for selective black and white techniques.

Create new channels with the Magic Wand

When you save a selection as a new channel, you can adjust it any way you like at any stage. To save a selection, go to Select>Save Selection. In the dialog box, set the Document option to your current image and give the channel a new name. Hit OK, and the new channel will appear in the Channels palette. By selecting its layer, you can then use the Brush or Eraser tools to add or subtract the selection. It works in a similar way to the Quick Mask mode.

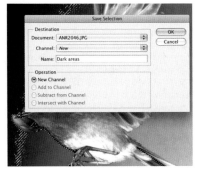

High Dynamic Range

Combine several exposures with Photoshop's Merge To HDR feature

ON THE DISC

::::: HDR source images

Tip

Image capture tips

Use a tripod and choose a lens focal length, then stick to it for each image. If you have a zoom, this means being careful to avoid knocking it!

 othing has created as much of a buzz in the digital imaging world as High Dynamic Range imaging. HDR describes the process of combining several exposures to record the full range of highlight and shadow detail in a high contrast scene that's beyond the capabilities of an ordinary camera sensor.

Our night-time image is a perfect example. A single exposure would leave us with burnt-out highlights or a near-black sky with zero detail beneath the pier. Combining exposures is the only way of having and guzzling our shadow and highlight cake!

In truth, HDR has been used to produce more cartoon-like effects by being used in low contrast scenes where it's not strictly required (via programs like Photomatix Pro). Unless you're keen on that eye-watering look, it's far better to use it on scenes like these that truly deserve it. Other examples you can try that are ordinarily beyond the limits of a camera sensor include sunsets where the foreground will usually turn to silhouette, and interiors where there's a window in frame that would ordinarily clip to pure white. With the HDR technique you can show all the wonderful foreground detail in a sunset shot and every little outdoor detail through an interior window pane. Magic!

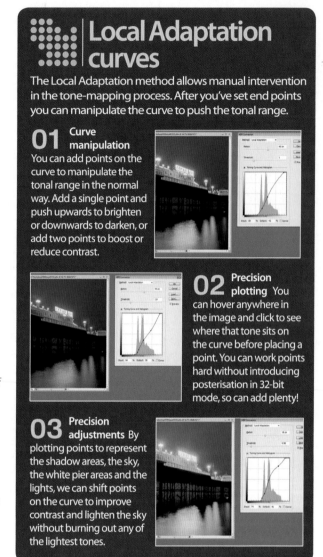

::::: Local Adaptation curves

The Local Adaptation method allows manual intervention in the tone-mapping process. After you've set end points you can manipulate the curve to push the tonal range.

01 Curve manipulation You can add points on the curve to manipulate the tonal range in the normal way. Add a single point and push upwards to brighten or downwards to darken, or add two points to boost or reduce contrast.

02 Precision plotting You can hover anywhere in the image and click to see where that tone sits on the curve before placing a point. You can work points hard without introducing posterisation in 32-bit mode, so can add plenty!

03 Precision adjustments By plotting points to represent the shadow areas, the sky, the white pier areas and the lights, we can shift points on the curve to improve contrast and lighten the sky without burning out any of the lightest tones.

::::: Must-know facts about HDR

Photoshop Merge To HDR can produce a 32-bit HDR image, but a pic in this format isn't a lot of use, as it can't be correctly displayed by current monitor technology. Instead, our images are usually converted from HDR back to low-dynamic range using a process called tone-mapping, which cherry picks and adjusts certain tones so there's detail in the shadows and highlights where none was previously present. So, although our final images may be the product of HDR imaging, our finished images are actually LDR.

::::: Exposing for ordinary scenes

The easiest way to capture several exposures is to switch to Aperture Priority mode, select an aperture and fire a frame. Check the LCD to see if exposure looks correct, then change the metering mode and try again if not. Once your exposure is bang on, you can use your camera's Exposure Compensation mode to take another frame one stop underexposed, and a third two stops under, then one stop over and another two stops over, giving you five frames in total. Check the darkest and lightest frames to see if all detail is recorded. A four-stop additional range is usually enough to record most outdoor scenes.

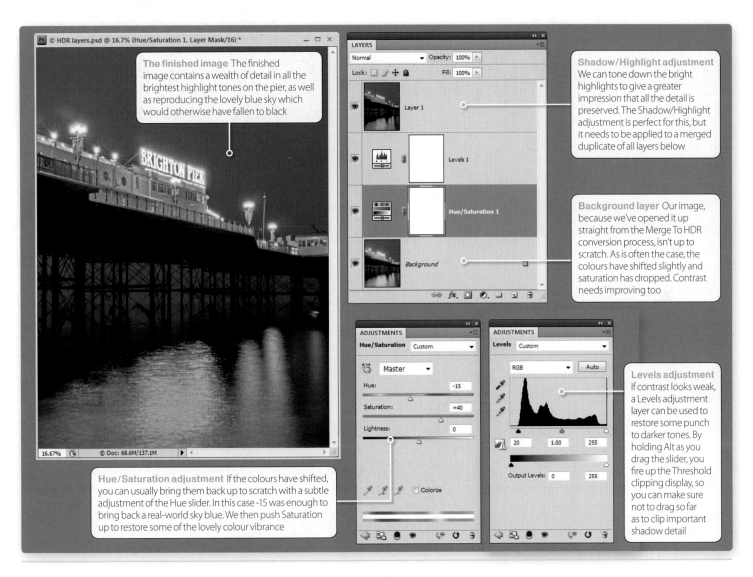

The finished image The finished image contains a wealth of detail in all the brightest highlight tones on the pier, as well as reproducing the lovely blue sky which would otherwise have fallen to black

Shadow/Highlight adjustment We can tone down the bright highlights to give a greater impression that all the detail is preserved. The Shadow/Highlight adjustment is perfect for this, but it needs to be applied to a merged duplicate of all layers below

Background layer Our image, because we've opened it up straight from the Merge To HDR conversion process, isn't up to scratch. As is often the case, the colours have shifted slightly and saturation has dropped. Contrast needs improving too

Hue/Saturation adjustment If the colours have shifted, you can usually bring them back up to scratch with a subtle adjustment of the Hue slider. In this case -15 was enough to bring back a real-world sky blue. We then push Saturation up to restore some of the lovely colour vibrance

Levels adjustment If contrast looks weak, a Levels adjustment layer can be used to restore some punch to darker tones. By holding Alt as you drag the slider, you fire up the Threshold clipping display, so you can make sure not to drag so far as to clip important shadow detail

Exposing for super high contrast scenes

If you are capturing an indoor scene with windows showing outdoor light, or a scene with a light source in shot – be it the sun at sunset or an artificial light source like a lamp – a four-stop range won't be enough. You'll need two- or three-stop increases rather than a single stop. To achieve this,

switch to Manual mode, dial in the Aperture and Shutter speed that gave you correct exposure, then alter the shutter speed to give you two more frames either side using two- or three-stop increments. This will give you an additional range of either eight or 12 stops.

More about aperture and shutter speed

If you're baffled by all this talk of exposure stops, just imagine stops as the amount of light you let into your camera. In aperture terms, exposure goes like this (from more light to less): f/1.4, 2, 2.8, 4, 5.6, 8, 11, 16, 22. In shutter speed terms, the numbers roughly halve for each stop (from more light to less). For example: 1 second, 0.5, 1/4, 1/8, 1/16, 1/30, 1/60, 1/125, 1/250.

TRANSFORM AN IMAGE USING HDR IMAGING
Combine several exposures to create a dramatic effect

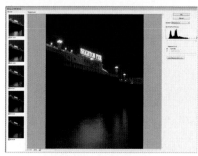

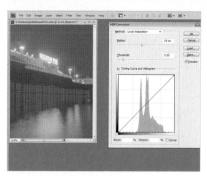

01 **Open the files** Go to File>Automate>Merge To HDR and select your files via the Browse dialog by Cmd/Ctrl-clicking each one (our source files are on the disc). Check the Align box and hit Open. The Merge To HDR preview window appears with all of the images arranged in terms of exposure on the left-hand side.

02 **Check the detail** Moving the White Point preview slider right the way across the histogram left and right, gives you the chance to check that you've captured all the detail necessary in the shadows and highlights. If it's not there, you may have missed an image when browsing, or you might need to shoot the scene again.

03 **Local Adaptation** Change Bit-Depth from 32-bit to 16-bit and click OK. Select Local Adaptation from the drop-down menu and click the button underneath the sliders to reveal the Curves dialog. Note the two points at either ends of the curve line. We'll be working those next.

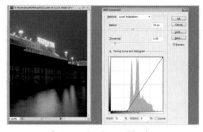

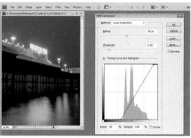

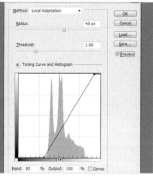

04 **Set up shadows** The histogram shows the range of information from shadow to highlight. To guarantee good contrast, we need to drag our end points inwards to meet that information. Click and drag the shadow point on the bottom of the histogram first, dragging rightwards to meet the edge of the histogram information.

05 **Set up highlights** Now we need to examine the highlights. We've still got space at the right of the histogram, so we click and drag the highlight end point inwards until we reach the edge of the histogram information. It needs less movement than the shadows.

06 **Sliders** Play with the Radius and Threshold settings, which control the tone-mapping. When either is set to 0, the other does nothing. High settings bring more contrast but not much detail. Low combinations can look too soft. We used Threshold 1.0, Radius 40px.

Merge To HDR settings 1

Local Adaptation uses a blurred version of the RGB channel as a mask to adjust tonality by calculating the amount of correction needed for local brightness regions in the image. The Radius and Threshold sliders control this mask. The Radius slider specifies the size of the local brightness regions, and the Threshold slider how far apart two pixels' tonal values must be before they're not part of the same brightness region. The tonal curve lets you make contrast alterations in the usual way. This is the daddy of all PS's Merge To HDR options and the only one you should use. Be sure to click the button below to make the Curve dialog visible.

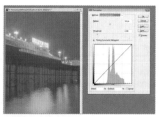

Merge To HDR settings 2

Exposure and Gamma doesn't really perform tone-mapping of any sort at all. It's identical to the display shown in the Merge To HDR preview dialog and simply shows how your HDR data appears on an LDR output source without any form of compression. The sliders will perform as you'd expect, but the highlight and shadow detail contained in your HDR image won't be condensed as required. It's only of use if you choose to work in Photoshop in 32-bit mode and then want to convert to 16-bit after the fact, and can be ignored by the vast majority of users.

07 **Manipulate the curve** You can now work the curve with extra points in the usual way. We add a single point and push upwards to brighten a touch. We could use a second point to boost or reduce contrast, pushing down from the shadows and up from the highlights, but we leave as is.

08 **Shift the hue** Once you're done, click OK and the 16-bit image will open up in Photoshop. You can now apply all your normal edits. If the colour has shifted (purple skies, for example) you'll need to add a Hue/Saturation adjustment layer using the button at the Layers palette base. Shift Hue to -15 to get a more accurate colour rendition.

09 **Increase saturation** The colour saturation also looks a little weak, which is another common by-product of the HDR process. Using the same adjustment layer, you can push Saturation up anywhere between +20 and +40. The sky and lighting are now enhanced and much more dramatic.

Using Raw files

To get the best possible quality during the HDR to LDR conversion process, PS requires source files to be in the RAW format. The images included on the cover disc are JPEG for copyright reasons, and decent results can be achieved in this way, but if you're attempting HDR work with your own images, try to capture in RAW where possible. You'll find that Photoshop will warn you when using JPEGs or TIFFs, that RAW files are the better option.

10 **Set black point** Despite the fact that we have good detail under the pier, the blacks look a bit weak. We add a Levels adjustment layer, hold down Opt/Alt and move the Black Input (top) slider inwards until black information starts to appear on the white background: setting 20. The blacks are now punchier yet no detail is clipped.

11 **Merged duplicate** The highlights are still a little bright, so we can knock them back a little with Shadows/Highlights. With the top layer selected, use Cmd/Ctrl+Opt/Alt+Shift+E in order to create a merged duplicate. Next, go to Image>Adjustments> Shadows/Highlights.

12 **Knock back the highlights** Set Shadows to 0% Amount, then Highlights to 35% Amount, 50% Tonal Width, and 100px Radius. Reduce Tonal Width and increase Amount if you get banding in the sky. Press Enter. We finish with some sharpening. Go to Filter>Sharpen>Unsharp Mask. Set Amount to 300% and Radius to 0.5.

Merge To HDR settings 3

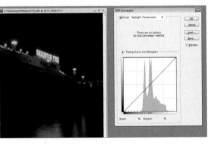

Highlight Compression performs a crude form of automatic tone-mapping compression, turning the brightest pixels to a value of 255 and converting the rest in a logarithmic way. It's the best method if preserving highlight detail is an absolute priority, but images usually appear very dark. If you're willing to go the semi-automated route with Local Adaptation, you can still ensure all highlight detail is present.

Merge To HDR settings 4

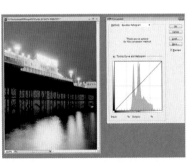

Equalize Histogram is another automated tone-mapping option with no further controls. It works in a vaguely similar vein to Auto Levels, attempting to maximise visual contrast. It finds the peaks in the histogram and spreads these out locally, ensuring that the majority of pixels receive a contrast boost. The effect is striking but tends to crunch the range at both ends together, producing heavy looking shadows and highlights that often appear a little weak. Again, Local Adaptation is a better option.

The Opacity settings

Use Opacity sliders to command the clarity of every layer and stroke

O pacity deals with an object's transparency, whether it's a layer or a tool. It's an essential adjustment that complements painting, photomanipulation and retouching to give degrees of subtlety.

The Opacity adjustment appears throughout Photoshop in a number of menus and palettes. It's an important control for many brushes, gradients and layer styles. Without the Opacity adjustment, it wouldn't be possible to fade subjects over others to create images that visually work better. Give a layer an Opacity of 100%, and it's at the maximum visibility with nothing visible underneath, but at an Opacity of 0% a layer turns completely see-through, revealing all that lies beneath.

Different tools in Photoshop have their own Opacity adjustments too. Take the Brush tool for example – you have many sliders to change the properties of the brush tip, such as Hardness, Size, Flow, as well as Opacity. A careful mixing of all these will make the perfect brush tip for you to paint with.

But the Opacity slider is also important when you use blend modes with a layer. Most blending modes at 100% Opacity look harsh or overcooked, but by lowering the opacity it makes for a more pleasing effect to the eye. It's a simple feature in Photoshop that's attached to nearly every tool, but can easily be missed.

Different tools The Brush tool has its own Opacity slider in the Options bar. Lowering the percentage of opacity, you can reduce thick strokes of paint to become fainter ones, for a finer way to paint

---

⣿ Controlling individual layers and objects

The Layers palette comes with its very own Opacity adjustment, and lets you change the transparency of any editable layer. Changing the opacity of your background layer will reveal the chequered canvas underneath. But by applying the Opacity adjustment to layers on top of each other, you can reduce the impact of the layer on top. Using the Quick Selection tool you can pick out an object in your image and place it on a new layer by going to Layer>New>Layer Via Copy. Once the layer has been created, you can edit the object with a blend mode, or with the Brush tool to give it a new colour. Whatever you decide, use the Opacity adjustment in the Layers palette to alter the strength of this object.

⣿ Adjust the strength of styles with opacity

The Opacity adjustment appears with every layer style, and is a great way to tweak the impact a style has on your image. To apply a layer style to your image, simply double-click a layer. The Opacity slider works on a scale of percentages, so it can be tweaked in minute variations. Whether you're applying a drop shadow or an inner glow effect, the Opacity adjustment makes all the difference to how powerful the final effect looks. The opacity of a drop shadow, for example, helps to indicate the intensity of the composition's lighting.

Flow: 100%

Options bar The Options bar holds the Opacity slider for various tools. This slider works separately from the slider in the Layers palette to give a greater control over the strength of a tool

LAYERS

Overlay | Opacity: 60%

Lock: | Fill: 100%

Background copy

Background

Before

Layers opacity
The Opacity slider in the Layers palette controls the individual layers, and when combined with a blend mode you can tweak the strength of the effect to suit your image

Tip

Shortcut keys

To control the opacity of a layer with shortcut keys, use the numbers 1 through to 0 to change the percentage of the Opacity slider in the Layers palette. You'll see a change on your chosen image.

Enhance colour in photos

Combine the Brush tool with the Opacity adjustment, and add a blending mode to the mix to change the colour of an object in your image.

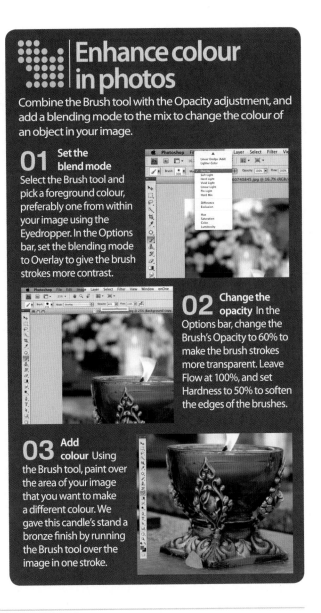

01 Set the blend mode
Select the Brush tool and pick a foreground colour, preferably one from within your image using the Eyedropper. In the Options bar, set the blending mode to Overlay to give the brush strokes more contrast.

02 Change the opacity
In the Options bar, change the Brush's Opacity to 60% to make the brush strokes more transparent. Leave Flow at 100%, and set Hardness to 50% to soften the edges of the brushes.

03 Add colour
Using the Brush tool, paint over the area of your image that you want to make a different colour. We gave this candle's stand a bronze finish by running the Brush tool over the image in one stroke.

Opacity and the Brush tool

Combining the Brush tool with the Opacity adjustment is easy, and changes the transparency of each paint stroke. The Opacity slider is found in the Options bar when the tool is selected. It's one of the many sliders that come with the Brush tool, and others include Hardness, Size and Flow. The Opacity adjustment is especially useful with the Brush tool to make sure whatever is underneath is visible, and you can use it to build up layers of paint in gradual steps rather than painting with solid strokes each time.

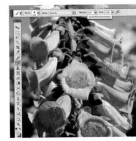

Opacity with image adjustments

When applying an adjustment layer to your image, such as a Gradient map, the effect at first looks overcooked. This shouldn't put you off applying the effect, because the opacity enables you to lighten it. Practise overdoing an adjustment layer and then using the Opacity slider to control its strength. For every new adjustment layer, the Opacity slider refreshes back to 100%, enabling you to experiment and adjust the transparency of each layer for the perfect result.

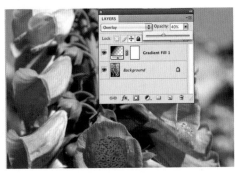

The Texture filters

Digital paintings and manipulations can sometimes appear a little flat

In this month's Big Technique we will be looking at Photoshop's Texture filters and how we can use them within our projects to add impact.

In real life, textures are all around us and we use them to visually distinguish how things would feel to the touch; for example, if we look at tree bark we know it will be rough to the touch. We can then use this knowledge to our advantage and assess the dangers of a situation. This also means we don't have to trudge across the park to feel the tree in the first place.

In Photoshop art we can use textures to give the impression of how things should feel, making the picture speak to its audience in ways beyond just the subject matter.

Photoshop filters are very handy and can be used to make some great art – although the overuse of them can very easily ruin a picture. The 'less is more' philosophy should always be kept in mind when delving into the Filter menu. The Texture filters come in six different flavours: Grain, Craquelure, Mosaic Tiles, Stained Glass, Patchwork and Texturizer. Each has its own unique result and set of options. For more information about the Texture filters, please refer to the boxes at the bottom of the page.

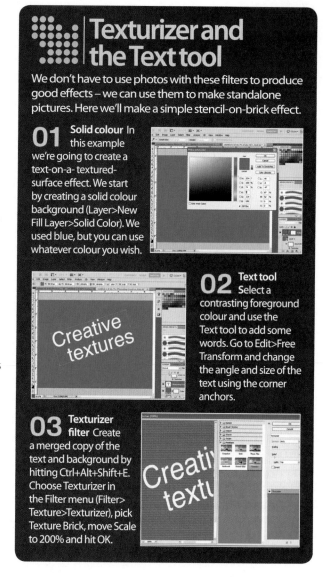

Texturizer and the Text tool

We don't have to use photos with these filters to produce good effects – we can use them to make standalone pictures. Here we'll make a simple stencil-on-brick effect.

01 Solid colour In this example we're going to create a text-on-a- textured-surface effect. We start by creating a solid colour background (Layer>New Fill Layer>Solid Color). We used blue, but you can use whatever colour you wish.

02 Text tool Select a contrasting foreground colour and use the Text tool to add some words. Go to Edit>Free Transform and change the angle and size of the text using the corner anchors.

03 Texturizer filter Create a merged copy of the text and background by hitting Ctrl+Alt+Shift+E. Choose Texturizer in the Filter menu (Filter> Texture>Texturizer), pick Texture Brick, move Scale to 200% and hit OK.

The six texture filter types

In real life everything has texture, not only in the feel of an object but also in the look (eg, if you look at a brick you know how it'll feel to pick it up). You can add texture to photos using blend modes and layer masks, but PS also has six Texture filters (Filters >Texture). When applied to pics they can add depth, effects or an organic feel to projects. The filters available are Craquelure, Grain, Mosaic Tiles, Patchwork, Stained Glass and Texturizer. Each creates a different effect and can be used in combination with the others.

Grain texture in detail

When we take photos a certain amount of grain is usually present. This happens when we set the ISO to a high number, eg for night photography. The rule of thumb usually is the higher the ISO the greater the grain. The Grain texture simulates different types of film grain and applies it to an image. There are a number of grain types: Regular, Soft, Sprinkles, Clumped, Contrasty, Enlarged, Stippled, Horizontal, Vertical and Speckle.

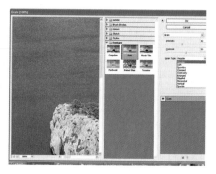

Filter on filter In our example here, we have applied multiple filters on top of each other. You don't have to use different filters on each layer, though. Strengthen an effect by applying it multiple times

Filter Library Photoshop's Filter Library allows you to cycle through the different Photoshop filters with ease. With the Texture filters we can easily see the six different varieties available to us and have the ability to change our minds without having to undo changes. Not all filters are available within the Filter Library

Filter Gallery With the introduction of CS, Adobe introduced the Filter Gallery which can be used to access filters and adjust their settings on the fly. Filters have also changed from CS4 onwards – where you can now have 'Smart Filters' that work like adjustment layers

Filter options The Texture filters all have different options which can be adjusted to suit your needs. Within this window we can adjust the effects by moving the sliders or in some cases selecting options from drop-down menus

Filter layers As well as being able to change filters on the fly, the Filter Gallery also allows you to combine different filters together using the Filter layers. In this window we can add more filters, rearrange them or delete them – very much as you would within Photoshop's Layers palette

Preview window This window shows you the effect the filter is having on your layer. We can adjust the zoom so that we can see a close-up preview of the effect or zoom out and see how it looks overall

Craquelure texture filter options

The Craquelure filter produces a plaster effect that is mapped to the image via a network of 'cracks' to duplicate the effect time has on oil paintings, where the surface will crack slightly. Evidence of this can be seen in museums and photos of old masterpieces. This filter can be manipulated to produce different effects. The options available are Crack Spacing, Crack Depth and Crack Brightness. This filter can also create an interesting cracked skin effect in photomanipulations.

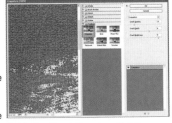

Mosaic Tiles texture, make more of less

Mosaic pictures are made up of a number of different coloured chips or tiles to produce an overall image – this is a bit like how monitors and printers work. With the Mosaic Tiles filter we can produce an effect that looks like a picture has been built out of small chips or tiles that have been grouted together. The filter allows us to customise the tile size, the grout width and how dark the grout is (Lighten Grout).

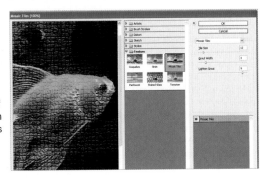

CREATE GREAT TEXTURE IN YOUR PROJECTS
Learn to make the most of the Texture filters

Homegrown textures

With the Texturizer filter we have four ready-made textures to make use of, but we can also create our own within Photoshop to use with this filter, although it would have to be PSD format. An easy copyright symbol can be made by creating a 200 x 200-pixel document, then using a bold font such as Arial, writing the letter 'C'. Surround this with a stroked elliptical selection and save as a PSD. Set Relief to a high number.

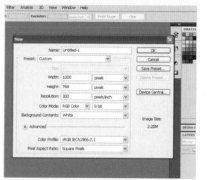

01 New project Create a new Photoshop document with a Width of 1000 pixels and a Height of 768 pixels. If you want to print your project then set the PPI to 300; if not, 72 is fine. Save this document as 'project.psd'.

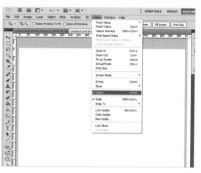

02 We rule We now want to divide the canvas into five equal sections, and we do this by first making sure we have the rulers visible (View>Rulers) or by pressing Cmd/Ctrl+R together. The top and left of the screen will now have visible rulers. Ctrl/right-click on one of these and select Pixels.

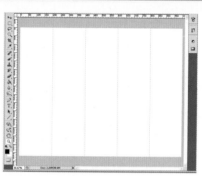

03 Set guides We need to make sure we can see our guidelines. We do this by going to View>Extra and making sure it's ticked. Next, select the Move tool from the Toolbox, and follow this by clicking and holding the left ruler. Drag a line out and drop it at the 200-pixel mark.

04 Flower power We repeat this for the 400, 600 and 800-pixel marks to get four guidelines and five sections. We want to fill each section with a photograph. We haven't supplied the start files for this, as it works on any image. Open up five photos and load the first one in Photoshop.

05 What a drag In the Layers palette drag the thumbnail of the photo to the New Layer icon (a square within a square) while holding the Opt/Alt key. A dialog will open asking you where you want to copy the layer to. Select Project from the list and name the layer. Finally, click OK.

06 Load and lock We can close the photo document and go back to our Project document. Drag it so it occupies the first section – feel free to move it around until you are happy with it. Next, we want to draw a selection around this section, but to make sure it snaps to the guides we need to check the Snap To option.

⣿ Texturizer filter, add texture quickly

This filter instantly adds texture to PS documents, with depth, shadows and highlights. It comes with a number of texture presets available from the filter's drop-down list, namely Brick, Burlap, Canvas and Sandstone. Scaling can be adjusted from 50% to 200%. Relief (darkness of the lines) and light direction can also be edited within this filter for different effects. We can use these

presets to easily change the feel of a picture, eg using the canvas texture will give the effect of something printed on canvas. We can also add our own textures to create other effects.

⣿ Patchwork texture options

The Patchwork filter works by breaking up the picture/selection into a series of squares. These are filled with that square's main colour. The filter also randomly reduces or increases the tile depth to produce shadows and highlights. You can also change its options – for example, adjusting Square Size to a larger number will produce larger

squares but will have the effect of fewer square blocks being produced. If we change the Relief option we can change the darkness of the lines that make up the picture.

07 **Snap!** Go to the View menu and locate the Snap To submenu (View>Snap To). Make sure that Guides is ticked, as well as Snap in the same menu. Choose the Rectangle Marquee tool and draw a selection around the flower. The Selection tool should snap to the edges of the guides.

08 **Put your mask on** We will now mask out the unwanted areas of the photo by using a layer mask. The good thing about making a selection beforehand is that anything inside the selection will not be masked – but everything else will be. We can do this by going to Layer>Layer Mask> Reveal Selection.

09 **Rinse and repeat** Repeat this again for all photos, putting each one in its own section and on its own layer. When you are finished you should have five sections with a slice of photo in each one, as in the picture above.

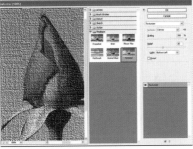

10 **Craquelure and Grain** Time for some effects! Locate the first photo layer and access the Craquelure filter (Filter>Texture>Craquelure). Set Crack Spacing to 15, Crack Depth to 6, Crack Brightness to 9 and hit OK. On the second photo use the Grain filter with Intensity 40, Contrast 50 and Grain Type Contrasty.

11 **Mosaic and Stained Glass** Choose the third photo and go to Filter>Texture>Mosaic Tiles. Make Tile Size 12, Grout Width 3, Lighten Grout 9 and hit OK. Reset to default colours by pressing 'D', then choose the fourth photo and select the Stained Glass filter (Filter>Texture> Stained Glass). Choose Cell Size 7, Border Thickness 2, Light Intensity 1.

12 **All good things** Finally, choose the last photo. Select the Texturizer filter from the Filter menu (Filter>Textures> Texturizer) and set the options to Texture Canvas, Scaling 200, Relief 20, Light Bottom Left. Remove the guides by using the Move tool to pull them off the canvas.

Stained Glass texture

The Stained Glass texture filter is a bit like the Patchwork filter, but builds an image of single-coloured cells. The cells are bordered by the foreground colour. The image is broken into areas of the predominant colour and arranged in a honeycomb style. The cell size, border size and light intensity can be changed to produce various effects. We can use this filter to make an easy stained-glass window effect, especially for the border.

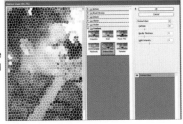

Stacks of effects in the Filter Gallery

These collected textures are great for creating quick effects, and it can often be useful to combine two or more of them. Luckily, Photoshop gives us the option of combining filters using the Filter Gallery. When we use one of the Texture filters we are given a window with options and previews. On the right-hand side under the options we have a window where we can add more filters or remove them – a bit like the Layers palette.

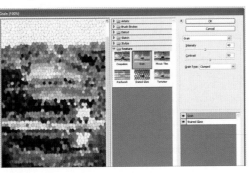

Marquee tool masterclass

Use the Marquee tools to give your images an exciting new look

T

he Marquee tools are a group of basic shapes used to make a selection. They are very simple to use but have endless possibilities.

The Magic Wand or the Quick Selection tools quickly introduce marching ants around a subject, whereas the Marquee tools have transformable dimensions, which can be a set size, perfectly round or a row of pixels, depending on the intended use. Not only that, but essentially being a selection, a marquee can have a layer mask attached to it and even a touch of feathering around its edges to soften its effects. Or it can be mixed in with a stew of marquee selections to create interesting and varied shapes.

There are four Marquee Selection tools in all, starting with the Rectangular Marquee and followed by the Elliptical, Single Row and Column tools. They are all represented on your image as dotted lines and can be used to cut out an area, revealing the layer underneath. They are like ordinary shapes but with no fill colour, so you can customise their contents with whatever you like, for example an adjustment or filter.

Have a read through of this guide to understand the difference between the Marquee tools and what they can offer the creative Photoshop user. There is lots of fun to be had with a little experimentation.

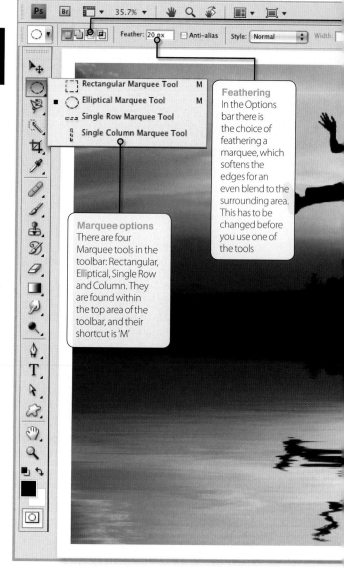

Feathering
In the Options bar there is the choice of feathering a marquee, which softens the edges for an even blend to the surrounding area. This has to be changed before you use one of the tools

Marquee options
There are four Marquee tools in the toolbar: Rectangular, Elliptical, Single Row and Column. They are found within the top area of the toolbar, and their shortcut is 'M'

∷ ## A rectangular window

The Rectangular Marquee tool is what it says, right? Not entirely, as there's a lot more to the tool than first meets the eye. Draw a rectangular border with this, and you can soften its edges, bend its shape or even make it a mask on a layer. To combine a layer mask with the Rectangular Marquee tool, draw your rectangle on an editable layer and click the Add Layer Mask button. This creates a window over your canvas showing only what's in the layer beneath. You

can freely move this window around by deselecting the chain link in the Layers palette found between the image's thumbnail and the layer mask. With the Move tool you can show different parts of the image by dragging it across your image.

∷ ## Fading out with the Elliptical Marquee

The Elliptical Marquee tool is perfect for designing albums, as you can fade out each picture with a circular frame. With your image open, create a new layer and drag it to the bottom of the layer stack. On this new layer go to Edit>Fill and choose white, then hit OK. Select the Elliptical Marquee tool, go to Feather in the Options bar and enter a value of 50px. Hold the Shift+Opt/Alt keys to draw a perfect circle over the subject in your image. Now select the original image layer and click on the Add Layer Mask button in the Layers palette.

Selections' behaviour Add, subtract or intersect multiple selections to create a unique shape. They have the shortcut keys Opt/Alt, Shift and Opt/Alt+Shift, and can be used to take off sharp corners of a square

Layers palette In the Layers palette you can apply a layer mask with a selection to single out an area around a subject. This layer mask can be manipulated just like any other selection

Tip

Remember to right-click
To open up a lot more options when using the Marquee tools, Ctrl/right-click does the trick. Give it a go and experiment with adjustments such as Feather, Refine Edge (CS3 and newer), Stroke and Fill.

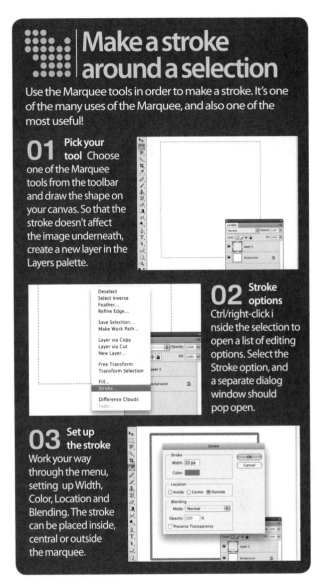

Make a stroke around a selection
Use the Marquee tools in order to make a stroke. It's one of the many uses of the Marquee, and also one of the most useful!

01 Pick your tool Choose one of the Marquee tools from the toolbar and draw the shape on your canvas. So that the stroke doesn't affect the image underneath, create a new layer in the Layers palette.

02 Stroke options Ctrl/right-click inside the selection to open a list of editing options. Select the Stroke option, and a separate dialog window should pop open.

03 Set up the stroke Work your way through the menu, setting up Width, Color, Location and Blending. The stroke can be placed inside, central or outside the marquee.

Quick Mask mode and the Marquee tool

The best thing about the Marquee tools is that they are just like any other Selection tool, and can be manipulated using the Quick Mask mode. After drawing the marquee over your image, press the 'Q' key on your keyboard (for the shortcut). By default a red opaque layer coats everything outside the selection. With the Eraser and Brush tools, paint or remove this red layer, and when you press 'Q' again the marquee changes. This is especially good for reaching difficult areas of a subject that you simply want to select.

Selecting pixels by row

This is really easy to do, and is an effective way to select just a row of pixels in your image. It's a technique that's otherwise quite tricky to achieve. In the Marquee set of tools there are the Single Row and Single Column tools. With one selected, simply click anywhere on your image to apply a selection. Try holding the Shift key to add more lines of single pixels. When the lines are set, go to Edit>Clear and whatever is underneath comes right through.

Edit your images for stock

Polish your pictures' pixels and earn you money as stock photos!

f you've been using a digital camera for a few years, you may have a valuable resource. By uploading your best shots to sites such as **www.istockphoto. com** you can supplement your income with a regular cash flow.

Designers are desperate for content to illustrate web pages or printed articles, and many download shots from stock photography sites because it's cheaper than commissioning a photographer or illustrator to produce work from scratch.

It's free to upload your photos to a stock site, but each image will be inspected for quality and content before being approved. There are many reasons why a shot might be rejected. JPEG compression, over-filtering in Photoshop and chromatic aberration are just the tip of the rejection reason iceberg! We'll demonstrate ways to edit to banish colour fringes, remove noise, reveal hidden shadow detail and even hide copyright logos. You'll also learn how to fake a shallow depth of field effect to blur unwanted details in the background.

You'll then find the process of editing and uploading stock photos much less frustrating, as more of your edited images will be accepted and you will be making more money on a regular basis.

⠿ Fake depth of field in your shots

Stock sites won't accept a shot if it has a person who hasn't signed a model release form in it, making it a challenge to shoot in city streets. Here's a quick trick.

01 Make a selection Open 'DepthofField_ before.jpg' from your cover disc. Grab the Magnetic Lasso tool. Draw around the edge of the foreground taxi to select it, then draw around the background to add it to the selection. Click the last point on the first.

02 Modify the selection Press 'Q' to activate Quick Mask mode. The taxi will turn red. Grab the Brush tool and spray a black brush to add missing bits of taxi to the selection. They will turn red. Use a white brush to remove bits of background from the selection.

03 Blur it Press 'Q' to exit Quick Mask mode. You'll see a modified marquee selection. Go to Filter>Blur>Gaussian Blur. Set Radius to 7.0 pixels and click OK. The background will become blurred, while the foreground taxi will remain sharp.

⠿ Depth of field texture effects

Your stock photos can't show shop fronts in a street scene due to copyright. People in a shot's background can't be recognisable if they haven't filled in a model release form. To hide unwanted elements you can select the background with the Marquee tool and use the Gaussian Blur filter to blur the selection. This fakes a shallow depth of field so that the background (and offending logos or people) becomes blurred, while the main foreground remains sharp. This mimics the effect of shooting with a wide aperture and stops the shot from being rejected. Check out our three-step walkthrough to see how you can apply a shallow depth of field effect to an image and hide unwanted elements.

⠿ Lose the logo from clothing

Logos or trademarks on clothing will get a shot rejected, so they need to be removed before the shot can slip through the inspection net. In this shot the skateboarding boy's cap features a green logo. In many cases the Spot Healing brush provide a quick way to remove unwanted logos. Simply click on the logo to replace it with a clean bit of texture. Alternatively, grab the Brush tool, press Opt/Alt to sample an adjacent clear pixel (like the boy's dark cap) and spray the sampled colour over the unwanted logo. This brush-based technique is good for removing car number plates as well.

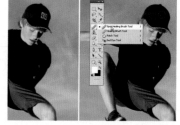

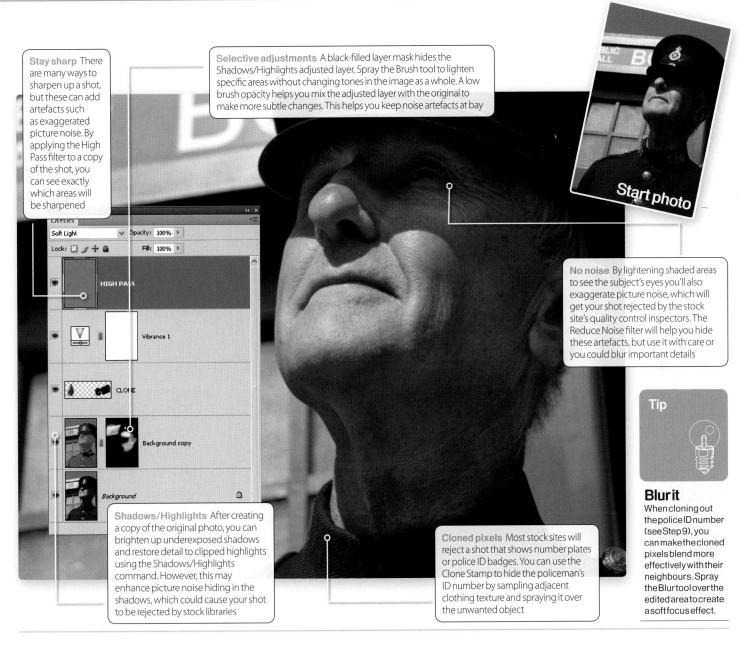

Start photo

Stay sharp There are many ways to sharpen up a shot, but these can add artefacts such as exaggerated picture noise. By applying the High Pass filter to a copy of the shot, you can see exactly which areas will be sharpened

Selective adjustments A black-filled layer mask hides the Shadows/Highlights adjusted layer. Spray the Brush tool to lighten specific areas without changing tones in the image as a whole. A low brush opacity helps you mix the adjusted layer with the original to make more subtle changes. This helps you keep noise artefacts at bay

No noise By lightening shaded areas to see the subject's eyes you'll also exaggerate picture noise, which will get your shot rejected by the stock site's quality control inspectors. The Reduce Noise filter will help you hide these artefacts, but use it with care or you could blur important details

Tip

Blur it
When cloning out the police ID number (see Step 9), you can make the cloned pixels blend more effectively with their neighbours. Spray the Blur tool over the edited area to create a soft focus effect.

Shadows/Highlights After creating a copy of the original photo, you can brighten up underexposed shadows and restore detail to clipped highlights using the Shadows/Highlights command. However, this may enhance picture noise hiding in the shadows, which could cause your shot to be rejected by stock libraries

Cloned pixels Most stock sites will reject a shot that shows number plates or police ID badges. You can use the Clone Stamp to hide the policeman's ID number by sampling adjacent clothing texture and spraying it over the unwanted object

Blown highlights be gone!

In bright lighting conditions you may encounter overexposed highlights that have lost colour. In the unedited version of the shot the yellow coat's highlights where white, as the colour had been bleached out. To restore colour to clipped areas, grab the Brush tool. Opt/Alt-click to sample the yellow from a correctly exposed area. Create a new layer and set its blending mode to Darken. Now spray the pink brush over the blown-out white highlights to turn them yellow. You can also boost the colour saturation to make the shot look more attractive.

Add more drama with a sky replacement

Overcast skies can make a shot look drab and boring. Enhance the shot by adding a more dramatic-looking sky to the original. Copy a suitably dramatic cloudscape and paste it onto your main photo. Now blend the transplanted sky by setting its blending mode to Overlay (or Soft Light) and reducing its opacity. Add a layer mask to the sky layer. Draw a white to black linear gradient on the mask to make the new sky fade and blend with the original.

RAW format

If you shoot in JPEG format, the camera throws away some information about the shot's colours and tones. This makes it harder to adjust colour and tone without adding artefacts to the shot. The best way to produce artefact-free stock photos is to shoot in Camera Raw format. You can then use the Adobe Camera Raw editor to fix colour and tonal problems more effectively, which gives your shot a better chance of being accepted as a stock photo.

:::: EDIT THE IMAGE
Remove any reasons for rejection by fixing colour, content and tone

01 Open image You'll find our unedited source file 'Police_before.jpg' on your cover disc. Open it in Photoshop. There are several reasons why this is unacceptable as stock. The angle of the sun has hidden his eyes in shadow, which could cause the shot to be rejected due to poor lighting. The background highlights are blown out, and his ID number needs to go.

02 Duplicate layer It's always worth copying the image onto a new layer so you can access an unedited version of the shot if required. Go to Window> Layers to open the Layers palette. Drag the background layer's thumbnail to the Create a New Layer icon to duplicate it.

03 Fix lighting Go to Image> Adjustments>Shadows/Highlights. Set Shadows Amount to the default 50% to reveal the subject's eyes. Set Highlights Amount to 21% to reveal detail in the blown-out background highlights. Hit OK. These settings tweak the tones in the entire shot and cause the shadows on his hat to lack contrast. We'll fine-tune the lighting later.

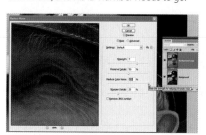

04 Reduce noise Grab the Zoom tool and click to take a closer look at his eyes. By lightening this underexposed area we've added picture noise. Noise artefacts will get the shot rejected. Go to Filter>Noise>Reduce Noise. Set Strength to 7, Preserve Details to 50%, and whack Reduce Color Noise up to 100%. Click OK.

05 Add layer mask The shot looks a bit washed out due to the lighting adjustments. You can limit the adjustments to specific areas such as his shaded eyes. Target the top layer (background copy) and click the Add Layer Mask icon. Now click on the mask's white thumbnail. Press Cmd/Ctrl+I to invert the mask. It'll turn black and hide the layer's content for the moment.

06 Edit the mask Grab the Brush tool ('B') and set the Tools palette's foreground colour to white. From the Brush Preset picker choose a soft-edged brush with a diameter of 500 pixels. Set Opacity to 40%. Click on the mask. Now spray over the subject's face in order to lighten it. Spray over the blown-out background highlights to darken them. The rest of the shot's tones can remain untouched.

:::: Rescue backlit subjects

If your location is backlit by the sun, the camera may set the exposure for the brightest part of the scene (the sky), so you might not be able to see much detail in the landscape's foreground features. By using a Levels adjustment layer you could try pushing the grey Midtone slider

to the right to brighten the underexposed midtones, but this will add lots of nasty picture noise to the lightened areas. Instead of trying to reveal detail, use the Levels command's black Shadow slider to darken the shadows and create a striking silhouette. This helps emphasise the shape and form of objects in the scene and gives the shot a better chance of being accepted as stock.

:::: Classy black and white images

Sometimes a shot's lighting can be too dark, causing colours to look desaturated. You could try boosting the midtone levels and increasing the colour saturation, but this can add nasty noise artefacts that will cause the shot to be rejected. It's often easier to make a shot with disappointing colours look more acceptable by converting it to monochrome. For effective high contrast mono conversions, go to Image>Adjustments>Black and White. You can lighten or darken specific objects in the scene

by dragging the appropriate colour slider. Black and white shots also stand out among a page of colour thumbnails.

07 **Limiting artefacts** By using masks and brush tips to target and tweak the tones in specific areas, we are able to reduce the chance of adding noise artefacts to the shot as a whole, which increases the image's chances of slipping past the eagle eyes of the stock site's quality control inspectors.

08 **Lose identity** The police officer's ID badge makes him identifiable, which could cause the shot to be rejected (even with a signed model release form). To remove the numbers click the Create New Layer icon in the Layers palette. Select the Clone Stamp tool from the Tools palette. Set it to Sample All Layers in the Options bar, and set Brush Size to 60.

09 **Clone** Zoom in to 100% Magnification and target the top layer. Move the cursor over a clear patch of clothing near the unwanted ID number, then press Opt/Alt to sample it. Place the cursor over the badge. Click to spray the clothing over the badge. Take several samples from various areas to hide all of the silver ID number.

10 **Boost colour** The shot is a little desaturated. You could boost the colour by increasing the Saturation strength, but this runs the risk of creating red-looking skin tones. CS4/CS5 has a handy Vibrance adjustment layer that boosts weaker colours but leaves stronger colours untouched. It's also very gentle when tweaking skin tones.

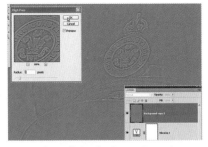

11 **Stay sharp** By sharpening a shot you run the risk of adding halos, enhancing noise and blowing out highlights. Duplicate the original background layer and drag it to the top of the stack. Choose Filter>Other>High Pass. Set Radius to 2 and click OK. Set the blending mode to Soft Light. This limits the sharpening to key details.

12 **Save it** Most stock sites require images in JPEG format. Go to File>Save As and select JPEG from the Format drop-down menu. To keep compression artefacts to a minimum, make sure you save the file at a maximum quality of 12 in the Image Options command window. This gives you the best quality result.

Stand out from the crowd

Anyone can shoot and upload scenic photos, but by using Photoshop's commands to produce more imaginative work you can create unusual shots that should sell more successfully than standard snapshots. Here we created an atmospheric night-time shot from a daytime source file. To produce this type of effect, add a Hue/Saturation adjustment layer to your source photo.

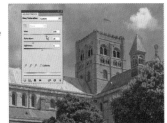

Tick the Colorize box to tint the shot. Drag the Hue slider to around 236 to turn the midtones a nocturnal blue, while preserving the blackest shadows and whitest highlights.

Banish chromatic aberration

Magenta or cyan colour fringes clinging to high contrast edges will get a file rejected as unsuitable for stock. If you're editing in the Camera Raw editor then the Lens Corrections tab's Chromatic Aberration sliders will do a great job of removing fringes. In the standard editor you can add a Hue/Saturation adjustment layer to a problem shot. Go to the

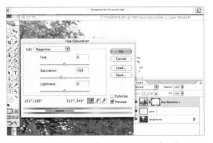

appropriate colour channel (such as Magenta) in the drop-down menu and reduce the strength of the Saturation slider to hide the fringes.

Swatches

Make your own unique Swatches palettes to help you create beautifully coloured work

S watches are great for collecting various colours together in one neat group and using them in your artwork and designs.

Imagine you've been asked to design a new logo for a company that uses set colours in all its publicity materials. By loading these set colours into a swatch and using them in the logo, you can be sure it will be accurately coloured to suit the company brand.

Another example of when swatches are useful is when you're painting a picture in Photoshop and you want to depict a certain kind of mood or season. By preloading a swatch full of rich, autumnal colours for example, you can be sure your painting comes to life – and you'll find it's much easier to have them all in one swatch.

The Swatches palette is the box containing colour swatch groups that you can use in Photoshop. To view the palette, just go to Windows>Swatches and it will appear on your screen. You can alter the default swatch and load alternatives by clicking the small black arrow in the top right corner of the palette and choosing a new swatch from the drop-down menu.

This guide will show you how to load and save your own swatches and put them into practice in your work.

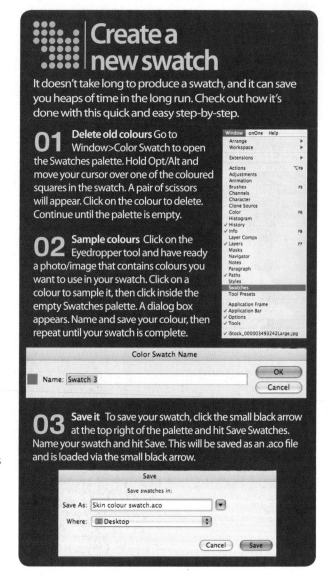

⣿⣿ Create a new swatch

It doesn't take long to produce a swatch, and it can save you heaps of time in the long run. Check out how it's done with this quick and easy step-by-step.

01 **Delete old colours** Go to Window>Color Swatch to open the Swatches palette. Hold Opt/Alt and move your cursor over one of the coloured squares in the swatch. A pair of scissors will appear. Click on the colour to delete. Continue until the palette is empty.

02 **Sample colours** Click on the Eyedropper tool and have ready a photo/image that contains colours you want to use in your swatch. Click on a colour to sample it, then click inside the empty Swatches palette. A dialog box appears. Name and save your colour, then repeat until your swatch is complete.

03 **Save it** To save your swatch, click the small black arrow at the top right of the palette and hit Save Swatches. Name your swatch and hit Save. This will be saved as an .aco file and is loaded via the small black arrow.

⣿⣿ Deleting the current swatch

Before you create a new swatch, you need to delete all the current colours in your swatch. Rather annoyingly, there's no 'Clear All' button, so we must delete the colours one by one. To do this, hold Opt/Alt and hover your cursor over a colour square until a pair of scissors appears. Now click on each of the coloured squares (still holding Opt/Alt) to delete them. Keep going until the palette is empty. If you place your cursor in the middle and click continuously, you will quickly delete the colours squares.

⣿⣿ Select individual colours for your swatch

In order to add new colours to your swatch you'll need to use the Eyedropper tool. The keyboard shortcut for this is 'I'. Open a photo that contains the colours you want to save and use the Eyedropper to click on a colour. Your colour will appear in the Foreground Color box at the foot of the toolbar. To set this to your swatch, click within the Swatches palette, name your colour and hit OK. Repeat this process for the whole swatch. If you prefer, you can hold down the mouse button when choosing colours with the Eyedropper to see a rolling preview of the various shades. Release the mouse and the colour is selected. This is a good option if you're unsure of which colours to pick.

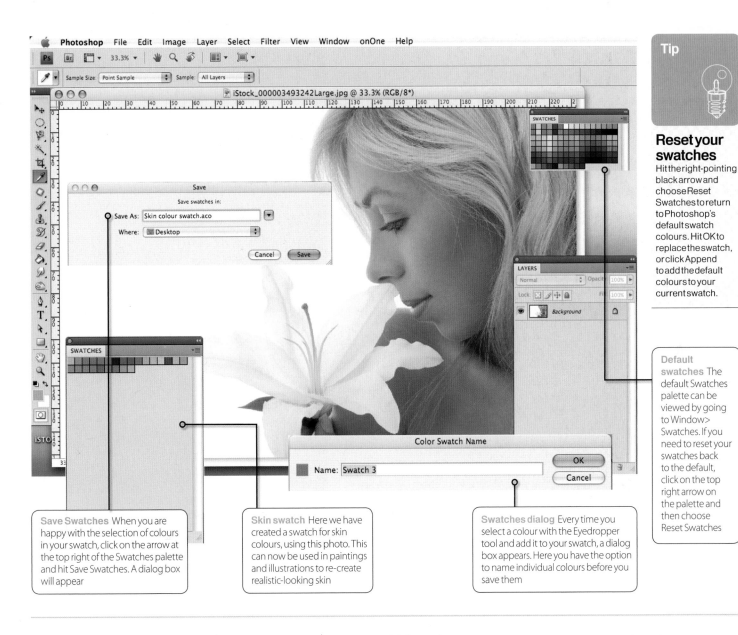

Tip

Reset your swatches

Hit the right-pointing black arrow and choose Reset Swatches to return to Photoshop's default swatch colours. Hit OK to replace the swatch, or click Append to add the default colours to your current swatch.

Default swatches The default Swatches palette can be viewed by going to Window> Swatches. If you need to reset your swatches back to the default, click on the top right arrow on the palette and then choose Reset Swatches

Save Swatches When you are happy with the selection of colours in your swatch, click on the arrow at the top right of the Swatches palette and hit Save Swatches. A dialog box will appear

Skin swatch Here we have created a swatch for skin colours, using this photo. This can now be used in paintings and illustrations to re-create realistic-looking skin

Swatches dialog Every time you select a colour with the Eyedropper tool and add it to your swatch, a dialog box appears. Here you have the option to name individual colours before you save them

The fast way to select colour

If you know you want to select all the tones from a single image, you can convert this easily into a swatch of its own. Open a photo and go to Image>Mode>Indexed Color. Set the Palette to Local (Perceptual), Colors to 256, ensure Transparency is checked and set Dither to None. Now go to Image>Mode>Color Table. The colours from your photo are picked out individually. Name it and save it. This is saved as an .act file (not a .aco file), which can be loaded into your Swatches palette.

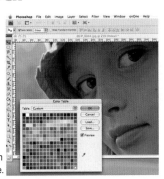

Swatch ideas and when to use them

It's a good idea to create a number of swatches to suit the scenes you wish to paint or the items you wish to design. For example, you may want to paint a rich autumn landscape or a pastel-based springtime landscape. You can create a colour swatch for each of these scenes. If you love to paint portraits you might find it helpful to create various skin swatches to help paint skintones. Swatches are great for keeping your artwork focused, rather than having an inconsistent mass of colour. Look online for plenty of free ready-made swatches such as at **http://freephotoshop.org/swatches/**.

Create realistic shadows

Use Displacement maps to create convincing shadows

iStock_
2204360.jpg
(courtesy of
RapidEye, www.
istockphoto.
com/RapidEye)

iStock_
5454448.jpg
(courtesy of
MBPHOTO,
INC, www.
istockphoto.
com/DNY59)

615072.jpg
(courtesy of
**elvissantana.
com**)

hadows create mood and atmosphere, while adding dimension and meaning to an image. Without them, images are rendered impotent, flat and lifeless.

The interplay between light and dark will enhance any image, which is why photographers have always striven to capture the perfect shadow that interacts with their subject. Thankfully, Photoshop has numerous tools that allow us to swiftly apply this dimensionality after the photograph has been taken.

In this feature we'll take a look beyond the ubiquitous Drop Shadow layer style and explore some more advanced techniques of how to add convincing shadows to your images. We'll use the often misunderstood Glass filter in conjunction with a greyscale Displacement map to conform our shadow to the uneven surface of a brick wall. We'll also investigate how the Glass filter's close relative, the Displace filter can be used to push and pull shadow pixels in a similar fashion. You'll also learn how to reproduce nature's 'image-based' shadows, as well as how the Lighting Effects filter is capable of producing some great results. Finally, we'll make full use of Photoshop's blending modes and layer masks to enhance selective light and shadow areas. Once you've mastered these techniques, you'll never want to settle for a plain old layer style again!

Exploring the Displace filter

The Displace filter is very similar to its cousin, the Glass filter. It works in a similar way using the brightness values of one image to shift the position of pixels in another.

01 **Background** Try exploring how shadows react to different environments. When you get to step 7 in the tutorial, add the metal shutter as a different background. The image is smaller, so you'll need to crop the canvas.

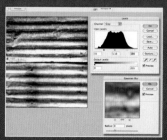

02 **Displacement adjustments** Copy the background to a new greyscale document. Add a Levels adjustment (blackpoint: 55, midpoint: 1.10 and whitepoint: 194). Add 5px of Gaussian blur. Save as 'MetalDisplacement.psd'.

03 **Apply** On the Shadow layer go Filter>Distort>Displace. Type 50 in the Scale field. Check Stretch To Fit and Repeat Edge Pixels. Add a masked duplicate of the Metal layer set to Screen. Clip a Levels adjustment to the Figure layer.

Image-based shadows

Adding moody atmospheric lighting to an image is fairly straightforward – the trick is to get the objects' shadow to interact with your subject. Here we transformed a fairly ordinary lit image into something much more dramatic by projecting shadows through a sunlit window. First, a separate black

and white stripe layer was dropped in and set to Multiply and its Opacity reduced, then various degrees of Gaussian Blur were applied. A mask was then used to hide the lower portion, and finally the shadow was displaced using the Displace filter with the same technique detailed in the boxout at the top right. Try using other objects as shadows, like tree foliage.

Let there be light... and shadow

The Lighting Effects filter works in a similar way to the Glass and Displace filters, but allows control over light and shadow. First create some blurred text and store it within an Alpha channel. Go to Filter>Render> Lighting Effects. From here you can load the channel using the drop-down Texture Channel menu, and adjust its depth up or down accordingly. You'll also find settings for Light Type, Intensity, Focus, as well as various Light Property options. By experimenting with these settings and adding different multiple coloured lights, you can create some interesting shadow interactions.

Keep it real Build your shadows up on separate layers and use varying degrees of opacity and Gaussian blur to achieve realism – remember, shadows in the real world exhibit light diffusion, meaning that they are much darker and sharper at their base than at their ends

Shadow displacement Save a modified greyscale version of your background to use in conjunction with the Glass filter. This filter will displace the shadow, conforming it to the contours of the wall. The displacement uses greyscale information the same way as 3D applications use bump maps to add texture to 3D objects

Figure isolation Create a Bezier path with the Pen tool to isolate the figure. You can then generate a path-based selection and add the figure as an independent layer over different background environments such as the brick wall or metal shutter

Start photos

Match light sources When comping different images together, always look for ways to make their lighting consistent. Here we've used a simple but effective method of flipping the background image horizontally to match the lighting of the figure

Set the mood By applying Transform functions such as Skew, Distort and Perspective to your shadow, you'll instantly create atmosphere. The position and strength of the lighting will also determine the mood of the scene

Tip

Add some noise
If your image is destined for print, add a small amount of noise to your shadow. This simple technique will make your shadows appear all the more real in print.

Add a splash of colour

It always pays to study nature and how natural or artificial light produce different shadows. Shadows in the real world exhibit light diffusion, so they are more intense closer to the base of the object. Also, light refracted through a transparent object such as glass or a liquid will reflect interesting colour hues besides monotone in their shadows. The Impressionist painter, Renoir is quoted as saying, "No shadow is black. It always has a colour". The original and retouched images illustrate this point perfectly.

Add realism to illustrations

Shadows not only play an important role in conventional photography – product designers also need to make their concept visuals as lifelike as possible. This illustration for a hand-held mobile device was created from scratch in Photoshop. To make the product plausible, a glossy reflection was added. While this is not technically a shadow, the same principles apply. Without the shadow, the image would lack dimension. It's this attention to detail that really does make a difference to the final image.

149

Tip

The Glass filter explained

The Glass and Displace filters work by aligning the upper left-hand corners on both the image to be filtered and the file used to create the displacement. Therefore both files need to share the exact same pixel dimensions. If you have any excess image areas extending beyond your canvas, you'll get some strange results. This is because the filters take this additional image information into account. You can overcome this by choosing Select All>Crop before applying the filters.

::::: MOVE YOUR SHADOWS ONTO NEW SURFACES
Get to grips with Displacement maps

01 Pen precision Open the model image. We need to isolate him so he can be placed on a different background. The Pen tool is really the only option for this image, so set it to Paths, zoom in and carefully plot your points around the figure. When you're done, Cmd/Ctrl-click your path thumbnail to generate a selection.

02 New layer Hit Opt/Alt+Cmd/Ctrl +D to add a 1px Feather. Copy and paste into the wall image as a new layer. Go to Layer>Matting>Defringe and use a 2px setting. Name the layer 'Figure' and hit Cmd/Ctrl+T to position it bottom right. Double-click the background layer, rename it 'Wall' and Edit>Transform>Flip Horizontal.

03 Skew the shadow Cmd/Ctrl-click your Figure layer to generate a selection, then drop a new layer underneath it and label it 'Shadow'. Hit Cmd/Ctrl+T again, then right-click to select Skew and pull the top-middle handle to the left. Feel free to apply the other Transform functions such as Distort and Perspective, then elongate towards the top of the canvas.

04 Fix problem areas If you zoom in and examine the edges of the shadow around the figure's left hand, you'll notice some areas that look unnatural – this will vary, depending on the degree of distortion you applied to the shadow. Fix these problem areas by setting the Eraser tool to a small hard-edged brush to remove them.

05 Shadow mask Soften the Shadow layer with a Gaussian Blur of 2px. Set your foreground colour to black and add a layer mask. Now Shift-drag a 45-degree Linear gradient from the top-left of your canvas on the mask using the Foreground to Transparent preset.

06 Depth Duplicate the Shadow layer, target the Shadow Copy mask thumbnail and hit Cmd/Ctrl+I to invert – you'll now have a reversed mask, revealing the top shadow area. Add a Gaussian Blur of 40px to the Shadow Copy layer. The two shadow layers now have depth, as areas closer to the light source will naturally have more focus.

::::: Add shadows the fast way

The great thing about layer styles is their relationship to the actual layer content; because the style is layer-linked, it will continually update as the layer content is edited or moved. Also, effects are easily adjusted at any point, making them

non-destructive. Once you've created a layer style, you can save it directly into the Styles palette. For more control use the Preset Manager found under the Edit menu. Here you can create your own layer style libraries to load as required.

::::: Independent shadows for precision

Using a Drop Shadow layer style has its limitations because the shadow shape is identical to the shape of the source layer. If you require more control over its appearance, go to Layer>Layer Styles>Create Layer. This will release the style onto its own independent layer. It can now be manipulated as required using the Transform tool's Skew, Distort and Perspective operations to create a cast shadow, then a mask added for extra depth. If your initial layer had multiple layer styles, the Create Layer command will also place them on individual layers.

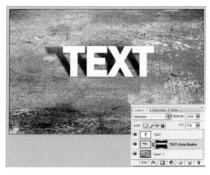

07 Merge the shadow Target your Shadow Copy layer and press Cmd/Ctrl+E to merge down, accepting Apply in the next window. Add a fresh mask to the merged layer, then click the Color Picker and enter C: 0, M: 0, Y: 0, K: 50. Add a Foreground to Background Linear gradient as before, then set the layer to Multiply and its Opacity to 90%.

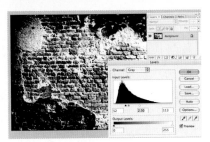

08 Displacement map Select all the content of the Wall background layer and Copy>Paste into a new document, accepting the Clipboard preset, and select Greyscale under Color Mode and Flatten. Now hit Cmd/Ctrl+L for Levels. Input settings: blackpoint 52, midpoint 2.30, whitepoint 113. Save it as 'Displacement_map.psd'.

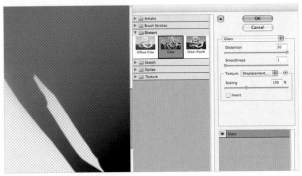

09 Conforming shadow Target your Shadow layer, then go to Filter>Distort>Glass. Set Distortion to 20 and Smoothness to 1. Now click the triangle icon next to the Texture menu to load your 'Displacement_map.psd' and leave Scaling at 100%. The effect is subtle, but you'll see the shadow follows the wall contours.

10 Wall light Now to add some light source to the background. Duplicate the Wall layer and set its mode to Screen at 70% Opacity. Add a layer mask, set your foreground to black then drag a Foreground to Transparent Linear gradient from the left of the canvas.

11 Clip an adjustment layer Let's add some selective tonal modifications. Target your Figure layer, then press Option while selecting Levels from the drop-down Create New Fill or Adjustment Layer icon at the foot of the Layers palette. In the next window, check Use Previous Layer to Create Clipping Mask. Move the blackpoint Input slider to 6 to darken the figure's darkest areas.

12 Refinements Add a Black & White adjustment layer using the Maximum White Preset, set it to Multiply at 57% Opacity. Add a Hue/Saturation adjustment layer using these Saturation settings in the Edit menu: Red -51, Yellow -54, Cyan -70. Now readjust Shadow Opacity to 75%.

Drop Shadow styles and settings

The Layer Style dialog box has various settings. The Angle sets the direction of the shadow. The Distance field determines how far the shadow will fall – you can also click in your document window and manually drag the shadow into position. The Spread setting affects how hard or soft it appears. The Contour setting is probably the most misunderstood and powerful feature. From here you can apply a multitude of different effects using the built-in presets, or even create your own settings within the Contour Editor.

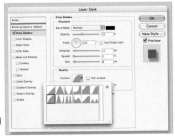

Adding more than one shadow

Multiple light sources will produce multiple shadows. If you've ever watched a floodlit football you'll have noticed this – sometimes up to four shadows are visible. Each light will cast its own shadow, with overlapping areas appearing multiplied. This is also noticeable when an image is exposed to both natural sunlight and artificial light or lights. You can achieve the same effect by simply flipping or rotating your shadows to match the light sources.

The Knockout blend feature

Discover this simple way to punch clean, digital holes through layers

T he Knockout blend feature in Photoshop is found inside the Layer Styles menu, and under the heading Advanced Blending options.

It's described as a layer style because it affects the way one layer interacts with other layers below it. When a Knockout blend is applied, it turns a layer into a floating, keyhole-like window. It will then move over the top of an image to show the layers below. A Knockout blend reveals layers underneath in two stages, Shallow and Deep. If a Deep Knockout blend is applied to a layer, it punches through multiple layers, whereas the Shallow blend only goes through one layer.

Over the next two pages we show you the ins and outs of Photoshop's Knockout blend. The Knockout blend has either a Shallow or Deep effect, and this is perfect for dealing with multiple layers and even when images are in groups. Applying a Knockout to a layer lets you move the shape freely across the canvas, and this shows different parts of the layers underneath.

So whether it's revealing layers underneath or creating your very own digital keyhole, it's time to get to know the Knockout blend a bit more personally.

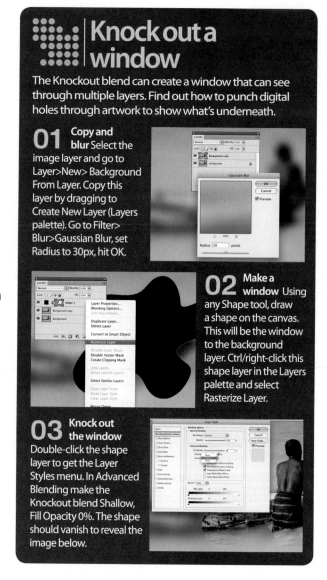

Knock out a window

The Knockout blend can create a window that can see through multiple layers. Find out how to punch digital holes through artwork to show what's underneath.

01 Copy and blur Select the image layer and go to Layer>New> Background From Layer. Copy this layer by dragging to Create New Layer (Layers palette). Go to Filter> Blur>Gaussian Blur, set Radius to 30px, hit OK.

02 Make a window Using any Shape tool, draw a shape on the canvas. This will be the window to the background layer. Ctrl/right-click this shape layer in the Layers palette and select Rasterize Layer.

03 Knock out the window Double-click the shape layer to get the Layer Styles menu. In Advanced Blending make the Knockout blend Shallow, Fill Opacity 0%. The shape should vanish to reveal the image below.

A Knockout blend needs a background

For the Knockout blend to work it needs the bottom layer to be set as a background layer. The background layer should contain the image you want to show through when the Knockout blend is applied. To make an image into a new background layer, go to Layer>New>Background From Layer. This will automatically send the layer to the bottom of the Layers palette, and lock it as the background. If there isn't a background layer when you apply the Knockout blend, all that will appear are grey and white canvas tiles and no image. You can double-click a background layer to convert it back into an editable one.

Get a clearer Knockout blend

When you double-click a layer, the Layer Styles menu opens. The Knockout blend is found under the Advanced Blending options inside the menu, and its Fill Opacity is found here too. The Fill Opacity will alter the transparency of the Knockout blend, and when reduced to 0% Fill, the background layer is completely visible. Reduced to 50% Fill, it'll give you a Color Overlay effect, where the shape and its colour are partly visible over the other layers. You can also change the Fill Opacity from inside the Layers palette by using the Fill slider.

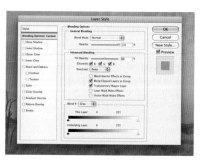

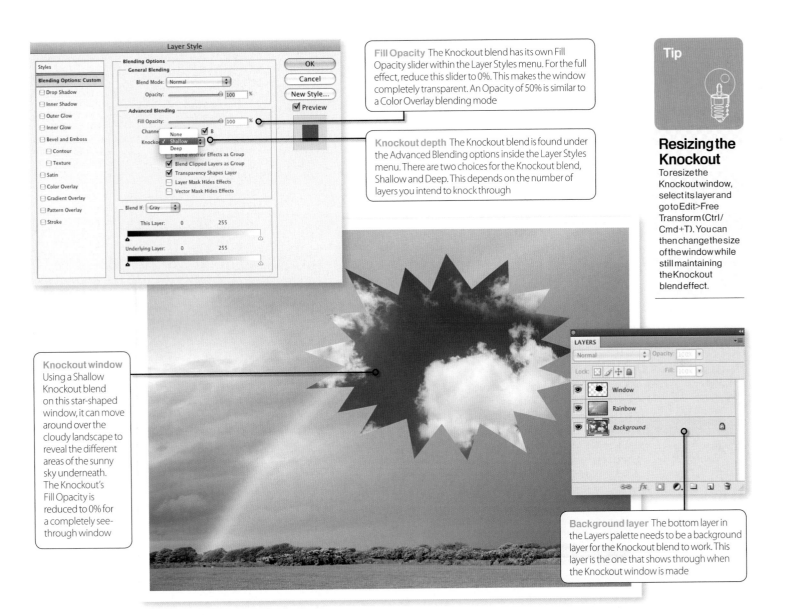

Fill Opacity The Knockout blend has its own Fill Opacity slider within the Layer Styles menu. For the full effect, reduce this slider to 0%. This makes the window completely transparent. An Opacity of 50% is similar to a Color Overlay blending mode

Knockout depth The Knockout blend is found under the Advanced Blending options inside the Layer Styles menu. There are two choices for the Knockout blend, Shallow and Deep. This depends on the number of layers you intend to knock through

Knockout window Using a Shallow Knockout blend on this star-shaped window, it can move around over the cloudy landscape to reveal the different areas of the sunny sky underneath. The Knockout's Fill Opacity is reduced to 0% for a completely see-through window

Background layer The bottom layer in the Layers palette needs to be a background layer for the Knockout blend to work. This layer is the one that shows through when the Knockout window is made

Tip

Resizing the Knockout
To resize the Knockout window, select its layer and go to Edit>Free Transform (Ctrl/Cmd+T). You can then change the size of the window while still maintaining the Knockout blend effect.

Knock out a window using multiple layers

Using the Link Layers button with the Knockout blend, you can make a window that moves freely across the canvas. It's a tidier way of cutting one layer out from another. Make two shape layers, with the smallest shape on top, and make sure there's a background layer underneath these. Double-click the smallest shape layer and set the Knockout to Shallow with a 0% Fill Opacity. Highlight both shape layers and select the button called Link Layers in the Layers palette. Both of the shapes will now move together.

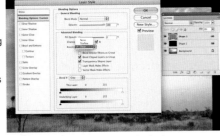

Using the Knockout with a group

The Knockout blend can be applied when multiple layers are in one group. An important point to remember when using a group with the Knockout is to set the group's blend mode to Pass Through. The blend modes are found inside the Layers palette. This makes sure that the Knockout blend accounts for all the layers outside the group. A Knockout blend can be set to two different strengths, Shallow or Deep, and both these will be taken into account.

153

Explore Smart Filters and Smart Objects

Learn to work 'smart' with two powerful non-destructive features

efore PS introduced Smart Filters, their effect was permanent – you only had one chance to get it right and apply blending modes via the Fade filter in the Edit menu. If it all went wrong your only saviour was the History palette, or the Undo feature if you were lucky!

With the introduction of Smart Filters (CS3), that's all behind us. They work in conjunction with Smart Objects (available from CS2 upwards). Any layer that's converted into a Smart Object can be scaled, rotated and warped many times without losing any of its original pixel info. Smart Objects can also have Smart Filters applied. Smart Filters work non-destructively – they remain completely malleable and can be revisited, removed or hidden at any point in the image creation process. Smart Filters also come with their own blending modes and opacity settings, completely independent of the Smart Object layer. Most Photoshop filters can be treated as a Smart Filter – except Extract, Liquify, Pattern Maker and Vanishing Point. Just be sure you're working in RGB mode.

Here we'll apply various Smart Filters and explore blending modes on Smart Object layers and their Smart Filters. We'll show how vector-based Smart Objects created in other apps can be incorporated into your workflow. You'll wonder how you ever managed before!

:::: Using Smart Blur Filters

Using Smart Filters, we can add a sense of speed to fast-moving objects on a static photo shot with a high or fast shutter speed. Here we'll add a Smart Radial Zoom Blur.

01 **Clone** Copy a selection of the car to a new layer, called 'Car Isolated'. Copy base layer, call it 'Background Blur'. Now clone the road into the front of the car. Now make a rectangular selection, pull down by transforming into the car.

02 **Smart Zoom Blur** Convert the Background Blur layer to a Smart Object via the fly-out menu (in red). In Filter>Blur>Radial Blur, drag the Amount slider to 12, check Zoom, place the Blur Centre so it radiates from the far right horizon

03 **Smart Radial Blur** Isolate the front wheel from original, copy to a top layer. Make it a Smart Object; generate a layer-based selection from the wheel. Add a Radial Blur of 19, check Spin, move Blur Centre to suit. Repeat for rear wheel.

:::: A quick filter fix for smooth skin

Smart Filters are ideal for retouching because of their non-destructive nature. Open 'Model.jpg' on the CD. The first thing is to remove obvious blemishes. Drop in a 'retouch' layer and use a combination of the Clone and Spot Healing tools set to Current & Below. Now create a composite image by first adding an empty layer at the top of the stack, then choosing Image>Apply Image. This composite layer can now be treated

to a small amount of Median or Gaussian Blur, then its opacity reduced to suit. Areas such as her eyes, lips, hair, eyebrows, eyelashes and jewellery can be brought back into focus by painting on the filter mask with black.

:::: Edit RAW settings within Photoshop

If you import a RAW file into Photoshop conventionally, all your conversion settings created in Camera Raw (for example) will be irreversible. Also, if further edits are carried out in PS and you later want to alter your initial Raw conversion settings, you have to start from scratch. To preserve your settings, open the RAW file as a Smart Object. Because Smart Objects support RAW files, you can modify their settings any time by double-clicking the Smart Object thumbnail. The ability to swiftly alter these directly from PS is a real time-saver.

Non-destructive edits Pixel-based Smart Objects remember their original pixel information. They can be scaled, rotated and warped multiple times without losing any of their original quality. A Smart Object can also be edited and updated on-the-fly by double-clicking its layer thumbnail

Vector-based Smart Objects Logos created in Illustrator can be placed as vector-based Smart Objects. These can be edited in their native application (if you've got it installed) by double-clicking the layer thumbnail to open a 'child' document. Once you've amended and saved the file, the Photoshop Smart Object will automatically update

Work 'smart' Smart Filters let you experiment with a multitude of effects without compromising pixel data. As Smart Filters are non-permanent, they can be tweaked, removed or hidden at any time. When you apply a Smart Filter, a filter mask appears, so areas can be hidden

Start photos

Tip

Smart is big
If you've venumerous Smart Objects in a document, the file size will grow. When you've edited the Smart Object you can go Layer>Smart Objects>Convert to Layer or go to Layer>Rasterize> Smart Object.

Experiment Smart Filters allow for almost limitless creative effects. Like most things Photoshop, it's worth experimenting with different filters and blending modes. Remember, Smart Filters can be revisited at any point, as long as your file remains unflattened

Hidden features The old Fade filter features are now built into the Smart Filter sub-layer. To access them, simply double-click the double triangle icon next to the filter name. From here you can choose different blending modes, as well as adjust the filter's opacity

---

Save time with live, multiple updates

Because PS embeds a Smart Object into the document, it can be edited on-the-fly by double-clicking its layer thumbnail – this will open it as a temporary, 'invisible' file. After making alterations such as Color Balance and then saving, it's automatically updated. If you have several duplicates (or instances) of the same Smart Object that were created by dragging the original over the Create New Layer icon or by selecting Layer>New Layer Via Copy, your edits will also be reflected on these layers.

Preserve your filters on replaced files

You can easily replace any Smart Object with another image. First target the Smart Object layer you want to replace, then go to Layer>Smart Objects>Replace Contents and navigate to the replacement file. Here we replaced the 'Snowboarder' layer with the 'Model.jpg'. When the image is replaced it also updates any duplicates – in this case the 'Snowboarder copy' object layer. Also, any scaling, warping or filter effects you've applied to the old Smart Object are preserved.

155

⣿ REACH NEW HEIGHTS
Go further with Smart Objects and Smart Filters

Multiple filters

It is possible to apply more than one Smart Filter to a Smart Object – but the drawback is they must share the same mask. Also, if you apply one or more Smart Filters by selecting Filter>Filter Gallery, they will appear as a group under your Smart Object and simply be called Filter Gallery. Although you can still edit these filters, it's best to add specific named filters so you can keep track of them.

01 **Blue skies** Create a new RGB landscape document at 30 x 20cm. Set Resolution to 300ppi and Background Content to white. Add the 'mountain' image as a new layer, then hit Cmd/Ctrl+T to transform and stretch horizontally. Don't worry about the sky falling short – we'll fix that next. Label the layer 'Mountain/Sky'.

02 **Non-destructive cloning** Add a new top layer – we'll use this layer to repair the sky. Set the Clone tool to Current & Below and clone in the missing sky area. It's always good practice to carry out any retouching on a separate layer because it's non-destructive to the original. When you're done, hit Cmd/Ctrl+E to merge down.

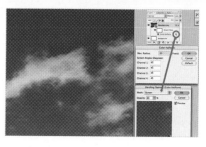

03 **Filter options** Target your merged layer and convert it to a Smart Object using the fly-out menu in the Layers palette. Go to Filter>Pixelate>Color Halftone, set Radius to 10 and all Channel Angles to 45 degrees. Double-click the double triangle icon to the right of the filter name to access its blending options (circled in red); set Mode to Screen, Opacity to 21%.

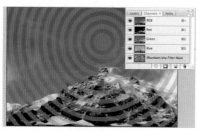

04 **Concentric circle mask** Open 'Circles.jpg' from the CD and go to Select All>Copy. Back in your project file, ensure the Mountain/Sky layer is targeted, then switch to your Channels palette. A temporary channel called 'Mountain/Sky Filter Mask' should be visible. Activate its visibility, target it, then paste in your selection.

05 **Stamp filter** Deactivate Visibility. In the Layers palette the mask is applied to the Smart Filter. Copy Mountain/Sky layer by dragging its thumbnail to Create New Layer. Drag Color Halftone filter to trash; apply Stamp filter to copy, using Light/Dark Balance 17, Smoothness 5. Change blending to Multiply.

06 **Remove the snow** Open 'Snowboarder' on the CD, switch to the Paths palette to see a supplied clipping path. Cmd-click its thumbnail to get a selection, then add a 'Retouch' layer. Zoom in; pick a small clone brush to remove snow particles. Just work in the selected area; don't worry about the rest.

⣿ Keep your text layers 'smart'

To keep text live and editable in Smart Object mode, first convert its layer to a Smart Object. Apply any filters needed. You can add layer effects as with a conventional layer. To edit the text, double-click its thumbnail to open the temporary 'invisible' file. From here you can amend it and change the font, but if your text is pushed beyond the canvas, you'll need to extend it with the Crop tool or go to Image>Canvas Size. When you save/close the temporary file, your text will update.

⣿ Open or import Smart Objects

1 Select File>Open As Smart Object – this is the best choice when you want to use a Smart Object independently.
2 Select File>Place, then navigate to your chosen file. It can be an image file, a Raw digital camera file or even a vector file such as an Illustrator PDF. This technique is best used when you want to add a Smart Object to your active document.
3 Copy a graphic from an open Illustrator document to the clipboard, switch to PS and Paste As>Smart Object. For this option, you'll obviously need Illustrator installed.

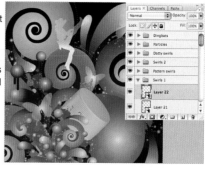

07 **Modify** Merge the Retouch layer. We will selectively colour change the snowboarder, so copy the background layer and go to Select>Color>Range. Hit Quick Mask in Preview and click the jacket. Drag the Fuzziness slider, using the window as a guide so the background stays black. Hit the Plus Eyedropper and click the trousers.

08 **Colour corrections** Hit OK – an active selection appears. Hit Ctrl/Cmd+U to access Hue/Saturation. Check Colorize using Hue 69, Saturation 52, Lightness +4. Set the duplicate background layer to Soft Light, and merge. Make a path-based selection and go to Select>Modify> Feather. Enter 1px and copy to the clipboard.

09 **Defringe the layer** Paste as a new layer at the top of the stack within your project file. Now go to Layer>Matting>Defringe: 1px – this removes any white halos picked up from your initial selection. Next, convert the layer to a Smart Object, position centrally and name it 'Snowboarder'.

10 **Smart Stamp filter** Duplicate the Snowboarder layer, then apply the Stamp filter to it using the following settings: Light/Dark Balance 25, Smoothness 5. Now set the Snowboarder Copy layer to Overlay and change the blending mode of the Stamp filter to Color Burn.

11 **Modify mask** Set the original Snowboarder layer to Screen. This gives the snowboarder a lighter look, but now the halftone pattern shows through. To fix it, Cmd/Ctrl-click the Snowboarder thumbnail to make a layer-based selection. Target the Mountain/Sky Smart Filter mask. With white set as the foreground colour, hit Delete to fill the selection with black.

12 **Vector graphic** Lastly, we'll add a vector graphic created in Illustrator. Go to File>Place and navigate to 'Snowboard_logo. ai' on the CD. Check Photoshop PDF Format; hit OK in the next window. The logo is imported as a Smart Object, which you can position top left.

Transform with confidence

If you repeatedly reduce and enlarge the content of an ordinary layer, its pixel quality will eventually be beyond repair. Pixel-based Smart Objects overcome this by remembering their initial dimensions at the point they're converted to Smart Objects. This allows room for manoeuvre, especially if you aren't sure how big an element will appear in the final design. You can make it very small and enlarge it again knowing it'll remain crisp, provided you don't exceed its original dimensions.

Non-destructive adjustments

There are a couple of hidden Smart adjustments you won't find in the Filter menu: Shadows/Highlights and Variations. The reason you won't find them there is that they're not classed as true filters – they're both adjustments users have requested be made non-destructive. You'll find them in Image>Adjustments. The Shadows/Highlights adjustment is a great way to recover lost detail in shadow or highlight areas, and Variations lets you do simple colour corrections quickly.

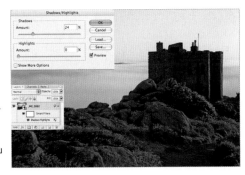

Blur tool techniques

Fine-tune each pixel with the help of the Blur tool

T he Blur tool is a fast and easy way to recreate the photographic effect, depth of field. It can also blend the edges of a subject into the layer underneath it.

If you're handy with the Brush tool, then the Blur tool is going to be second nature. With the Blur tool, you can zoom into your image and apply blurring to individual pixels. It performs in the same way as the Brush tool, which means you can paint a blur into your image. You can also change its size and even its strength, which is very useful for creating depth as well as movement in an image.

If it's not depth of field that you're looking to create, you can always use the Blur tool for smoothing out edges. When a layer needs to be blended with a layer underneath, you can do this with the Blur tool. By choosing a small brush size and zooming close into your image, simple apply a gentle blur to the edges of your subject.

It's a tool that can easily be overlooked or pushed aside by the Blur filters in Photoshop, but this shouldn't be the case. There are four examples below describing how to use the Blur tool. Whether it's combined with a selection or a blend mode, the only thing that can hold you back is not using your own creativity!

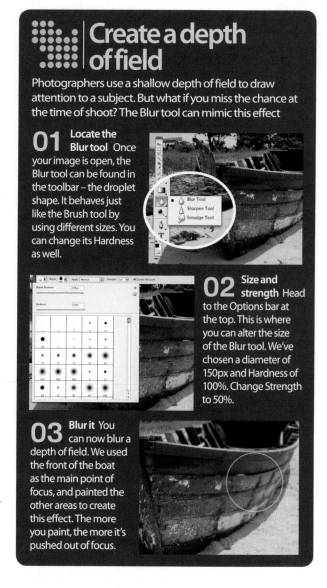

⠿ Create a depth of field

Photographers use a shallow depth of field to draw attention to a subject. But what if you miss the chance at the time of shoot? The Blur tool can mimic this effect

01 Locate the Blur tool Once your image is open, the Blur tool can be found in the toolbar – the droplet shape. It behaves just like the Brush tool by using different sizes. You can change its Hardness as well.

02 Size and strength Head to the Options bar at the top. This is where you can alter the size of the Blur tool. We've chosen a diameter of 150px and Hardness of 100%. Change Strength to 50%.

03 Blur it You can now blur a depth of field. We used the front of the boat as the main point of focus, and painted the other areas to create this effect. The more you paint, the more it's pushed out of focus.

⠿ Working with selections

Making a selection is great for choosing specific parts of your image and protecting them from being blurred. You can use any of the Selection tools along with the Blur tool. If your subject is in the centre of your image, you can use the Magic Wand tool or any of the Marquee tools to make a selection around it. You can then modify that selection (Select>Modify) in a number of ways – Expand or Contract are just a few. A Feather modification will affect the amount of blur that bleeds over the edge of a selection. Possibilities are endless; you can also use the Pen tool to make precise selections around a subject that doesn't want to blur.

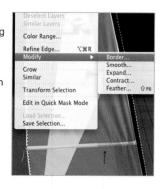

⠿ Use the Blur tool with blend modes

The Blur tool, like any individual layer, has its own blend modes. When these are applied to the Blur tool they change its properties. It will still blur the image, but it also affects the pixels in a more artistic way. There are seven modes in all, ranging from Saturation to Hue. The Normal blend mode is the one to stick to if you're creating a depth of field in an image. The difference between the Blur tool's blend mode and the ones you find in the Layers palette is simply that there are fewer of them.

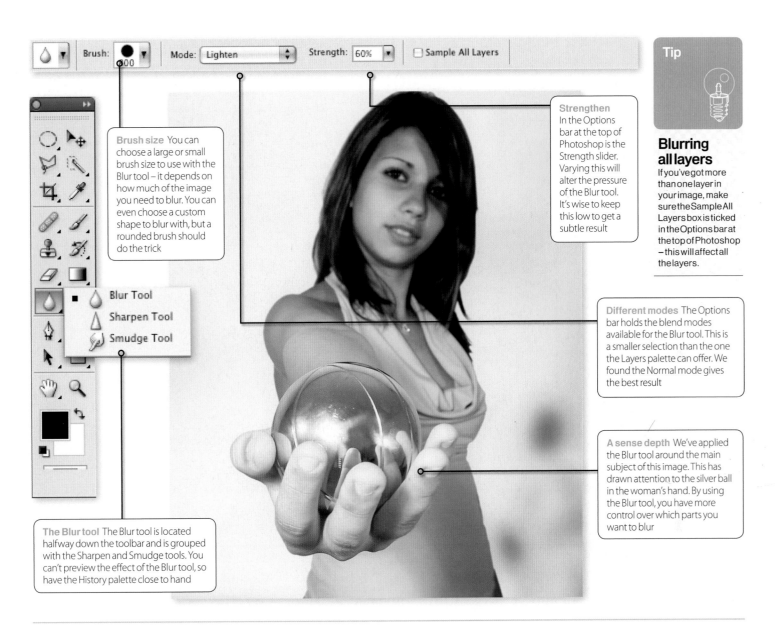

Brush size You can choose a large or small brush size to use with the Blur tool – it depends on how much of the image you need to blur. You can even choose a custom shape to blur with, but a rounded brush should do the trick

Strengthen In the Options bar at the top of Photoshop is the Strength slider. Varying this will alter the pressure of the Blur tool. It's wise to keep this low to get a subtle result

Blurring all layers If you've got more than one layer in your image, make sure the Sample All Layers box is ticked in the Options bar at the top of Photoshop – this will affect all the layers.

Different modes The Options bar holds the blend modes available for the Blur tool. This is a smaller selection than the one the Layers palette can offer. We found the Normal mode gives the best result

A sense depth We've applied the Blur tool around the main subject of this image. This has drawn attention to the silver ball in the woman's hand. By using the Blur tool, you have more control over which parts you want to blur

The Blur tool The Blur tool is located halfway down the toolbar and is grouped with the Sharpen and Smudge tools. You can't preview the effect of the Blur tool, so have the History palette close to hand

Blur Tool
Sharpen Tool
Smudge Tool

Experiment with the Blur filters

Photoshop has many Blur filters. That's why we're not going to neglect to mention them in this Focus On. They're found under Filter>Blur and are a fantastic alternative to the Blur tool. You have the choice of a Gaussian blur, Lens blur, Motion blur and lots more. These filters will allow you to preview the blur before applying it, which you're not able to do with the Blur tool. So if you can't achieve the effect you're after, head to the Blur filters.

Give the Blur tool more power

You can intensify the effect of a blur by adjusting the Strength slider. This is found in the Options bar at the top of Photoshop. It's similar to the Brush tool's Flow adjustment, which changes the density of paint with each click. The Blur's Strength adjustment acts in the same way by altering its intensity. This is handy when creating a sense of depth in an image: by changing the strength of a blur, from the foreground to the background, you can emphasise distance.

Final image

Before image

Daytime effect

Paint with light

Transform a plain image with this simple method

ainting with light can be done with a camera, a steady hand, a long exposure and a torch. However, this is a bit of a long process, so why not turn to Photoshop instead?

Using your software is a great alternative, and it requires little more than the standard Brush tool. The technique gives the impression that a torch was used to light the subject in front of you, taken with a long exposure to capture the torch's path. But waving a touch around in the right areas is a tricky thing to get right. Photoshop is a real time-saver.

The strips of light in this tutorial are created using the Brush tool on layers with different blend modes. The highlights are treated separately from the shadows, and unlike using a torch in real life, in Photoshop you can control both aspects of light and shade.

Understanding the nature of light and how shadows react is important when making any composition work, so check out the tips over the page to find out more.

The night sky in this tutorial was made to look as though it's behind the window with the help of a layer mask and the Pen tool to make the initial selection. This particular element brings the composition together, rather than leaving it with just the foliage outside.

Using adjustment layers, you can give the whole image an overtone of light blue, to reflect the tone of light coming from the moon. The teddy bears are taken to an entirely different time of day, overlooking the calm sea at night.

essentials

SKILL LEVEL
Beginner
Intermediate
Expert

TIME TAKEN
1.5 hours

ON THE DISC

Teddy Bears.jpg
Night sky.jpg

KEY SKILLS COVERED
What you'll learn

BLEND MODES
BRUSH TOOL
PEN TOOL
LAYER MASKS
ADJUSTMENT LAYERS

BUILDING UP THE LAYERS PALETTE
Blend modes can create mask-like layers

01 The setup Open 'Teddy bears.jpg' on your disc. As we're not making any adjustments to the image itself, we don't need to duplicate. Add two blank layers in the Layers palette above the original by clicking twice on the Create a New Layer button.

03 Goodbye layers The Highlights and Shadows will act like a layer mask. On the Shadows layer change its blend mode to Color Burn. On the Highlights layer alter its mode to Color Dodge.

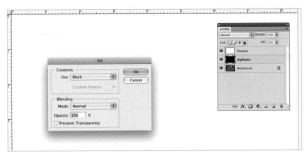

02 Black and white fills Name the top layer 'Shadows'. With this layer selected, go to Edit>Fill and choose white for Contents. Set layer Opacity at 100% and hit OK. Select the other blank layer and name it 'Highlights'. Hit Edit>Fill, and use black for Contents. Hit OK.

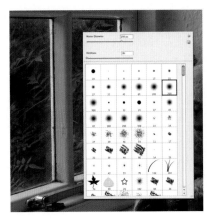

04 Prepare the Brush tool Select the Brush tool, which will be used for painting the light onto the teddy bears. Go to the Options bar at the top of Photoshop and set its Opacity to 10% for a light touch. Choose a Brush size of 200px, and reduce the Hardness to 0% for a soft edge.

Tip

The right image
Choose your image wisely for painting with light. It works best on an image that has flat colours and is low in contrast, and also has no bleached white or dark black areas. This way, the detail that's already there is enhanced and you get better results. If you need to, dull down the original image before painting with light.

THE BEHAVIOUR OF LIGHT

Placing the light in an image is tricky. Note where the light source is, and where highlights and shadows will fall. Shadows have two parts, a dark inner area and faint outer shading – not always noticeable.

The light sources Think not only about the obvious light sources in your image, but also about a light source that may be hidden out of the frame.

Soft shadows Use soft, blurred areas for curved surfaces, and harsh and strongly outlined shadows for areas such as the ground.

Highlighting For highlights, accentuate subject edges with a glow by increasing the intensity of brush strokes. Take into account objects blocking light.

Surfaces Think about which surfaces would be more affected by the light source, and make this distinction with a darker shadow on edges further away from it.

Long shadows Don't be afraid to paint on long shadows that stretch across the ground. This shows the light source is low to the ground.

::::: CONTROL THE EFFECTS OF LIGHT
The Brush tool is perfect for painting beams of light

05 Painting light Select the Highlights layer and set the Brush tool's foreground colour to white. Gently apply the Brush tool to the leaves outside, making them glow. Dab light onto the bears' heads, legs and arms, making them look high-contrast and vibrant with glowing light.

06 Beams of light Make sure the wall between the bears and the window has highlights to show the light streaming in. Flick the Brush tool to and from the two. If areas appear to be bleached out, make the foreground colour black to add detail back in.

07 Paint the shadows Select the Shadows layer and set the Brush tool with a foreground colour of black. Change the Brush's Opacity setting to 5% in the Options bar. Paint over the existing shadows around the edges of the bears, and darken the parts of the window frame that are facing into the room.

08 Tidy up Look for bleached or overly dark areas. Switch the foreground from white to black for the Highlights layer and vice versa for the Shadow layer. Touch up areas to bring back the detail.

09 Window Select the image's layer. Choose the Pen tool and zoom in to 300%. Make a selection (a path) on one of the four panels in the window. When complete, hit Ctrl/right-click inside the selection and choose Make Selection. Add no Feather Radius. Repeat for all four sections, but pick Add To Selection in the dialog.

TEDDY BEARS AT MIDNIGHT
Use a layer mask to add another element to the composition

10 New channel When all the four panels have 'marching ants' around them, go to Select>Save Selection, name the new channel 'Window Panels' and hit OK. The selection saves into the Channels palette so it can be called up at any time. Hit Cmd/Ctrl+D to remove the marching ants.

11 The night sky Open 'Night Sky.jpg' (don't worry about the colours of the sky and moon). Drag the image onto the canvas of the teddy bears, and move its layer to the top of the layer stack. Hit Cmd/Ctrl+T to shrink the night sky to fit neatly over the window frame.

12 Layer masking Open up the Channels palette. While holding Cmd/Ctrl, click on the thumbnail of the Window Panels channel. The selection will become active. Go back into the Layers palette and on the Night Sky layer hit the Add Layer Mask button.

13 Position the sky Unlink the Night Sky layer from its layer mask by clicking the chain link between them. Click on the image thumbnail to freely move the night sky to a good position. Hit Cmd/Ctrl+T if you need to make it smaller or bigger.

Layer structure
How we layered up the light

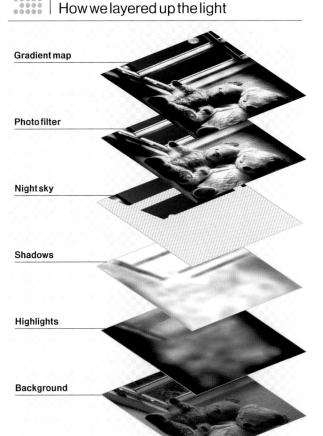

Gradient map

Photo filter

Night sky

Shadows

Highlights

Background

14 Cooler light To match the colour of moonlight, add the adjustment layer Photo filter (from the bottom of the Layers palette). Use the Cooling filter (82), because it's a light blue colour, and set its Density to 30%.

15 Gradient Map Add the Gradient Map adjustment layer. Inside the Gradient Editor menu, select a light blue-to-white gradient. Hit OK and change the blend mode of the layer to Color Burn. Lower the Gradient Map's layer Opacity to 50%, and your composition is complete.

Lasso Tool   L
Polygonal Lasso Tool   L
Magnetic Lasso Tool   L

Ultimate guide to selections

Your one-stop guide to achieving perfect selections in whatever you do

Selections are at the core of Photoshop's power, and are the foundations that have made Photoshop stand out from the competition – it is quite a challenge to squeeze the subject into ten pages!

Selections come in all shapes and sizes, and it's handy to know which ones work best for the task ahead. That's why we've split the following feature into sections involving composites, creative projects and photo-retouching, all with selections and their techniques at the top of the agenda. By working your way through each section you can pick up tips and techniques to translate into your own projects.

We show you the basics of each tool, and break down into steps the processes involved in setting and applying each one. Take our personal favourite as an example – the Pen tool – as this has the unique trait of allowing you to stay in full control as you work your way around a subject to form a selection. You can tweak the tool's path, and edit it at a later stage if it's not right. But this is

not the quickest Selection tool out there. For speed and accuracy, the winner is the Quick Selection tool, which we demonstrate on a complex subject such as our image of the Lander.

It's amazing just how big a role selections play in Photoshop, and how Photoshop (and digital art for that matter) couldn't exist without them. They are rarely the main focus of a project, but get them wrong and you can ruin an otherwise perfect scene. So it's important to spend some time getting used to their ways.

Hopefully you can find the selection technique you've been looking for all this time! Check out the collection of images on your disc for trying out our tutorials, so you can follow along with us.

"Selections are at the core of Photoshop's power, and are the foundations that have made Photoshop stand out from the competition"

165

Composites

Seamlessly combine images

You may often have seen two images and thought they'd look great together, but found the idea of laboriously drawing around a subject enough to burst that bubble.

You can make the task easier to swallow with a handy tool named Quick Selection, a cousin to the Magic Wand. One reason the Quick Selection tool is so helpful is in the way it can spread across a busy area of an image and detect the defining edge between subject and background. This proved perfect for our image of the Lander, where other selections methods would have taken much longer.

The Pen tool is also handy in the quest for composites, but does require skill: the trick is making a seamless edge between subject and background. In our example, the Pen tool selected the boundaries of the window in our cockpit. You'll learn how to manipulate the tool's anchor points, made as you form a path. The path can then be saved and used to combine multiple selections into one layer. Access the cockpit image from your disc, courtesy of Quasi Modo at **www.sxc.hu/profile/easternmar**, and the desert image, donated by Julia Starr at **www.sxc.hu/profile/night_fate**.

Compositing two images can present new vistas to the viewer and unlimited possibilities to the digital artist

Before

> "The Pen tool is also handy in the quest for composites: the trick is making a seamless edge between subjects"

A change of view

How to set up and apply the Pen tool for making a frame and replacing the contents

01 **Set to Path** Open the cockpit image from your disc. For creating a path to turn into a selection, select the Pen tool and make sure that the Paths symbol (second box in the Options bar) is ticked. The selection should appear as a simple outline.

04 **Complete the path** When the path is joined up, Ctrl/right-click in the area and pick Make Selection. Go to Select>Save Selection, and hit OK. This saves it as a new Alpha channel. For every new path, pick Alpha 1 from this menu and tick Add To Channel.

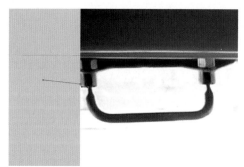

02 **Begin the selection** Hit the 'F' key to give the canvas a grey background behind your image. As the window of the cockpit is against the edge of the image, drag the image to one side using the Spacebar. With the Pen tool, begin your path on the grey canvas.

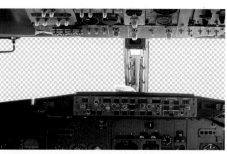

05 **Finished selection** When the entire window has been selected, go to Selection>Inverse (Cmd/Ctrl+Shift+I) and add a layer mask, showing only the inside of the cockpit. Click the layer mask's thumbnail in the Layers palette and go to Filter>Blur>Gaussian Blur. Set Radius to 1px. Open the landscape image on the disc and drag onto the canvas to complete.

03 **Manipulating the path** Work your way around the edges of the window, bending the path as you go using the anchor points. After each bend, Opt/Alt-click on the manipulated anchor point to continue laying the outline with straight lines.

Duplicating paths

When a path has been completed and joined together using the Pen tool, select the Direct Selection tool and hold Opt/Alt. Hover over the path, and a plus symbol should appear under the tool's pointer. Click and drag the path to duplicate and move.

Refine Edge

Refine Edge came onto the scene with PS CS3, and it gives more options and control over editing selections. To use it with the Pen tool, after drawing around your subject and completing the path, Ctrl/right-click in the path and hit Make Selection. Select one of the Marquee Selection tools and the Refine Edge option should appear in the Options bar. Open this menu and you'll see Radius, Contrast, Feather and Contract/Expand. Adapt these for an even better selection. CS5 has further improved this feature, with new Edge Detection options and a Decontaminate Colors adjustment for fine, crisp selections.

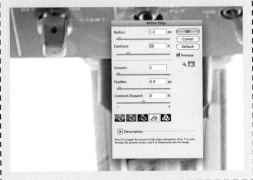

Create your own optical illusion quickly and easily using the Quick Selection tool

"The Quick Selection tool can detect the defining edge between subject/background"

Magnetic control

With the Pen tool selected, choose the Freeform Pen box in the Options bar and tick the Magnetic box. This changes the behaviour of the Pen tool and it attaches itself to the edges of the subject. Try zooming in to 300% and moving slowly around the edges to ensure a good selection. This method offers an alternative to the normal use of the Pen tool, where you need to click and adjust each point of the path as you go. This way can also prove quicker than the normal method, although results are slightly harder to control. It's worth trying both ways if you find yourself struggling with a particular one. Depending on how good you are at drawing freehand, you can uncheck the Magnetic option for complete freedom of making a selection.

Inhabiting planets
Using the Quick Selection tool, you can create composites quickly and effectively

01 Speedy take-off Quick Selection, found with Magic Wand, offers a fast way of selecting complex areas. The Options bar has a brush setup for Quick Selection. The bigger the brush, the larger the selection.

02 Easy as click and drag! Open the images of the Lander and desert from your disc, and zoom in to 200%. Set the Size of the tool to 8px with 100% Hardness. From the outside in, click and drag over the Lander to make a selection.

03 Soften selection If you stray outside the object, Opt/Alt-click to remove the selection. For thinner areas of the Lander, decrease Brush Size to 4px. When the selection is complete, double-click the layer and add a layer mask. Select the mask, go to Filter>Blur>Gaussian Blur, apply 1px to soften edges.

04 Satellite Download the satellite dish pic 'IMG_0813_s.jpg' from **Morguefile.com**. Zoom to 25% and use Quick Selection set to 50px Diameter in the Options bar to select the main area. Zoom in to 200%, make Diameter 16px and select the dish's support poles. Add a layer mask and drag onto the desert image with the Lander cutout.

Using selections creatively

How to use them for those small but important elements

When it comes to selecting objects for creative uses, you can get away with simpler techniques, as the selection will often be covered or masked by the creative process being applied. This means you get to enjoy the Marquee and Lasso tools. They suit tasks such as scrapbooking perfectly due to their 'sketchy' appearance and haphazard results.

The Lasso tools can be applied to your image with very little effort, and their freehand style gives you a selection that may not be exact but could be the style you're after. For our scrapbook design here, we've built up the page furniture using the Rectangular and Elliptical Marquee tools, and placed each new shape on its own layer. This way, we could give different layer styles and blend modes to each one, to add depth and texture.

Follow our step-by-step on creating a custom shape using the Marquee tools, which could then be applied to your scrapbook for a unique design. Find out how to form clouds, and maybe a sky that could be used as your scrapbook's background...

Cloud formations

Build up some fluffy shapes

One of the many uses of the Elliptical Marquee tool is creating simple shapes. These could be used as part of a scrapbook, poster, card design or even on a website. To perform this particular task, you need to head to the Options bar to change the setup of the tool. With the Elliptical Marquee tool selected, click on the second option from the left in the Options bar, called Add To Selection. Now, whenever an oval selection is drawn, you can add to it simply by drawing another one overlapping. This enables you to build up oval upon oval, forming the fluffy nature of a cloud. When one cloud is made, hold Shift to continue drawing more.

Creating a custom shape

Using the Marquee tools for designing shapes

There are a vast number of custom shapes in PS, from arrowheads and signposts to musical notation and outlines of animals. They let you quickly draw simple outlines on the canvas, and can be resized using Edit>Free Transform. They're also editable once drawn on. Selection tools can be used for creating custom shapes of your own, and using the Marquee tools you can form the shape of nearly anything. Here's how to use the Rectangular and Elliptical Marquee tools to create a frame for using around an image, which can be saved and used repeatedly.

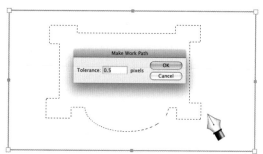

02 **Turn into a path** When your frame design is complete, Ctrl/right-click inside the selection and choose Make Work Path from the list. In the pop-up menu set Tolerance to 0.5px and hit OK. Your selection should now be a solid path.

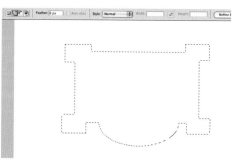

01 **The frame** Select the Rectangular Marquee tool and draw a rectangle selection on a blank white canvas. Click Add To Selection in the Options bar, and hit the Elliptical Marquee tool. Begin to elaborate the design of your frame by overlapping oval selections.

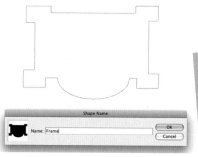

03 **Save shape** Go to Edit>Define Custom Shape, and in the Shape Name field give your frame a name. Hit OK, select the Custom Shape tool (U) and search for your frame in the Options bar.

Design a scrapbook with the Marquee and Lasso tools

Create the border Using the Rectangular Marquee tool, draw the outline of your scrapbook and go to Edit>Fill (F5). Select a colour and hit OK. Now choose the Brush tool and set it to a Chalk tip. Click on one corner of the background, hold Shift and click on another corner.

> "The Magnetic Lasso tool is ideal for making fast selections around your subject"

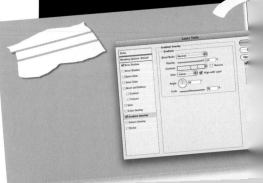

Photo corners Select the Polygonal Lasso tool and set Feather to 0 in the Options bar. Draw a small photo corner by holding Shift to create se vertical and diagonal lines. When complete, go to Edit>Fill and choose black.

Create a scrapbook

Selections with the Lasso tools

The Magnetic Lasso tool is ideal for making fast selections around your subject. Set a number in the Frequency in the Options bar (a higher number is more accurate), and zoom 300% into your image for a closer inspection of the pixels. Click on the edge of your subject and drag the selection around the area to form points along a path. Left-clicking as you go places points manually. Join up the two ends to complete your selection.

Car Show

Day Out

The show's oldest runner and still looking good

In the showroom - caught in the headlights!

Beautiful weather for beautiful cars

Me!

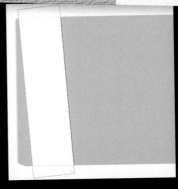

A thrilling experience - my next car!

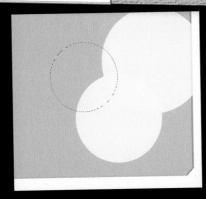

Make scrap paper
With the Lasso, draw a selection of a torn piece of paper. Edit>Fill with white and double-click its layer to open the Layer Style menu. Add a subtle drop shadow and a gradient overlay. Set the gradient to two blue lines in the Gradient Editor.

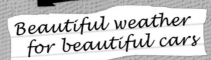

Add decorations The Elliptical Marquee tool is great for making perfect circles and filling with colour. Decorate your scrapbook with circles of various sizes (hold Shift while making a selection) and set the blend mode to Screen for each one.

More decorations The Rectangular Marquee tool can also make good page furniture. On a new layer, draw a tall and thin rectangle across the entire canvas and fill with white. Use Edit>Free Transform to rotate slightly to use it as a banner.

"The main consideration with selecting hair is asking yourself what its final use will be"

Using the right tools means this task is not too difficult

Before

Masking hair
Using channels for one of the trickiest jobs in PS

Photo-retouching
Focus on the crowning glory

R etouching images is an art in itself, and takes just as much dedication as is required with forms such as painting.

Depending on the task, some selection methods will work better than others. One task is the challenge of selecting hair accurately – a daunting prospect. Here we show you how to make the most of the Channels palette for making selections around hair, and how choosing the best channel can make all the difference.

The main consideration with selecting hair is asking yourself what its final use will be. A quality cutout lies not just in the selection process but in the touch-up process too. We demonstrate various ways to edit on both a white and a black background, to give you different ways of editing after the selection is made. If using CS5, you can benefit from an improved Refine Edge menu, making selections around hair easier.

Selections can help retouch a cityscape with the use of a long-standing member of Photoshop, the Magic Wand tool. With areas of foliage or grey buildings, you can set up the tool to make a selection spreading across your image, to pick out just one colour.

01 **Pick channel** Download '1167491.jpg' from **www.sxc.hu**. Open the Channels palette (Window>Channels) and click the Red, Green and Blue channels. Pick the channel with most contrast – blue works well. Ctrl/right-click the channel, hit Duplicate Channel then OK.

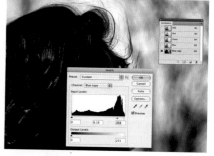

02 **Adjust Levels** Click on the duplicated channel (making sure it's the only one visible) and go to Image>Adjustments>Levels. Slide the midtones point to the right to darken the hair. Make sure the strands of hair are completely black, and hit OK.

03 **Create a mask** Using the Brush tool set to black with 80% Hardness, paint black over the subject's face and body. Use the Eraser tool set to white to remove leftover background, roughly going around the hair, to create your mask.

04 **Load the selection** Cmd/Ctrl-click on the thumbnail of the duplicate channel to load as a selection. Hit Cmd/Ctrl+Shift+I to inverse the selection. Go into your Layers palette and drag the background layer onto the Create New Layer button and apply a layer mask.

Rescue a cityscape
The Magic Wand tool is ideal for retouching

Before

After

01 Sky Open the cityscape image on the disc (from Charlotte Pickering) and pick the Magic Wand. In Options set Tolerance to 10, tick Contiguous. Zoom in 100%, click the grey sky. Using Opt/Alt- and Shift-click, remove/ add areas. In Select>Modify>Feather enter 1px. In Layer>New>Layer Via Copy place sky on own layer.

02 Select greenery Uncheck the Contiguous box in the Options bar and set Tolerance to 50. Click multiple times on a tree and the selection should select all green parts in the image. Hit 'Q' for Quick Mask mode and use the Brush and Eraser tools to edit the selection accurately. Select the background layer, Feather by 1px and go to Layer>New Layer>Layer Via Copy.

03 Select the rest To select the remaining area, Cmd/Ctrl-click on the sky layer's thumbnail and then Ctrl/right-click in the selected area with the Magic Wand tool. Choose Save Selection and hit OK to save it as a new channel. Do the same with the tree layer, but select Alpha 1 in the dialog box and tick Add To Channel. Hit OK.

04 Final selections In the Channels palette Cmd/Ctrl-click the thumbnail of Alpha 1, then go Select>Inverse. With the selection active, Feather by 1px, click the background layer and go to Layer>New>Copy Via Layer to complete the three-way dissection of the cityscape. For each segment, use adjustments such as Levels and Saturation to boost colour and contrast.

Improving your mask – white background

Creating a spotless selection around hair depends on the use of the image, and also the background it's going on. For a white background, after adding the layer mask around your subject, create a new layer and position it in the middle of the layer stack. Go to Edit>Fill, set it to white and hit OK. Click back on the layer mask, and with the Brush tool set to black at 30% Hardness, tidy the edges of the hair. Some strands may need sacrificing, but using the Eraser tool set to white, errors can be undone on the layer mask. The model should now be against an entirely white background with wispy hair. Save a layered copy of the image, and then go to Layer>Flatten Image to continue to edit the model in the desired way.

Use the Eraser tool to achieve a precise hair cutout on white

Removing 'halo' edges

If, after making the selection, you place the image on a black background, you may see a halo effect, or a muddy distinction between the background and the hair. These are areas left over from the background. To darken these areas, click on the image's thumbnail to the left of the layer mask in the Layers palette and zoom in to 100%. Select the Clone Stamp tool and set its mode to Luminosity in the Options bar. Using Opt/Alt-click, apply the Clone Stamp along the edges of the hair. The result is a darker edge with darker strands of hair. Against a white background this stands out, but as we're using a black one behind our subject, the effect isn't noticeable. The way the image is going to be used, or the colour background it's going to be placed against, will decide the touch-up methods.

If you have a darker background, use the Clone Stamp to tidy up

Tricks

The best of the rest
Ten techniques for making and editing selections

Lasso Tool   L
Polygonal Lasso Tool   L
Magnetic Lasso Tool   L

Paint a selection

If you have a steady hand and take the opportunity to paint whenever you can, you can use the Brush tool to make a selection. With your image open, double-click its layer to make it editable. Add a layer mask to the image and select the Brush tool set to black. Paint over the areas of the image you want to hide, and hold Shift while clicking for straight edges.

Custom shape cutouts

Custom shapes can be used to make selections, offering a variety of outlines and cut-out shapes. With the Custom Shape tool selected, head to the Options bar and pick your shape. Draw the shape over the image, and in the Layers palette Cmd/Ctrl-click the layer mask's thumbnail to load as a selection. Hit Backspace to remove the layer contents and the layer itself, leaving just the selection outline. Use the Move tool to cut out the shape.

Defringe

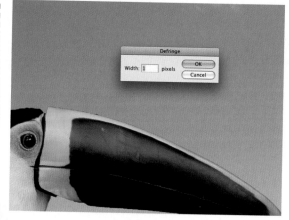

After you've made your selection and replaced what's behind with a new image, an outline of one or two pixels can sometimes occur from the last background. You can remove this thin strip of colour from the edges by using Photoshop's Defringe command, found under Layer>Matting>Defringe. Make sure that a layer mask has not been placed on your image about to be defringed.

Selecting colour with Color Range

If you're looking to make a selection of one colour, the Color Range command could quite possibly be your best bet. Select the Magic Wand tool and Ctrl/right-click on your image. Choose Select>Color Range, and click once on the colour to form a mask (in the preview window). Click on the Add To Sample eyedropper to add areas that have been missed.

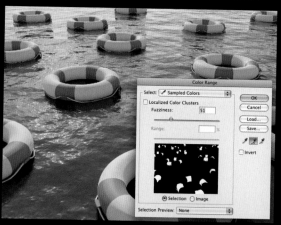

Extract filter

The Extract filter is another method for removing a subject from its background, and is especially helpful for selecting hair in portrait images. For Photoshop CS4 users, the filter is downloadable from **www.adobe.com/downloads**, and goes straight into the Filter menu. Once loaded up, paint around the edges of your subject and use the filter's Paint Bucket tool to fill, then hit OK to extract.

Constraining a selection

You can set a selection to a certain size using the Options bar field's Width and Height. Alternatively, when making a selection, holding down the Shift key will keep the Rectangular Marquee tool perfectly square and the Elliptical Marquee an exact circle. To draw a selection from the cursor outward, hold the Opt/Alt key. Combining Shift with Opt/Alt creates a perfectly centred square or circle.

Hiding selections

One of Photoshop's helpful shortcut combinations is Cmd/Ctrl+H. This quickly hides any selections on your canvas in the event that they obstruct your view. The important point to always keep in mind is that when a selection is hidden it's still active and is affected by any adjustments being made.

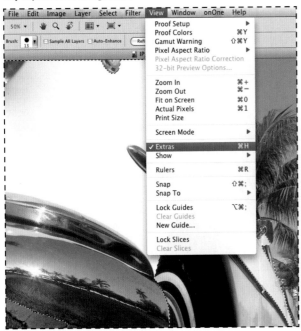

Resizing selections

Photoshop allows you to transform a selection using the Select>Transform Selection command. You can tweak a selection by rotating or reshaping, depending on the shape and size of your intended new background. With the Transform controls active, Ctrl/right-click and open a menu of other options such as Perspective, Warp and Skew. This way, you're only applying transformations to the selection area and not the image.

Refine Edge in CS5

If you're using Photoshop CS5 then you have the blessing of an improved Refine Edge menu, helping to remove subjects with even more precision. In this menu, new Edge Detection option Smart Radius lets you accurately pick out thin edges, with the control of its Radius slider – a big improvement every artist will benefit from. Also, the Decontaminate Colors option removes leftover colours from a removed background.

Modify commands

Accessed through Select>Modify, these commands include Feather, Contract, Expand, Smooth and Border. These are selection aids, helping to make your selection cleaner and more accurate. When creating photo-composites, try applying the Feather command with 1px to an active selection before cutting out a subject, to soften the edges of the area.

Fixes

176-253

We all have photos that we resign to the trash can because there is something wrong with them. Well, no more, as we unveil a whole host of nifty tips that help you to perfect any photo and fix any problem. We explore everything from giving old photos new life to modern retouching effects for perfect shots each and every time. So let's get started!

176
Fix your photos
Remove dust and scratches, and many other common problems with this in-depth feature to common problems and how to fix them!

Before

Before

After

Before

After

242
Change hair colour
Brunette to blonde with no bleach!

Fix your old photos

Remove fade, colour casts, rips, folds, cracks, dust and scratches from precious family photographs

T his guide is all about repairing, restoring and retouching images sourced from original negatives, slides or photographs that have been damaged or have deteriorated in some way.

Many of the examples we've used are relatively aged photographs, but photos of any age can deteriorate given the right conditions. Direct sunlight, high humidity and gases like paint vapour can bring any photograph or piece of film to a rapid demise in the right quantities –

and that's before we've even considered accidental damage. The most common problems you'll encounter include dust, rips, scratches, folds and cracks, as well as fading, yellowing and colour shift. Nothing we can't handle, you'll be glad to know!

Restoring contrast to faded photos and removing colour shift are fairly straightforward tasks. Removing dust, scratches, cracks, folds and suchlike is a bit more challenging. The technique basically centres on using good areas

of the image to replace bad areas, and the Spot Healing Brush tool ('J') and the Clone Stamp tool ('S') are the staple tools for the job. While using the former is a mostly automated affair, using the latter requires a bit more thought about where you source the information from. It needs to be from somewhere with a similar pixel makeup so it all blends nicely, making sure that no cloning patterns are obvious. Check out the information on the following page to see when and how to use each tool.

Add colour tone

Remove cracks

The Spot Healing brush is unrivalled for removing blemishes in areas of even tone, such as the sky here

Where information starts to get a bit more detailed and complex, the Clone Stamp tool is the safer bet

Healing and cloning

When to heal and when to clone

The Spot Healing brush and Clone Stamp tool will be the tools you'll use most in the majority of repair situations. Spot Healing removes blemishes by using nearby information and blends to match. Clone Stamp just copies directly from one area to another. The general rule is to use the Spot Healing brush over Clone Stamp unless you're working near edge detail. In these situations you can find the Spot Healing brush ends up blurring detailed edges, or that colour spills over into areas it shouldn't. Here, the Clone Stamp is the better choice. The Clone Stamp may also perform better in the case of images that contain a lot of blemishes like fungus, dust or scratches which Spot Healing can end up replicating, especially when focusing on larger blemishes such as tears, folds and cracks. It's best to have a go with the Spot Healing brush in even tone areas and see the sort of results you get. If they're not good, you've got no choice but to stick with the Clone Stamp tool throughout.

The Clone Stamp tool is perfect for replacing missing areas of an image with information from elsewhere

In severe cases of dust and scratches, the dedicated filter is better than healing and cloning

Scanning advice

Scan in RGB mode not greyscale, and set your desired output size at a given resolution (240ppi is good for print). Work any exposure controls to ensure the image isn't overly light or dark. Select Adobe RGB rather than sRGB colour space unless your image is for web only.

Fade and colour casts

Eliminate odd colours in your shots

The Photoshop Auto Contrast and Auto Color adjustments are a great place to start for removing fade and colour casts. In most cases they'll get you at least very close to where you want to be, and you've got the option of adding a Levels adjustment layer to tweak as desired. Where problems can occur is if fade or colour casts aren't uniform across the image; perhaps either one is restricted to a single corner or area. In this case the Auto adjustments will be fooled and you'll have no option but to work manually. In this scenario you'll also need to make use of the layer masks attached to any Levels layer in order to localise your adjustment changes. For example, if you were correcting for fade that was only in one corner of the image, you'd need to take a large black brush and brush out the adjustment in the remaining area where contrast was okay. In some cases you might need two Levels layers: one to remove the localised fade area and a second to establish good contrast for the image as a whole.

> "Where problems can occur is if fade or colour casts are not uniform across the image"

Before

After

After an initial try with the Auto Contrast function, we used a Levels adjustment layer to add contrast

Fight the fade, cull the cast

Photoshop provides Auto adjustments for removing fade and restoring decent contrast as well as removing colour casts from colour photographs. When the Auto functions don't work, you can use Levels to do the manual work instead. As always, be sure to use an adjustment layer rather than an adjustment directly onto layer content.

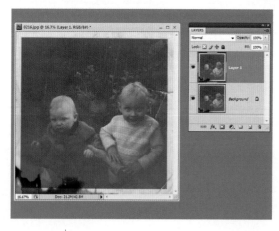

01 Try Auto Contrast Start with the Auto Contrast function to improve contrast and remove any colour casts. Duplicate your background layer with Cmd/Ctrl+J. Go to Image>Auto Contrast and look at the results.

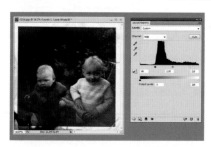

02 Levels manual contrast If Auto Contrast doesn't do the job, we need to work manually instead. Add a Levels adjustment layer and drag the black and white Histogram sliders inwards until the contrast improves.

*18.jpg @ 12.5% (Levels 1, Layer Mask/8) *

Doc: 34.7M/84.0M

Bring contrast and definition back using layer masks and simple editing tweaks

Brush it out
Sometimes areas of clipped information, like the sky here, can look worse with contrast changes. Brush the adjustment out with a black brush.

Use a layer mask
In this case there's patchy fade, so some areas look too dark with the contrast increase. We brush these out with a black brush and the layer mask selected.

Set contrast
We can usually ensure decent contrast to correct fade by dragging the black and white End Point sliders inwards to meet the edges of the histogram info.

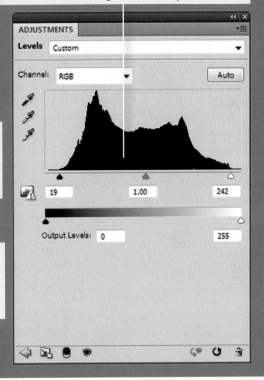

Boost contrast
We can increase contrast further without introducing clipping by adding a Curves adjustment layer and plotting a shallow 'S' to darken shadows and lighten highlights.

Desaturate
For non-adjustment layer corrections we start by duplicating our background layer – in this case to apply the Desaturate command to remove the yellowing.

03 **Try Auto Color** To remove a colour cast just use Image>Desaturate on the duplicate layer. For a colour photograph, use Image>Auto Color instead. Generally it does a good job of getting you a neutral result.

04 **Levels manual colour 1** If colour still doesn't appear totally neutral, add a Levels adjustment layer and click the drop-down menu that says RGB. Select Red and move the middle grey slider left to add red, and right to subtract.

05 **Levels manual colour 2** Next, select Green from the drop-down menu and repeat. Repeat again for Blue. You can also select RGB and use the middle slider to lighten or darken the image without affecting colour.

::: Fixes

Working on the right layer

A note on tool setup and using layers

Use the Spot Healing Brush tool and the Clone Stamp tool on blank layers rather than duplicates. Check the box Sample All Layers in the Tool Options bar for healing, or Current and Below for cloning.

An essential tip is to add the blank layer above the background and below any adjustment layers, making sure that you turn off any adjustment layers temporarily, using the eyeball icon, if you're performing healing (Sample All Layers will be checked). This way the repair work is done sampling the background layer only, ensuring that you can alter your adjustment layers at a later date without the repair work suddenly shifting in tone.

By combining cloning and spot healing techniques, we can repair the damage

To repair missing corners, add a new layer and use the Clone tool to add in the detail. Add adjustment layers above this

"Use the Spot Healing Brush tool and the Clone Stamp tool on blank layers rather than duplicates"

Creases and folds

Tears, scratches, folds and cracks are common with old photographs, and are best dealt with through the usual combination of Spot Healing Brush tool and Clone Stamp tool.

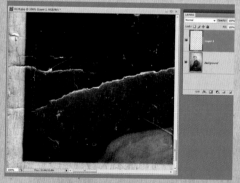

01 Duplicate and zoom Create a new layer then zoom in to 100% using Cmd/Ctrl+ Opt/Alt+0. Hold down the Spacebar and click and drag to where the problem begins.

Dust and Scratches

The Dust and Scratches filter does soften detail a little, so add a layer mask using the button at the Layers palette base, zoom in and use a black brush to rescue detail in important areas such as eyes.

04 **Multiple Undo** We use Multiple Undo with Cmd/Ctrl+ Opt/Alt+Z to reverse our healing work, and have a go with the Clone Stamp tool instead, sourcing first with Opt/Alt.

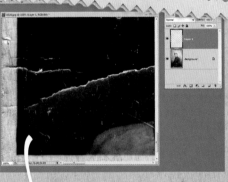

02 **Spot Healing brush** Now press 'J' to select the Spot Healing brush and use the '[' and ']' keys to size the brush to suit. Make sure Sample All Layers is checked in the Tool Options bar.

05 **Cloning work** The Clone Stamp tool works far better for this image, so we use it to slowly work away at the cracks, making sure to regularly re-source from nearby areas.

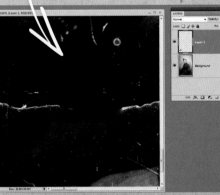

03 **Try healing** Now click a small section of the tear area and keep clicking along to see the result. We need several goes to remove the crack mark, but the result isn't great.

06 **Remove dust and scratches** Create a merged duplicate with Cmd/Ctrl+ Opt/ Alt+ Shift+E and run Filter>Noise>Dust and Scratches. Radius 6 and Threshold 16 does the job.

Top ten tips for vintage pics

Top tips on cleaning your photos and slides for scanning, as well as tips for handling, storing and restoring your photos!

Old photographs pose many challenges to the Photoshop user, but rest assured there is always a solution at hand. It's good practice to organise your old photographs on your computer, so they can be accessed quickly and easily. Remember to name them and even archive them by date, generation or family. This saves you lots of time when you need to search for them later on. Here we round up our essential advice on getting the best out of your images, no matter how battered they may be. Whether it's a case of getting the best possible scan or choosing a correct repair method, we show you how…

01 Replacing lost areas

If there's a piece of a photograph missing, all may not be lost. Look at your image and see if the missing bit can be made from other areas. For this image, we simply flipped the good side and used it to patch up the bad!

02 Scanning care

If you're scanning an image and want to include the border, try not to get any of the white scanner base underneath, as this will fool any Auto Contrast adjustments. If it's unavoidable, be prepared to use Levels to make your changes.

03 Removing dust

Far better to clean your photos or slides before scanning than to have to do lots of cloning work afterwards. Start by trying to shift dust with a can of compressed air or a purpose-designed soft brush.

04 Stubborn stains

For stains, fungus and other blemishes, you need to use a specialist cleaner like the widely available PEC-12 product, with either cotton swabs or non-adhesive wipes like PEC-Pads. PEC-12 is suitable for cleaning both film and prints.

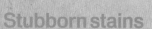

05 Clever cropping

If there's an area of an image that you don't feel confident about repairing, don't disregard the option of cropping the bad stuff out if you really want the image looking blemish-free.

> "If there's an area you don't feel confident about repairing, don't disregard the option of cropping the bad stuff out"

Fix your old photos

06 Good storage practice

Photo storage boxes, envelopes, sleeves and albums will all help protect your photographs, negatives and transparencies against light, dust, handling, air pollutants and rapid fluctuations in temperature and humidity. Never leave materials lying around loose.

08 Smart Sharpen

Photoshop's Smart Sharpen filter (Filter>Sharpen> Smart Sharpen) can do wonders to rescue blurry photographs. Try both the Gaussian Blur and Motion Blur settings, and experiment with both the angle and sliders.

07 Handling photos

Handle your photos, negs and slides as little as possible and use white cotton gloves to shield your materials from damaging fingerprints. Wash your hands first to avoid gloves getting contaminated with dust and dirt.

Bring back some definition to your photo using the Smart Sharpen filter

09 Toning old photos

Even if your image is a neutral monochrome, there's still nothing to stop you toning it to add something extra. Use a Color Balance adjustment layer with Midtones checked. Combine red and yellow for an old-looking sepia tone.

> "Even if your image is a neutral monochrome, there's nothing to stop you toning it to add something extra"

10 More on storage

Humidity and high temperatures are the greatest enemies of photographs, negatives and slides. Store your precious photographs and film in a place that's as cool and dry as possible – basements are generally too damp and attics are too hot.

Feel free to get creative with your old photos and add a nice warm tone

KEY SKILLS
COVERED
What you'll learn

BACKGROUND
ERASER TOOL
LAYER MASKS

Before

Use the Background Eraser tool

A quick way of extracting subjects from surroundings

essentials

SKILL LEVEL
Beginner
Intermediate
Expert

TIME TAKEN
One hour

hotoshop offers lots of ways to extract an element from its background. You can use paths to create a selection, select colour ranges and delete them, or even make clever use of channels and layer masks.

When we want a quick and easy way to get rid of parts of a layer, however, most of us tend to reach for the regular Eraser tool. The destructive nature of this approach aside, it's a lot of hard work to ensure you don't overlap edges, create halo effects and generally end up with a dog's dinner. Step up the Background Eraser tool. You use this tool in the same way as the regular Eraser, but behind the scenes Photoshop is examining the colour beneath your

eraser brush and sampling the pixels you brush over. When your brush is over areas of similar colour, Photoshop removes them. If, however, your brush also moves over an area that contrasts in tone, Photoshop will intelligently leave those pixels alone. The result is a far more precise way of removing backgrounds, while leaving fine detail in place that would be nigh on impossible to retain using the standard Eraser tool.

In this tutorial we'll look at extracting a beast from its surroundings. The Background Eraser does have limitations, so we'll look at how to cope with these and work around any problems. Finally, we'll learn how to ensure we're acting non-destructively.

SELECTING AND UNDERSTANDING THE TOOL
Find the Background Eraser tool and set it up for use

01 Open the image Open your starting image, then zoom in and examine the areas where the tiger's fur meets the background. We want to get a cutout that keeps the detail in this area but removes the background entirely. In the following steps it's worth coming back and checking that you're not removing the detail you see here.

02 Make a copy Select and drag the background layer onto the New Layer button at the bottom of the Layers panel to create a copy of the image. We want to keep the original in case we need to go back to it, so we'll work on the copy. Turn off the eyeball for the background layer and select the copy.

03 Select the Background Eraser The Background Eraser tool is hidden beneath the regular Eraser. To select it, click and hold on the Eraser tool in the toolbox. A fly-out menu will appear that contains the Eraser, Background Eraser and Magic Eraser. The Background Eraser tool has a pair of scissors as the icon; select it now. You can also press 'E' on your keyboard to cycle between the Eraser tools.

04 Give it a go Before you get down to using this tool in earnest, get used to how it works by selecting a nice big brush size and painting down the outside edge of the tiger's head. Make sure the + symbol inside the brush is in the black area, but the brush edges move over the edge of his head.

05 What happened? Photoshop is analysing the pixels as you paint. The + symbol is used to mark the spot that's used as the reference colour to be deleted. Anything that differs more than the threshold amount in tone is left intact, and everything else is removed. Undo your painting now by hitting Ctrl+Alt+Z or Cmd+Opt+Z until you're back to the point at which you started step 3.

Toolbar options
Gain fine control over the tool

Sampling has three erasing modes: Continuous reads tonal values under a brush, then decides what to erase; Once retains the first tonal value you click on, so only one tone is removed; Background Swatch limits pixels removed to those matching the selected background colour. Tolerance sets the tool sensitivity. Limits defines how the tool erases pixels: Discontiguous removes same coloured pixels; Contiguous only removes adjacent pixels of the same tone. Find Edges deals with inside pixels. Protect Foreground Color prevents pixels with the same colour as the foreground being erased.

Tip

Protect the foreground

Don't overlook the Protect Foreground box in the toolbar. It overrides any decision the tool makes to remove pixels where they match the foreground colour in the colour well. Hit 'I' to get the Eyedropper tool and pick up the colour of the tiger's fur, then return to the BE tool and check the Protect Foreground box where the difference between background/tiger is less pronounced.

Tip

Extract fine details such as hair

Most Photoshop users don't tend to immediately think of the Background Eraser tool as an obvious choice for removing pixels, but it can be incredibly useful where other tools just aren't up to the job. A great example for a practical use of the tool is where you want to retain fine hair detail. Cutting out the pixels in between individual strands of hair is next to impossible, but cautious use of the Background Eraser tool makes it child's play.

ERASE THE BACKGROUND
Make short work of a complex operation

06 Set the tool options Tolerance sets how much difference between two tones must exist before Photoshop keeps the pixels. Try varying the amount of tolerance and paint over the same area. If you pick a high tolerance, some of the tiger will be erased. Too low, and there will be a halo of background pixels around the edge of the tiger. Find the value that works best for you.

07 Start at the top Ensure that Contiguous is ticked and hit Sample Once. Start with a medium sized brush at the top right of the tiger's head and brush down the side of the face. Ensure the + symbol remains outside the tiger to avoid removing parts of his fur. You'll see pixels are left around. You'll mop these up later, so don't worry about them. We used a brush of 45, Tolerance of 75%.

08 Complete the head Continue working the head area. This shouldn't be a problem for the BE tool as there's plenty of contrast between background and tiger. As you move around the top of the tiger into the shadow area, you'll need to lower the tolerance and reduce the size of the brush for best results. One area that will cause issues is the left ear. It may be best to switch to the Eraser tool to mark out a line where you think the ear should fit.

09 Block out the top Now you have the head and back isolated, you can increase the size of your brush and quickly work over the remaining pixels at the top of the image. Temporarily switch to the Eraser and bulk erase pixels that aren't adjacent to the tiger. Remember to switch back afterwards!

10 Complex areas As you work your way down the tiger's body it'll become harder to get the right balance between brush size and tolerance. If you can't get the tool to cooperate, don't worry – we're going to fix any problems where too much has been deleted (or not enough) once we have finished.

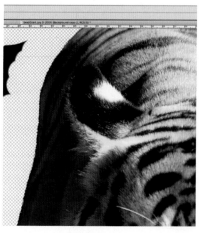

11 Paws for thought This area is especially tricky. As the fur is so similar to the background, we're going to have to use an extra control to capture the difference between the two. Press 'I' on your keyboard to select the Eyedropper tool, then click inside the tiger close to the border with the background. Now return to the Background Eraser tool and check the Protect Foreground checkbox. Adjust the Tolerance value down to 5 or 6 and continue painting around the edge.

12 Block out the sides You can now block out the sides of the image in the same way as you did for the top. You can also use the Eraser tool to help tidy up the edges in the area you've just been working on. There is some detail worth retaining but this is a particularly difficult area – so do what you need to achieve a nice edge.

13 Get context Complete both sides in the same way. When you're nearing the end, zoom out enough to get a clear view of the whole image. From this perspective you should be able to see any glaring pixels that you've missed while mopping up the side areas. When you're done, zoom back in for the final area at the bottom of the image.

14 **The final furlong** Once again, grab the Background Eraser tool and move to the very bottom of the image. This is the most difficult area of all, and will require a lot of patience to get right. Ensure you're zoomed in sufficiently to accurately move along the threshold between tiger and foreground. For the bottom of the paws you may have no choice but to use the regular Eraser tool.

16 **Check the image** Inevitably you're going to miss areas. Although we'll deal with these oversights in the final stages of our manipulation, the task will be easier if we get most of them now. Create a new layer below the Background Copy layer and fill with a magenta colour. Select the Background Copy layer and zoom in close. Hold down the Spacebar and pan over the image to check for areas where pixels still remain. The contrast against magenta makes it easy to spot and deal with these stragglers.

18 **Check for missed bits** Opt/Alt-click the mask to view it in the image area. You'll see pixels in areas you thought had been fully removed. The Background Eraser tool is good at what it does, but if there are pixels in the background that exceed the Variance setting you chose, they won't be removed. Paint with black over these pixels to get rid of them. Now click on the layer thumbnail to return to the Artwork view.

15 **The last gasp!** Okay, breathe a sigh of relief and use the regular Eraser tool to get rid of those last outlying areas of pixels along the bottom edge of your image. It's taken a while to achieve, but you're now the proud owner of a cut-out tiger with no background.

17 **Create a mask** Everything we've done so far has been destructive. We've been throwing away pixels of our image without worrying about it, but for flexibility it's better to keep all the pixels and mask out the ones we don't want to see. Duplicate your hidden background layer to create another copy of the complete image. Cmd/Ctrl-click the Background Eraser layer to load the pixels as a selection, then click New Layer Mask in the Layers panel for the duplicate background layer. You can now hide the Background Eraser layer.

19 **Mask refinements** If you're using CS4 or beyond, Photoshop offers you a number of ways to refine your mask and make it pixel perfect. If you are using an older version, however, you can still improve your mask. Zoom in tight and paint onto the mask with black to hide extra pixels, and white to reveal pixels where you've gone too far.

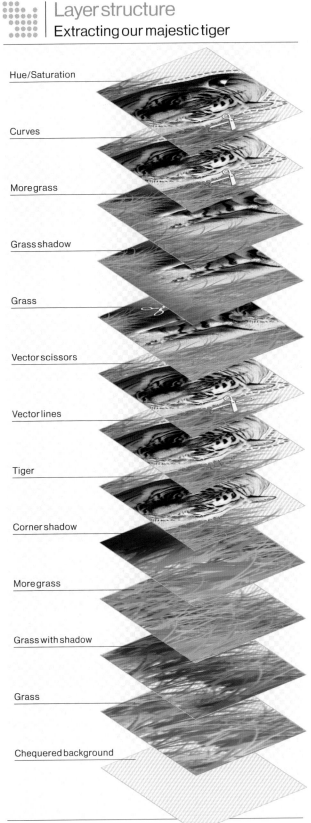

Layer structure
Extracting our majestic tiger

Hue/Saturation

Curves

More grass

Grass shadow

Grass

Vector scissors

Vector lines

Tiger

Corner shadow

More grass

Grass with shadow

Grass

Chequered background

Start image

essentials

SKILL LEVEL

Beginner
Intermediate
Expert

TIME TAKEN

30 minutes

ON THE DISC

Improve teeth and eyes source.jpg

VIDEO TUTORIAL

Teeth and Eyes video

Whiten teeth and eyes

Lighten and colour correct teeth and eyes with precision

T he eyes are always the first thing we're drawn to in a portrait, and this fact is something of a double-edged sword for Photoshop folk. On the one hand you can improve any portrait quickly and easily by retouching these most important facets.

On the other hand, bad retouching will obviously be just as quick; there's nothing like overly white eyes to send the viewer packing! So the message here is clear – do it, but do it well and leave it looking natural. The same goes for lightening and whitening teeth, another good method of improving your portrait, although you can usually get away with a shred more

work than is possible for eyes. In both cases, once you've done your work, it's good practice to zoom out and try reducing the opacities of the layers involved by half.

The techniques we're applying are a little more sophisticated than the standard Dodge and Burn approach. We're using a three-point Curves adjustment to make tonal changes to the pupils and whites of the eyes, while ensuring that the iris remains untouched (it receives a more suitable method of lightening via Hue/Saturation later on). And for teeth, we can target individual colour channels with a Levels adjustment layer to get them perfectly white and neutral. Both methods can produce natural results.

CLEAN UP THE EYES AND IMPROVE CONTRAST AND COLOUR
Clone Stamp, Curves and Hue/Sat are our tools for the eye trade

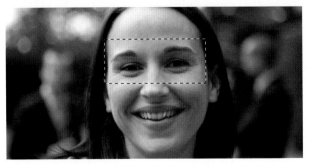

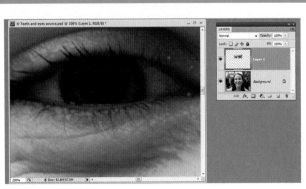

01 Select the eyes Start by selecting the Rectangular Marquee Tool ('M') and make a selection around both eyes. Float this to a new layer using Cmd/Ctrl + J. The first thing we want to do is remove any unsightly veins. This is best done with the Clone Stamp tool ('S') (set to Current and Below in the Tool options).

02 Clone out veins Zoom in close and use Opt/Alt to source good clean areas, then brush over the veins. It's important to source as close as possible to the destination points as there are a lot of subtle changes of tone in the whites that we need to preserve.

Tip

Precision colour correction
If you want to get an absolutely neutral white, you can use the Color Sampler tool ('I'). Click in three different areas to produce three sample points, then work the Blue and Red sliders in each Levels layer until the values of Red, Green and Blue are all as close as possible for each of the sample points. The values are displayed in the Info palette (Window>Info) – focus on the second set of numbers in each pair.

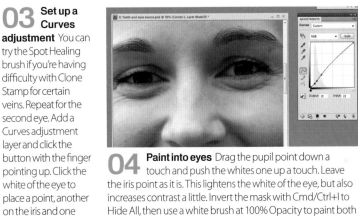

03 Set up a Curves adjustment You can try the Spot Healing brush if you're having difficulty with Clone Stamp for certain veins. Repeat for the second eye. Add a Curves adjustment layer and click the button with the finger pointing up. Click the white of the eye to place a point, another on the iris and one more on the pupil.

04 Paint into eyes Drag the pupil point down a touch and push the whites one up a touch. Leave the iris point as it is. This lightens the white of the eye, but also increases contrast a little. Invert the mask with Cmd/Ctrl+I to Hide All, then use a white brush at 100% Opacity to paint both eyeballs back in.

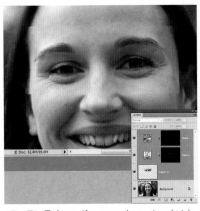

05 Bring out the colour Zoom out and check the effect. If the eyes look too light, drop the layer opacity – the change must be subtle. Next, add a Hue/Sat adjustment layer, boost Saturation by +15, Lightness to +7 and then invert the mask with Cmd/Ctrl+I. Paint into the iris and pupil with white to bring out the colour.

06 Enlarge the eyes An optional trick is to increase the size of the eyes. Cmd/Ctrl-click on the eye layer and the two adjustment layers and hit Cmd/Ctrl+T for a Free Transform. Enter 103% in the Width and Height box, and hit Enter twice.

07 Brush the mask Now add a layer mask to the eyes layer using the button at the bottom of the Layers palette, invert it and paint in the eye areas (including eyelids, lashes and eyebrows) using a soft white brush.

LIGHTEN AND WHITEN FOR THE PERFECT SMILE
Clever Levels adjustments do all the dentistry here

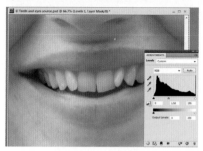

08 Levels adjustment layer Start by zooming into the teeth area. Next, add a Levels adjustment layer using the button at the Layers palette base. Move the middle slider leftwards to around 1.50 to lighten the tonal range. Now invert the layer mask with Cmd/Ctrl+I to Hide All.

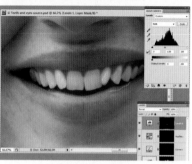

09 Brush into teeth Take a white brush and carefully brush into the teeth only, taking care to avoid gums and lips. Use black to brush back out if you make a mistake. Toggle layer visibility on and off to check you haven't missed any bits or gone into unwanted areas.

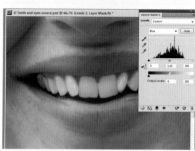
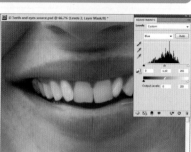

10 Reduce yellowing Cmd/Ctrl-click the layer mask to load it as a selection and add another Levels adjustment layer. It will load with a mask based on that selection. Select Blue in the Levels adjustment drop-down menu and move the middle slider leftwards until yellowing disappears from all parts of the teeth.

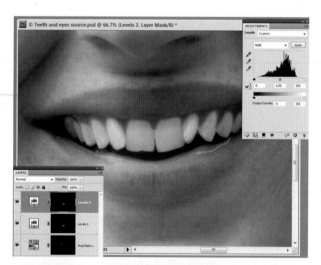

11 Knock back the blues You'll probably find now that some of the less yellow areas have taken on a bluish hue. Knock these back by brushing over with a black brush set to around 30% with the layer mask selected. Work over until you get a neutral white.

12 Another Levels layer Teeth also have a strong red tinge that we're going to try and tone down to hit a perfectly neutral white. Cmd/Ctrl-click the first layer mask to load as a selection again and add another Levels adjustment layer, this time selecting Red from the drop-down menu.

13 Reduce the red tinge Move the middle slider rightwards a touch to remove any red tinge. We only had to go to 0.94. Go too far, and you'll introduce too much cyan. Again, brush out any areas that have taken on a cyan tinge.

14 Reduce opacity Zoom out with Cmd/Ctrl+−, and take a good look at the work. Reduce the opacity of the first lightening Levels layer if the effect looks too strong. You can alter the opacity of the red and yellow colour removal layers too.

Control Unsharp Mask

Squeeze more from Unsharp Mask with Fade

5 minute fix

essentials

t is so easy to get caught up in controlling all the options available in an edit that you forget that it's possible to edit the edit!

The Fade command is a useful tool that allows you to reduce the intensity of an edit but still keep the essence of what you want to do.

One of the best ways to see this in action is to use it with the Unsharp Mask filter. We know how handy this is in sharpening images, but we also know that it can be a tightrope between getting the sharpness needed and ending up with loads of 'halos'. With the Fade command, however, you can ramp up Unsharp Mask and get rid of the halos later.

KEY SKILLS COVERED

What you'll learn

UNSHARP MASK FILTER

USING THE FADE COMMAND

REMOVE HALOS

Quick tip: The Fade command is available for a lot of tools and is always worth trying if your edit doesn't look quite right. It's much better than starting again...

BE A MASTER OF UNSHARP MASK

Don't let the halos ruin your edit!

01 **Apply the filter** Open up the image you want to edit and then pootle up to the Filter menu. Go down to Sharpen and then across to Unsharp Mask.

02 **Make the edit** Usually Unsharp Mask involves a dance between getting the sharpness you want and avoiding any halos. Don't worry this time – use the sliders to sharpen up your edges without fear of recrimination. Click OK when done.

03 **Bring it back** Go up to the Edit menu and pick Fade Unsharp Mask (this obviously changes if you have used a different tool). Now use the Opacity slider to bring back the halos but still keep the sharpness! You can try different blend modes for an extra finish.

Fixes

Before image

After

essentials

SKILL LEVEL

Beginner
Intermediate
Expert

TIME TAKEN

1 hour

ON THE DISC

CloneSourceFile.jpg
Cloud1.jpg
Cloud2.jpg

VIDEO TUTORIAL

View the video tutorial on the CD to see how the Clone Stamp tool can be paired with the Vanishing Point filter to clone in perspective

Fix your photos with the Clone tool

Learn how to convincingly clear clutter from your backgrounds using the Clone Stamp tool

he Clone Stamp tool is possibly the most frequently abused feature in Photoshop. It's the tool the tabloids use to their greatest advantage to edit photos to show what they want them to show.

While we don't condone the use of our favourite software to pester celebrities with ill-timed photos, we do fully encourage its use to enhance your own personal photos as much as you wish. The basic idea of the Clone Stamp tool is to copy pixels from one point of the image to another by way of a brush. This is accomplished by first defining a source point and then defining the offset by beginning a paint stroke. As you push the brush across the canvas, the source point moves with it accordingly. One of the most common uses for this tool is to remove unwanted elements from the background of a photo. This works particularly well when there are clear areas of the background to use as a source point. Elements such as sky, grass, ocean and forest are all usually pretty forgiving of cloning. Other things like crowds or buildings with easily recognisable features can be problematic in that the repetition will be more obvious.

In our example we'll take an image of three adorable little girls sitting in a field with a ball park in the background. You'll see how to use the Clone Stamp tool to remove the unwanted background elements and create the illusion the photo was taken in the middle of an empty field.

Tip

Clone Source panel

If you're using CS3 or above, the basic Clone Stamp tool has its own panel of features. The most useful of these is the ability to save source point definitions. The panel allows for up to five different source points, so you don't have to worry about losing a perfectly aligned source! The source points don't even have to be in the same document – you're free to source one open document and then paint in another.

CLEANUP ON FIELD FOUR!
Learn how to easily remove debris and other clutter from your snapshots

01 Image setup Open the image named 'CloneSourceFile.jpg' on the cover CD. Create guidelines (View>New Guide) at 950 and 2935 pixels for the vertical, and 420 pixels for the horizontal. These are the bounds for the final image. The photo is larger, so there's more source area to clone from.

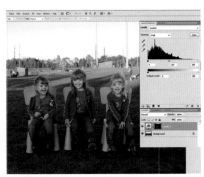

02 Levels adjustment Add a Levels adjustment layer and set the centre slider to 1.27 to lighten the midtones, especially the children's faces. Fill the adjustment layer's mask with black to completely hide the effect. Now use a soft-edged white brush on the mask to carefully paint the effect back in over the faces of the girls on the left and middle.

03 Commence cloning Create a copy of the background layer and grab the Clone Stamp tool. Select a soft-edged brush around 45 pixels wide. Opt/Alt-click to set the source, then begin painting to copy the source area pixels. Clone out the debris on the ground to the right and the running child in the background.

AUTOMATIC CLEANUP

A hidden gem of CS4/CS5 Extended is the ability to have Photoshop evaluate several images and automatically remove the elements that are different. It doesn't sound possible until you see it yourself…

One position, many photos
Take several shots from the same position (use a tripod!) of an ever-changing subject matter such as a Little League game.

A menu you've never used
Now go to a menu you may have never opened before: File>Script>Load Files Into Stack. It's really there, we checked!

Hit the proper settings
In the Load Layers window, load the images and then check both options at the bottom of the window.

Change Stack mode After PS loads the files, go to Layer>Smart Object>Stack Mode>Median. Watch as PS replaces unique pixels with common ones.

Slight touch-up Rasterize the layer and do some light cloning to remove any artefact from the process, then crop the image down as needed.

SPECTATORS OUT, TREES IN
Replace crowds with a peaceful forest tree line

04 Forest extension Pay attention to the crowd and dugout on the left. Carefully select your grass and tree line source points. It's helpful in this instance to deselect the Aligned box in the Options bar. This way each paint stroke uses the same source point instead of having it shift along as you paint.

05 Pole removal service The poles above the tree line are fairly simple to remove. Recheck the Aligned box and set your source point as the sky directly next to the poles. Position your paint point as level to the source point as you can; this ensures the slight gradient of the sky is preserved.

06 Repetitions If your clone work shows a lot of recognisably repeating patterns, lower the brush opacity and use multiple source points to paint over the repeating area. Another trick is to switch the brushes blending mode to Soft Light or Overlay. This adds more variation to the hues.

07 CS3 and above When working on areas that include objects which are symmetrical like trees or buildings, you can reduce clone repetition by having the cloned area flipped from the source. Open the Clone Source panel, unlink the Width and Height settings. Enter minus 100% in the Width field.

08 More cloning Using the same techniques, remove the ball field from the background at the right of the photo. The guidelines mark the edges of the finished piece, so don't worry about items outside of these. Keep that outside area in mind when looking for good source points to clone from.

09 Forecast calls for clear skies Clone in the sky areas to remove the light posts as before. With solid areas like this, Brush Opacity should be at a full 100%. Remember to try and keep the source point and the paint point level in order to retain the sky gradient.

10 **Field extension** The bottom grass area should be extended to cover the white space. Grab the Rectangular Marquee tool and set Feather to 25 pixels. Select the grass area below the girls' feet and press Cmd/Ctrl+T to bring up the Transform controls. Scale the selected area downwards until it completely covers the white bar.

12 **Greener grass** Add a layer on top; fill it with bright green. Set the layer mode to Soft Light and Opacity to 77%. Hold Opt/Alt and click the Add Layer Mask icon. This adds a black mask to conceal the effect. Paint with white on the mask to reveal the green only over the foreground and midground grass area.

14 **Is it 'partly cloudy' or 'mostly sunny'?** The CD also contains two cloud images, with thanks to **photoshopdaily. co.uk**. Load these images into Photoshop and copy and paste them into the project file. Position the cloud layers over the sky area. Set the blending mode for the Cloud1 layer to Darken with Opacity at 75%. For the Cloud2 layer use Overlay and 72% Opacity.

11 **Grass patch cleanup** The grass patch now includes some areas that appear obviously stretched or distorted. Use your new Clone tool proficiency to blend these areas out. Remember to adjust the brush opacity to avoid visible repetition.

13 **Insist on a beautiful blue sky** Create a Sky layer and a rectangular selection over the sky area. Use the Gradient tool to fill the selection with a white to bright blue linear gradient. Set the layer mode to Multiply and go to Edit>Transform>Warp. Set the Warp to Arc and manoeuvre the gradient into place according to your guidelines.

15 **Remove the excess** For the final step we'll crop the canvas down. But first, it's wise to save the file in case you need to get back to this point in the future. Then use the Crop tool to draw out a rectangle according to the guidelines. Hit Enter/Return, and you're done!

Layer structure
Creating cloned perfection

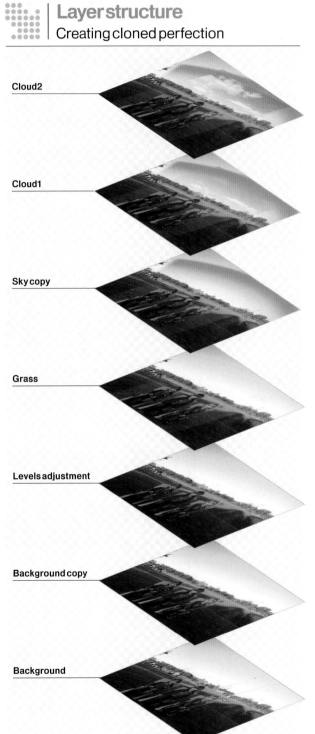

Cloud2

Cloud1

Sky copy

Grass

Levels adjustment

Background copy

Background

Before photo

Fix your hazy landscape photos

With a little help we can rescue detail from the haze

D igital cameras can produce some wonderful results. However, if the shooting conditions are tricky, you can suffer from washed-out hazy landscape photographs, where the foreground is sharp but the background looks dull.

This can be due to any number of reasons; for example, the air may be very humid or full of pollutants like exhaust fumes or dust. It might be possible to combat this by attaching equipment such as an ultraviolet filter to reduce haze and improve contrast. This minimises the amount of UV light that reaches the sensor.

An obvious Photoshop trick would be to use Unsharp Mask, but this has the effect of creating a halo between the original photo and the fixed background. Of course, this can be remedied using cloning and healing tools, but this would change the original photo quite a lot and add or remove elements we may not want.

So in this tutorial we'll examine how to reduce photo haze by isolating the background using the Quick Selection tool to reduce the halo effect, and also utilise the Multiply blending mode to make the colours darker. Multiply removes all the white elements from the layer and makes everything considerably darker.

CLEAR AWAY THE HAZE
Rescue the image using selections, blending modes and gradients

01 Let's begin We start our fix by opening the image in Photoshop – you will find it on the CD. As you can see, the foreground of the image is pretty sharp and clear, but the background is blurred and the sky is very washed-out.

02 Quick selections We want to isolate the sky and distant hills from the background. There are many different ways of doing this, but the Quick Selection tool is by far the easiest. Choose the Quick Selection tool from the toolbox – it may be hidden behind the Magic Wand tool. Now hit the Add To Selection option in the Options bar.

03 Small brush v big brush Reduce Brush Size to around 45px and begin to select the distant hills. Don't worry if the sea gets selected as well, because we'll sort that out soon. Once the hills are selected, move your attention to the sky – increase Brush Size to around 90px and select the sky.

Tip

Warm up with filters
This project will fix the hazy/soft feel of the sky and distant hills, but throughout the project the foreground has been untouched. The foreground colours are quite cold and could do with some subtle tweaking. With PS this is pretty easy; we can use a Photo Filter adjustment Layer. Go to Layer> New Adjustment Layer>Photo Filter and select Warm Filter (85) with Density set to 15, and drag this layer under the Sky layer.

04 Subtract From Selection If you have selected the sea along with the sky and hill, simply switch to the Subtract From Selection option in the Quick Selection tool, and brush out the sea until just the sky and hills are selected. Next, choose Select> Modify>Feather>50 pixels. Finally, copy the selection to a new layer by pressing Cmd/Ctrl+J.

05 Blending mode Rename the new layer 'Sky', then duplicate that layer and rename it 'Multiply'. Set the blending mode of the Multiply layer to Multiply in the Layers palette. The sky will immediately darken and become less washed-out. Next, make a new layer above the Multiply layer and name it 'Gradient'.

Tip

Remove some noise
We increased the contrast of a washed-out background using blending modes. The downside was an increase in noise. We can combat this by using a Surface Blur. First move to the top of the layer stack and press Cmd/Ctrl+Opt/ Alt+Shift+E on the keyboard to create a merged copy. Run the Surface Blur filter with a Radius of 9 and Threshold of 7. Reduce Opacity to 50%.

06 Looking to the sky We're going to use our Sky layer to make a selection. Hold Cmd/Ctrl on your keyboard and left-click the Sky layer. This puts a selection around the area we want to work on. Now press 'D' on your keyboard to return the swatch colours to the default.

07 Soft Light gradient While on the Gradient layer, select the Gradient tool from the toolbar and pick the Foreground To Transparent gradient. Drag out a gradient from the top of the selection to the bottom, then set the blending mode of this layer to Soft Light.

essentials

SKILL LEVEL

Beginner
Intermediate
Expert

TIME TAKEN

30 minutes

ON THE DISC

Before image

KEY SKILLS COVERED

What you'll learn

INSPECT CHANNELS

DUPLICATE A CHANNEL

USE SURFACE BLUR TO REDUCE NOISE

ISOLATE SKY WITH COLOR RANGE

SMOOTH WITH GAUSSIAN BLUR

BRUSH DETAIL BACK ON A MASK

Remove noise with Surface Blur

Tackle noise with Surface Blur and a surface mask

C rank up your camera's ISO to compensate for low light, and you'll get a proportionate increase in sensor noise – small grain-like detail often accompanied by larger blotchy areas that show up most in smooth areas such as sky.

It's enough to ruin a perfectly good picture, especially as you head to the higher ends of the ISO spectrum. The eye is drawn immediately to those speckled areas, and it's too easy to become distracted from the beauty of the image at hand. The solution is some form of noise reduction to smooth out those nasty noise areas. But noise reduction isn't a totally benign cure; it runs the

risk of smoothing out image detail, making everything appear soft. Photoshop's Reduce Noise filter provides a semi-decent compromise in allowing detail to be preserved, but you often end up with an image that can't be sharpened without horrible artefacts showing up.

A better solution is PS's Surface Blur filter used with a surface mask. This filter has a clever algorithm that attempts to focus on smooth areas only, although it isn't clever enough to handle the more pronounced noise cases. By combining the Surface Blur filter with our own surface mask, we double up detail protection, maximising noise reduction while minimising detail smoothing.

CREATE A SURFACE MASK TO START
Our surface mask conceals detail and reveals smooth areas

Tip

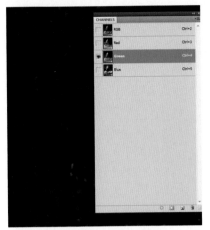

01 Check channel noise Open your image and use Cmd/Ctrl+0 to zoom in at 100%. Go to the Channels palette and inspect the Red, Green and Blue channels by clicking each one. Work out which channel has the least noise in smooth areas such as the sky.

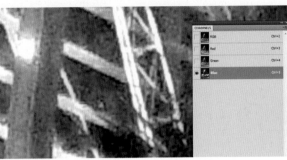

02 Choose your channel In this image, noise is least bad in the Green channel, so we can use this to make a surface mask. The mask will use differences in tonality to separate edge detail from smooth areas like sky – heavy noise in smooth areas can end up being recorded as detail, so it's important to pick the least affected channel.

More about Surface Blur
The Surface Blur Radius slider determines how much blur or softening will be applied, and the Threshold slider controls the number of tonal values that will be blurred. You'll find that as you increase the Radius setting, the Threshold setting will need increasing too. A Threshold setting of around double the Radius is normally a good figure to aim for. Without a surface mask, you'll struggle to go beyond Radius 5 and Threshold 10 without destroying detail. The mask lets you go much further.

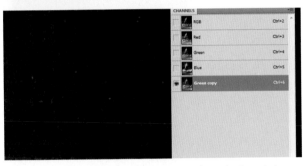

03 Duplicate channel With the Green channel selected, drag it down to the Create New Channel button at the bottom of the Channels palette (next to the trashcan). A new alpha channel called Green Copy will appear. Double-click the label to rename it to Surface Mask. This channel will be used to create our mask.

04 Find edges Now we go to Filter>Stylize>Find Edges to isolate the edges from everything else, as we want to preserve these when we apply sharpening. Edges appear as black, and smoother areas where noise is obvious appear white. Zoom out to see how it looks.

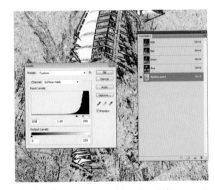

05 Increase mask contrast At present many of the edges are grey, which means they are partially exposed. We want them solid black, so we fire up Levels with Image>Adjustments>Levels. By dragging the Black slider in to around Level 200, we can turn our edges black. Go too far, and the noise in the sky starts to become protected too.

06 Blur mask Next, we go to Filter> Blur>Gaussian Blur and apply 2.0 pixels of blur to the mask to ensure the transition from blur to non-blur isn't too sharp. Our mask is now ready. Go back to the Layers palette and duplicate the background layer with Cmd/Ctrl+J.

07 Add surface mask The RGB channel will be selected again. Go back to the Channels palette and Cmd/Ctrl-click the Surface Mask channel to load it as a selection. A selection will appear based on the mask luminosity. Click the Add Layer Mask button at the bottom of the Layers palette to add a mask to the duplicate layer.

:::: | COMBINE SURFACE BLUR AND SURFACE MASK
We're now free to remove noise without destroying edge detail

08 Surface Blur Now we have a mask added based on the alpha channel. Zoom in with Cmd/Ctrl+0. We're safe now to increase noise reduction without ruining too much edge detail. Select the layer icon rather than its mask. Go to Filter>Blur>Surface Blur.

09 Sliders Let's work the Radius and Threshold sliders, toggling the Preview button on and off for comparison. Move the grabber hand inside the window to move the image around and have a look at the effect in smooth areas and edge detail areas.

10 Apply the blur We're looking to achieve a decent amount of noise reduction without softening edges or making the image look too impressionistic. We found that Radius 20 and Threshold 40 offers a compromise. It's fairly strong but you can always knock back the layer opacity. Hit Enter to apply your blur.

Tip

Sharpening softened detail

Some softening is inevitable for strong noise reduction, even with a surface mask. To reveal some of the softened detail, add another merged layer on top as before. Hold down Opt/Alt and drag the surface mask from the Surface Blur layer to the top layer. Invert this new mask with Cmd/Ctrl+I. Run Levels and drag the Black slider to 75 so no noise is sharpened in smooth areas. Select the layer icon, not the mask, and run Filter>Sharpen> Unsharp Mask, Radius 7.0 and Amount 50%.

11 Sky work Small-scale noise is reduced, but the sky is still blotchy. Solve this by focusing on the sky only for more work. Add a new merged layer above with Cmd/Ctrl+Opt/Alt+ Shift+E. Now go to Select>Color Range. Select White Matte from the Preview drop-down menu.

12 Isolate the sky Now select the Plus eyedropper and click an area of the sky. Keep clicking the white specks in the sky until they all start to disappear. You may need to increase the Fuzziness slider as well – at 30 most of the sky will be visible with little revealed below. Hit Enter to finish.

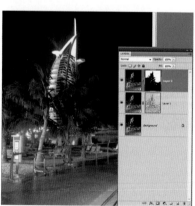

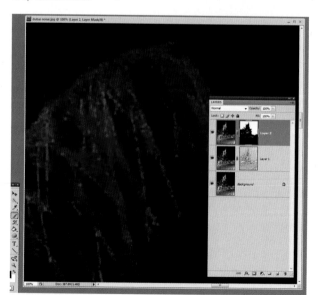

13 Add a layer mask We need to go hard with blur on the sky to remove the blotchiness. With the selection active from Color Range, click the Add Layer Mask button, with the new merged layer selected. A mask appears based on the selection.

14 Run Gaussian Blur With the layer icon, not the mask, selected go to Filter> Blur>Gaussian Blur and run 75 pixels Blur Radius. Look around your image carefully, select the layer mask, and brush out blur with a black brush at 100% in any unwanted areas such as tree edges.

Create a realistic tan

Paint the perfect tan using a layer mask and a boost of saturation

essentials

SKILL LEVEL

Beginner
Intermediate
Expert

TIME TAKEN

Five minutes

ur 5-minute fixes aim to give great Photoshop effects in the space of only five minutes.

Here we show you how to make skin look as though it is tanned It's the perfect technique for finding out how you'd look if you wanted to add a bit of colour to your skin. The Saturation slider is ideal for the job, as it takes every pixel and intensifies the skin colour that's there.

By using a layer mask you can work with a couple of layers to isolate the skin from the model's hair and the background in the rest of the image – it will only take you five minutes!

KEY SKILLS COVERED

What you'll learn

SATURATION
LAYER MASKS
BRUSH TOOL

Quick tip: For an alternative way of selecting the skin, use the Magic Wand tool and feather the selection for a smooth transition

Before

After

FAKE TAN HAS NEVER BEEN SO EASY
Put those layer masks into action

01 Warm things up Duplicate your image and click the eye in its layer to make it invisible. Select the background layer and go to Image>Adjustment>Hue/Saturation. Grab the Saturation slider and increase its value so the skin tones in your image turn to a tan orange.

02 Masking off Click on the eye of the duplicate layer to make it visible. This hides the layer underneath with the tanned skin tones, but to see the underlying layer hit the Add Layer Mask button on the above layer.

03 Painting a tan Select the Brush tool and make sure the white layer mask thumbnail is selected. Hit 'D' to reset your colour palette and begin painting over the model's skin to remove the layer mask. The tanned effect should come through from the layer underneath.

Final

KEY SKILLS
COVERED
What you'll learn

PEN TOOL
MASKING
SHARPENING
TECHNIQUES
HUE AND
SATURATION

essentials

SKILL LEVEL
Beginner
Intermediate
Expert

TIME TAKEN
1 hour

ON THE DISC
iStock_
7245267.jpg
(courtesy of
Maica, **www.
istockphoto.
com/Maica**)

1086187.jpg
(courtesy of
**www.sxc.
hu/profile/
sankla1**)

Before images

Add new reflections to your photos

Master Photoshop's masks to add new reflections to your images, adding lively context and detail to photographs

t's rare that you'll get a perfect photo straight from the camera. In fact, the more you use Photoshop, the more possibilities for improving your images will present themselves.

One improvement that can give an image a lift is the addition of new details reflected in shiny surfaces within your scene. The existing reflections might be nondescript, ugly even, or may simply fail to add anything of value to your composition. By choosing a nice image and using it as the basis for new reflections, you can add extra context, detail and help tell a story with your photograph – you can suggest undiscovered lands, open up the world around your subject and give a tantalising glimpse of what else might be just outside the shot.

In this tutorial we're going to look at how to add a fairly straightforward reflection to an image of some skiers. There are quite a few things to consider, even in this relatively easy example. We'll examine masks and the much dreaded but fantastically useful Pen tool, blending and layer styles. We'll also take a quick look at colour and Curves adjustments to help match our two images together, and finally, apply a sprinkling of sharpening and noise to create a coherent final image that looks realistic and fresh.

Using the Pen tool
It's not as scary as you think

The Pen tool is operated by placing points with the mouse. Photoshop joins these points with a line (or path). Click and then release to lay down points, and the lines between the points will be straight. Click, drag and release to create Bezier handles, which turn the straight line into a curved line. The handles control the degree and direction of the curve. Once you've released the mouse you can continue to edit the amount of curve by selecting the Convert Point tool from the Pen tool fly-out menu, or by simply holding down the Opt/Alt key while the Pen tool is selected. It may seem bewildering at first, but start by plotting some simple shapes and you will soon realise just how easy and useful the tool is.

BRING ON THE SNOW
Mask the goggles and bring the snow scene into the image

01 Open the image Locate the image 'Maica_istock7245267.jpg' on the disc, and open it in Photoshop. Zoom in to 100% and have a look at the areas around the goggle lenses to familiarise yourself with the area we're going to overlay our artwork onto. Notice how the edges closest to the frames seem to get darker – we'll use this to help make our photo sit naturally on the goggles.

02 Create a vector path Starting at one point along the edge of the goggle lens on the woman closest to the camera, click with the Pen tool to create a nodal point. Now select a point further along the lens edge and click-drag to create a curve between the two. Don't release the mouse until the curve accurately describes the edge.

03 Finish off the path This tool really takes some getting used to, so be patient and have a look at the 'Using the Pen Tool' box to learn more about how to get to grips with the curves and handles. Work your way around the lens using as few points as possible, until you have completed the path around the whole set of goggles.

04 Repeat for the other goggles Open the Paths palette and double-click on the path to give it the name of 'LH Goggles'. Click outside the path to deselect it, then repeat the exercise for the other set of goggles in the image. Don't rush these steps – it's worth spending the time to get a nice clean outline, as we're going to use this path to mask our photo and blend the edges in nicely.

05 Place your snow scene Locate and open 'snow_C_sankla1. jpg' then choose Select>All, Edit>Copy, and switch back to the main image before pasting onto a new layer (Edit>Paste). You should now have the snow scene positioned on top of the women. We're going to use two copies of the snow scene, so duplicate the layer and then hide the copy.

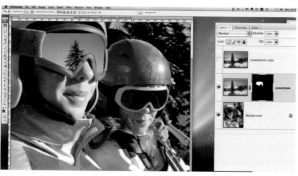

06 Set up the mask With the visible snow scene layer selected, open the Paths palette and Cmd/Ctrl-click on the LH Goggles path to load this as a selection (you could also click the icon at the bottom of the palette). Return to the Layers palette and click the Add Layer Mask button to use the selection as the basis of a mask.

07 Blend and fade Change the blending mode of the layer to Screen and reduce the Opacity to around 80%, allowing the original reflections to pass through. Unlink the layer and the mask by clicking on the chain icon between them, and reposition/resize the snow scene to create a nice composition in the goggle lens.

REFINE AND COMPLETE YOUR IMAGE
Add little touches to improve realism and bring out details

08 Bring out detail On the original image you can just make out an eye in the left goggles. Click the mask in the Layers palette and paint with a soft black brush set to 50% Opacity. Gently reveal the eye by masking out the image where the eye is. If you overdo it, swap to white to get the snow scene again. You can blur the edges of the mask in the same way.

09 Repeat for other goggles Repeat for the other goggles by using the copy of the snow scene you created in step 5. Scale down the snow scene to be smaller in this second copy, and position it so that more ground is showing. This will help reinforce the idea that the lady further away is looking down.

10 Add highlights... The goggles already look really good, but there's more we can do. Use the Polygonal Marquee tool to draw a rough shape over the top half of the left-hand goggles. Fill this with a black-to-white gradient on a new layer. Add a Gaussian Blur (Filter>Blur>Gaussian Blur) at something between 6 and 10, and set the blending mode to Screen, 35% Opacity.

11 ...and shadows You can darken the image too, to help reduce the artificial look. Add a layer style to the right-hand goggles image by choosing Layer> Layer Styles>Gradient Overlay. Choose a black-to-white gradient at 90 degrees, and set it to Multiply at 25%. This little addition makes a big difference to the final result.

12 Colour correction The colour on the original pic doesn't quite match the inserted artwork, but this is easy to fix. Click the background layer, then add a Hue and Saturation adjustment layer by clicking New Adjustment Layer at the bottom of the Layers palette. Reduce the opacity, and optionally reduce the amount of red in the image.

Layer structure
Beneath the snow

13 Sharpen Create a new layer at the top of the stack, and hold Opt/Alt, Ctrl/Cmd and Shift while opening the fly-out menu in the Layers palette. Choose Merge Visible; a composite of your layers will appear on the new layer. On this layer choose Filter> Sharpen>Unsharp Mask and play with the settings for best effect (we chose an Amount of 92%, a Radius of 3.7px and Threshold of 1).

14 Add noise and contrast Finally, the image could do with a little noise added consistently across the artwork to seal it all together. Choose Filter>Noise> Add Noise, and choose an Amount of 2%, Monochromatic and Gaussian to complete the transformation. If desired, add a Curves adjustment (or Levels if you prefer) above the other layers and increase Contrast a little.

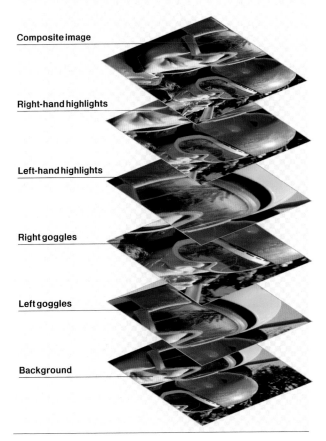

Composite image

Right-hand highlights

Left-hand highlights

Right goggles

Left goggles

Background

Fixes

essentials

SKILL LEVEL

Beginner
Intermediate
Expert

TIME TAKEN

10 minutes

ON THE DISC

start.jpg
(courtesy
of Krystle,
**morguefile.
com**)

KEY SKILLS COVERED

What you'll learn

DUST AND
SCRATCHES
FILTER

MASKS

ADJUSTMENT
LAYERS

Tip

Finer details
To really get a clean look, make sure you zoom in close to parts of your image when painting onto your mask. If you make a mistake and reveal too much of the image underneath, simply switch to white and paint the smoothness back in. Altering the size of your brush will help you get into the finer areas of the image.

Start image

After retouch

Create flawless skin

Give portraits a quick and easy makeover using masks

W e all want flawless skin, but in photographs our complexions can often look blotchy, red and patchy. Thankfully, Photoshop has just the tools to help us rescue any such skin scenarios, without the need for an intensive facial.

In this tutorial you'll learn how to create a smooth and even skintone, while maintaining facial details. The technique is very simple and can be applied to virtually any portrait image. You will make extensive use of the Noise filter to achieve a smooth base

layer for the skin. We will then follow this up by applying a layer mask and using a brush to paint finer details back in. By altering the opacity of our brush we can also give more form back to the face, reintroducing highlights and shape, for a natural feel.

f you are unfamiliar with masks, this is a fantastic introduction to the feature, providing a sense of just what it's capable of. You will learn how to apply a mask and use the brush to hide and reveal parts of the image with the mask.

Our start image came from **http://mrg.bz/3Y9gh4**.

MAKE EVERYTHING SMOOTH, THEN WORK BACKWARDS
Apply a filter and mask to the bits you want to reveal

01 Set up Open your image, then go to Image>Mode>CMYK. Drag the background layer onto the New Layer tab to create a copy. With the background copy layer selected, go to Filter>Noise> Dust & Scratches. Set Threshold to 0 and Radius to 6px. Hit OK.

02 Mask Click the Add Layer Mask icon at the foot of the Layers palette. Pick a big black brush and paint over the hair, background and clothing. Painting with black will reveal the sharpness below. Click the eye icon off the background layer to see the mask.

03 Smaller details Next, select a smaller brush (or hit the '[' key) and use this to carefully paint over the eyes and lips. Ensure you are still using black to paint with. You will now see the detail return to these areas.

04 Add detail The skin now looks a bit too smooth, so to add some realism pick a medium-size soft brush set to black, and lower the brush Opacity to 25% in the top Options bar. Sweep the brush over the main facial features, following the contours of the nose, eyebrows, chin, neck and cleavage.

05 Add some warmth To add some warmth to this photo, go to Image> Adjustments>Shadow/Highlights and enter 2% for Shadows and 4% for Highlights. Hit OK. You'll need to experiment with these amounts if you are using your own photo.

06 A little more refinement Now go to the Layers palette and reduce Fill to between 70% and 80%. This will give the skin a bit more texture without losing all the smoothness.

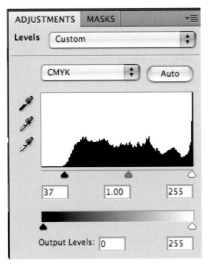

07 Level it out These final two steps are optional. To add a bit more punch to the image go to the Adjustment Layer icon at the bottom of the Layers palette. Pull the black slider inwards until it's in line with the start of the histogram information. Do the same with the white slider if you need to.

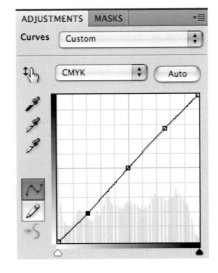

08 Curves Now add another adjustment layer and this time select Curves. Click on the top portion of the line (about a third of the way down) and pull it upwards just a little. Now click on the bottom third of the line and pull downwards a little. It creates a slight S-shaped curve to help boost contrast without clipping highlights or losing detail in the shadows.

Tip

Adjustment layers
You can tweak your photo with adjustment layers. Just click on the black and white icon at the foot of the Layers palette and choose from multiple editing options such as Levels and Curves.

essentials

SKILL LEVEL

Beginner
Intermediate
Expert

TIME TAKEN

30 minutes

KEY SKILLS COVERED
What you'll learn

COLOR BALANCE

ADJUSTMENT LAYERS

WORKING WITH MASKS

WORKING WITH BRUSHES

DODGE AND BURN

Start image

Boost colour using the Color Balance options

Learn to adjust colour in your photos to maximise their impact

 he Color Balance tool is one of the myriad ways of adjusting colour and light levels in Photoshop, and can be used to good effect for boosting the impact of images and recovering lost colour and light.

In this tutorial we'll be giving you a head start and showing you a few simple tricks to get the most out of your images using the Color Balance tool. Adjusting one image, we'll show you how to change colour to warm a picture up, how to add light by increasing the amount of RGB and how to adjust the colour of selected areas. We'll also demonstrate how to create a simple but pleasing vignette effect without resorting to filters. You'll also learn how to apply

effects using adjustment layers. Don't be deterred by technical jargon – using this tool is a relatively intuitive process because the results are immediately visible and it's often simply a case of choosing what looks right.

It's easy to get carried away when experimenting with colour in Photoshop, which is great fun when practising. For the finished article, however, take small steps and err on the side of caution, as you'll be surprised what a dramatic effect small changes can have when using this tool. You can practise using one of the free stock images on the disc, or use one of your own – just remember to save a copy before you undertake any dramatic experiments.

LIGHTEN UP
Introduce warmth and light

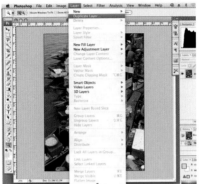

01 Select the image
Open your image. You might want to create a duplicate layer by selecting Layer> Duplicate Layer. This way, if your adjustments go too far it's easy to revert to the original. Name the layer 'Midtones'.

02 Add some warmth
Select Image> Adjustments>Color Balance. Make sure the Preserve Luminosity option is ticked. Starting with the midtones, take out some blue and a little magenta to bring a bit more warmth to the evening scene.

Tip

Greater accuracy
Often different parts of an image require different colour changes. Using the Mask tool and brushing out unwanted areas is one way of achieving this. However, creating paths with the Pen tool can afford greater accuracy – or if your original picture is well defined, experiment with the Magnetic Lasso tool.

03 Preserve Luminosity
Click OK to apply the changes and then return to the Color Balance tool by going to Select Image> Adjustments>Color Balance. This time however, deselect the Preserve Luminosity option.

04 Let there be light Using the Red/Green/Blue (light spectrum) sliders, we can reintroduce lost light into the image. Select the Highlights option and increase all three sliders by about 30%. This is a good opportunity to make use of the fields at the top to ensure all values are equal. Stay in the Color Balance panel for the next step.

Tip
Vintage photos
You can use the Color Balance tool to age photos as well as bring them back to life. Deselect Preserve Luminosity and select the Midtones button. Add a healthy dose of magenta (maybe -60) and some yellow (maybe -20). Now select the Highlights option and wash the image out by increasing red, green and blue.

FIGHT THAT WASHED-OUT LOOK
Add a bit of contrast

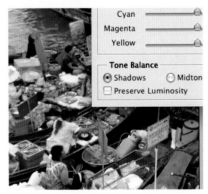

05 Add some contrast By boosting the levels of light there is a danger the image becomes washed-out. To counter this we can increase the contrast by selecting the Shadows option and reducing the amount of RGB. Don't click OK just yet.

06 Experiment with Luminosity
Before saving your changes, click the Preserve Luminosity option to observe the different effect that it creates. When selected, colour will change but tone will not; when deselected, an increase in RGB can give the impression of more light.

07 Adjustment layer Click the Create New Adjustment Layer icon in the Layers palette and select Color Balance from the drop-down menu. This creates an editable layer that's a little more versatile, and with the application of brushes will enable you to change specific parts of an image.

Fixes

Tip

Easy sunsets

Sunset photos can look even better with a little application of Color Balance. With Preserve Luminosity selected, add magenta to the shadows for a deep, rich contrast. Add cyan to the Midtones for a gentle blue sky, and a bit of red and yellow to the highlights to boost the warm light from the sun.

TRUE BLUE
Perfect the colour in your image

08 **Deep blue sea** In the Color Balance dialog box select Midtones and ensure that Preserve Luminosity is ticked. Add some blue, cyan and magenta to return the colour of the water to a nice rich blue. Click OK to save your changes.

09 **Paint out discolouration** As you can see, the rest of the image has become an unnatural shade of pink. Using the Adjustment layer mask we can paint this out. Make sure the layer mask thumbnail in the Layers panel is highlighted. Select black from the Color palette and choose the Brush tool.

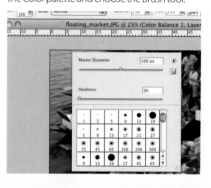

10 **Using brushes** Use a brush with a soft edge and set the Opacity and Flow values to about 75%. Using the brush on a layer mask is just like using an eraser, so paint out the parts of the image that have become discoloured (everything but the water). You may need to zoom in and use a smaller brush for the detail around the edge of the boats.

ADD A FINAL DRAMATIC TOUCH
Create a vignette effect

11 **Composite** Create a composite of your layers: highlight the top one in the Layers panel and hit Shift+Opt/Alt+E; name it 'Composite'. It's like adding a stop in the History panel: if things go wrong you can retrace your steps.

12 **Vignette effect** Create another adjustment layer, click the Create New Adjustment Layer icon in the Layers palette and select Color Balance in the drop-down menu. This time, deselect Preserve Luminosity.

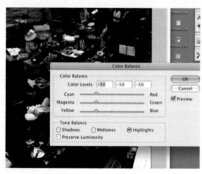

13 **Going to extremes** We are going to make the image very dark by reducing all the sliders to a value of -50. Do the same for Highlights, Midtones and Shadows. Now click OK to save the changes.

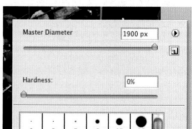

14 **Big is beautiful** Using the process we used in steps 8 and 9, we're going to remove the darkness from the central focus of the image. Leave the Brush Opacity and Flow settings at 75%. Again, the brush needs to be soft but also needs to be much larger – we used a brush measuring 1,900 pixels.

15 **Brush in light** Only a few applications of the brush are needed to return light to the central area, leaving the outer edges dark. This helps focus the viewer's eye and gives a professional look. Finding ways to create effects like this without using filters is important for maintaining as much info as possible, for a high quality result.

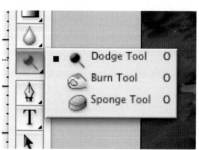

16 **Finishing touches** Create a final composite layer by pressing Shift+Opt/Alt+E; name it 'Final'. Using the Dodge and Burn tools, add highlights and deepen shadows for that extra bit of depth and interest to draw the viewer's eye.

Make a quick and easy halo

Whether you're a saint or a sinner, a halo can be yours

Make a quick and easy halo

essentials

SKILL LEVEL

Beginner
Intermediate
Expert

TIME TAKEN

Five minutes

This fun little tutorial will show you how to add a halo to your photos in minutes.

You'll begin by making a basic shape with the Marquee tools, turn it into a halo shape with the Transform tools, then colour it up with the help of Color Balance. It's quick, easy and a fun way to achieve a squeaky-clean image no matter how naughty you may have been! You can download the start image for free from **www.sxc.hu**, image number '218820', courtesy of Cop Richard.

KEY SKILLS COVERED

What you'll learn

ELLIPTICAL MARQUEE

IMAGE ADJUSTMENTS

TRANSFORM TOOLS

Quick tip: Use the Eyedropper to pick a light colour from the halo, and use a large brush (Opacity set to 25%) to brush over the top of the hair and face to give the impression of light reflecting from the halo.

5 minute fix

AN ANGELIC ADDITION

Turn your friends into angelic beings in minutes

01 Ring Using the Elliptical Marquee, hold the cursor in the middle of the face, hold Shift and Opt/Alt and draw a circle outwards. It should cover the head. Add another circle within this one: hold down Opt/Alt, hold the cursor within the first circle. Drag a new circle from top left to bottom right.

02 Transform Add a new layer called 'Halo'. Set the foreground colour to White and go Edit>Fill to fill the ring with white. Hit Ctrl/Cmd+T and drag the top and bottom of the box inwards to make a halo shape. Move it into position. Hit OK. Add a new layer and move it between your model and Halo layers.

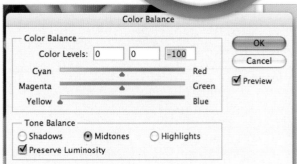

03 Colour it Go to Edit>Fill and pick Black. Now select the Halo layer and hit Ctrl/Cmd+E to Merge Down. Select Screen as the layer blending mode, then go to Filter>Blur>Gaussian Blur and enter 15px in the Radius box. Go to Image>Adjustments>Color Balance, check Preserve Luminosity and move the Yellow/Blue slider to -100. Do this for Shadows and Midtone, and experiment with the other sliders to achieve the best colour.

Perfect family portraits

essentials

SKILL LEVEL

Beginner
Intermediate
Expert

TIME TAKEN

One hour

ON THE DISC

Image1.jpg
Image2.jpg
Portrait.psd

Learn how to take the best parts from multiple images to create a family portrait where everyone looks happy

T aking a perfect family portrait isn't easy. As soon as you get more than three people in a group, especially if they're in the same family, you can almost guarantee that when you take a photo at least one person will have their eyes shut, be pulling a face or not looking at the camera.

The latest digital cameras are now shipping with face-detection algorithms that are designed to hold the shot until a smile is detected, but even these sophisticated programs can't cope with a family of five. Inevitably you end up with an image that would have been perfect if only that one person hadn't been picking their nose!

As ever, Photoshop can help you overcome these frustrations. The solution is surprisingly straightforward: take multiple photos, then blend the best bits of each together in a single image.

In this tutorial we're going to look at a typical family photograph, and we'll use two versions of the photo to create a final image where everyone is looking at the camera and looking completely natural. The most important part of creating a seamless image is ensuring that both the colour and the lighting match between

> ## "The most important part is ensuring the colour and lighting match between the photos"

the photographs you are blending together. This is essential, because as soon as you blend two images together that have a different lighting or colour balance, the inserted areas will become all too obvious.

At the end of this tutorial you'll have all the skills you need to create your own perfect portraits and group photos, and even be able to bring together people who were never standing next to each other. So, let's get started...

IDENTIFY THE IMAGES
Get your images aligned and colour matched

01 Examine your images It sounds obvious, but the very first thing you need to do is look through the images you have and identify a base image to work with, and also which frames (images) the individuals look best in. Make a note of the images you want to use for each person and, if you're using Adobe Bridge, flag them so you can quickly compare and contrast.

02 Create a master composition Open up the image that has the biggest overall area you wish to retain. You should always start off with a plan to do as little as possible to achieve an acceptable result. Starting with the best overall image will reduce the need to bring in elements from the other images, and save you time and headaches. Here we're starting with 'image1. jpg', so open that up in Photoshop.

03 Import and save Next, we're going to bring in our other image (or other images if you're using more than two). Each version of the shot will sit on a layer of its own. Choose File>Place and select 'image2.jpg'. If you're using a recent version of Photoshop, Image2 will be imported as a Smart Object, which is fine for this tutorial. Repeat the process for the remaining images you want to use, then save the overall composition as 'portrait.psd' to ensure you retain the original image unchanged.

Final image

Family Portrait

Before image 1

Before image 2

Tip

Add noise for aesthetic effect
Almost all images have a degree of grain or noise within them. On film cameras this comes from the individual grains of photosensitive material on the film; on digital it arises from the sensitivity of the CCD. A good way to disguise image joins is to deliberately add noise to your final composition by choosing Filter> Noise>Add Noise. Choose Monochromatic Gaussian at a low level for an aesthetic result that also ties the different parts of the image together under a single unifying effect.

UNDERSTANDING MASKS

By showing/hiding layer content we can create sophisticated effects. Masks work with tone, not colour. Black hides content, white shows it. Anything between will show/hide the layer to a greater or lesser extent.

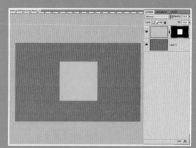

A simple mask
Here the top layer has a simple mask with a square area of black pixels that allow the layer underneath to shine through.

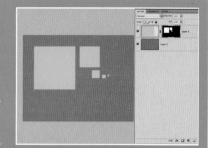

Multiple areas
This mask has multiple areas of black that hide the layer the mask is applied to. Opt/Alt-click on a mask in order to view it in the image window.

Shades of grey
Masks can contain any range of tone from black to white. A common technique is to use a gradient-based mask to layer a new sky onto an image.

Type as a mask
Masks can give you interesting effects. Here we have a copy of a layer that's been desaturated, and we typed text on the mask to show the layer below only where letters appear.

Complex masks
By combining many layers and masks you can reveal and hide multiple layers on top of one another. Here, three layers are blended differently according to their masks.

ALIGN, BALANCE AND COMPOSE
Make sure your images align and match perfectly

04 Perfect alignment If you took the photos with your camera on a tripod, you may find the images align perfectly already. Just to be sure though, it's worth running an alignment to save any additional work later. Double-click the background layer to convert it to a standard layer, then duplicate by dragging it onto the New Layer button.

06 Bring the primary image to the front Now we've got our images aligned nicely, drag the best image to the top of the layer stack so it's hiding the other layers. We're going to mask out the areas of this image where there are elements we don't like, so add a new layer mask by clicking on the New Layer Mask button at the bottom of the Layer panel.

08 Repeat for each area Repeat this process for each area you don't like in the main image. Add further layer masks to each of the layers underneath so you can choose which layer to show for each area. Remember that black paint on a layer mask hides that layer, and white paint shows it. If you paint with grey, you'll reduce the opacity of the layer so it's partially transparent.

05 Reposition Select all layers then go to Edit>Auto-Align Layers. In the Alignment options hit Reposition Only. If you had images with slightly different perspective you could use this function set to Auto or Perspective, but for our image we only need to reposition. Note you need at least three layers. This option is only available in recent editions of Photoshop, so if you can't see it you'll have to manually nudge each layer into position.

07 Paint out the bad bits Select the layer mask then choose the Brush tool. Set your brush colour to black, and choose a soft round brush at a medium size. Paint black onto the mask over the areas you don't like to reveal the layer underneath. If you make a mistake or remove too much of the layer, swap the paint colour to white and paint back over the area to reveal the top layer again.

09 Examine the edges You should now be able to see the right versions of the faces and bodies you want in the image, but unless you're very lucky there will still be a bit of work to do. Zoom in close to the image and look at the edges around the areas you've masked out. Tidy up imperfections by painting with a smaller soft brush onto the mask – black to reveal the layers below, white to hide them.

FINISH IT OFF
Spit, polish, sharpen and add noise

Layer structure
All in the family

10 Colour balance Depending on how you shot your source photos, there may be a slight shift in the hue and saturation of the different images. We used studio lights so the lighting is the same, but if necessary add a Hue and Saturation (Image> Adjust>Hue/Saturation) adjustment to individual layers to match them to the top one.

11 Merge Visible Layers Create a new layer at the top of the stack. Hold down Ctrl+Alt+Shift (Cmd+Option+Shift on a Mac) and open the fly-out menu on the Layers panel. Select Merge Visible Layers and release the mouse button, then the keys. You should have a merged version of the layers in the new layer. If your layers disappear and you end up with only one layer, undo (Cmd/Ctrl+Z) and then try again.

12 Clone out imperfections Now you have a single layer at the top to work on, you can use the Clone tool to remove imperfections such as spots and stray hairs etc. With the Clone tool selected, hold Opt/Alt and click to choose a source point, then paint to cover undesired areas with a copy of the source pixels. Keep this to a minimum to avoid creating an artificial result.

13 Add curves Add a new Curves adjustment layer at the top of the stack. Click and drag two points on the diagonal graph to create a subtle 'S' shape. This adds contrast to the image by changing the output tones across the image – we're increasing the black and decreasing the white to compress the tonal range.

14 Sharpen Duplicate the merged layer and select the copy. Choose Filter>Sharpen>Unsharp Mask. Zoom in to 100% so you can see the effect and adjust the sliders to suit. We chose an Amount of 113%, a Radius of 0.7px and a Threshold of 0. Generally, when you're planning to print an image you should aim to over-sharpen slightly. When you're happy, click OK to accept the changes.

15 Add noise and vignette Finally, go to Filter>Noise>Add Noise. Choose 2%, Gaussian and Monochromatic then hit OK. Add a new layer and draw a big oval selection. Click Add New Layer Mask with the selection active, then invert the mask by clicking it and hitting Cmd/Ctrl+I. Add a Gaussian Blur to the mask at 250px and fill the layer with black. Reduce the opacity of the layer to taste.

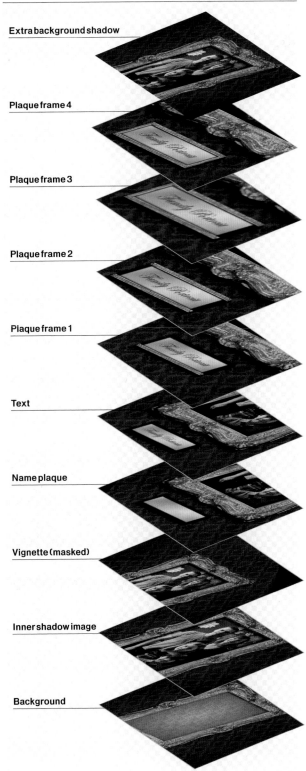

Extra background shadow

Plaque frame 4

Plaque frame 3

Plaque frame 2

Plaque frame 1

Text

Name plaque

Vignette (masked)

Inner shadow image

Background

Use the Color Replacement tool

Discover the possibilities of this hidden wonder

he extent of Photoshop's ability doesn't stop on the surface of what's there when you load it up. The toolbar actually contains many more tools than are visible, with sometimes two, three, four or more options than you first see.

The Color Replacement tool is one of these – hidden in the Brushes group ('B') because it performs in the same way as the Brush tool but with mannerisms of the Selection tools. This tool is used by taking a colour and painting over a subject to swap two colours. It's similar to the Color Balance and Hue adjustments, but you choose the colour. After the first spot of paint is applied, the tool ignores all other colours and only changes that particular one.

The best aspect of this tool is that it retains the lighting on the subject that you're colour swapping. This means that highlights and shadows are preserved. But the trick is to make sure the chosen colour for the replacement has the right brightness for the effect to look natural. Otherwise you could end up with a blotchy outcome. The Tolerance value is the most important aspect of the Color Replacement tool, because it controls how much paint is applied.

Follow our quick and easy tutorial on using the Color Replacement tool to give this bowl of fruit a funky makeover. You can try it out with the image we've provided on the disc, or grab your own picture and start practising your colour replacement skills!

THE BEST OF THE BUNCH
Use the Color Replacement tool to swap colours around

01 Set up the brush Open the image 'iStock_1289640.jpg' on the disc. Duplicate the layer so you have a copy with the original colours and select the Color Replacement tool. In the Options bar set Mode to Color, Sampling to Once, Limit to Contiguous, Tolerance to 100%, Size to 200px.

02 Test colours Open the Foreground Color picker, choose a colour, or one from a fruit, and use the tool to paint a small patch on one of the fruits. If it's too dark/light it looks blocky. When happy, in the Color picker hit Add To Swatches. Repeat for each colour on all the fruit, saving each colour as a new swatch.

03 Red bananas! Go to Window> Swatches to open the saved colours. For the bananas we chose red from one of the strawberries – but click on the swatch you saved for the bananas. Paint close to the edges using the Color Replacement tool, but make sure you don't go over them.

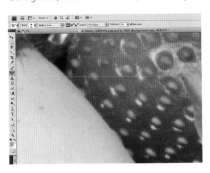

04 Edges Before we replace colours of the other fruits, touch up the banana edges. In the Options bar change the settings to Sampling Continuous, Limits to Find Edges, Tolerance to 20%. Lower the tool's Hardness to 0%. Zoom to 300% and paint to the edges. Don't worry if it's rough, we'll tidy up later.

05 Orange apple In the Swatches palette click on the colour you saved for the apple. As with the bananas, use a Brush Size of 200px and the settings in step 1 to paint the apple, leaving a thin strip of green around the edges.

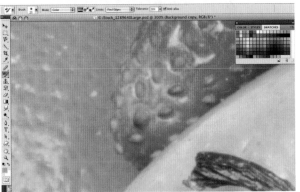

06 Finer details Zoom in to 300% and set the Options bar for painting the edges as we did with the bananas. Make the colour replacement around the edge of the apple and around the stalk. We'll correct imperfections later on.

07 Last but not least For the oranges, choose the colour you saved as a swatch to paint over the fruit. We chose the green of the apple. Paint each orange to the edges using the settings Sampling: Continuous, Limits: Find Edges and Tolerance 20%.

08 Tidy the layer mask On the layer with replacing colours click on the Add Layer Mask button in the Layers palette. Zoom in to 300% and use the Brush tool on the white layer mask thumbnail to erase any rough edges around each of the pieces of fruit.

essentials

SKILL LEVEL

Beginner
Intermediate
Expert

TIME TAKEN

One hour

ON THE DISC

Landscape
image

KEY SKILLS COVERED
What you'll learn

3D TEXTURE
WITH NOISE AND
EMBOSS FILTERS

PERSPECTIVE

GRADUATED
SELECTIONS
WITH QUICK MASK
MODE

FLIP A LAYER
ONLY USING
TRANSFORM

ADD GRADUATED
TINTS USING
LAYER MASKS

MOTION BLUR

DISPLACE FILTER

CONTROL MASK
STRENGTH
WITH LEVELS

Original

Displace filter

Create a realistic lake to flood any landscape scene

dding water to a landscape scene is not a new technique, and it usually involves duplicating the top area of an image, flipping it then adding a bit of Motion Blur.

But this version of the technique doesn't take just a step further – it actually takes more of a leap, and the end result really is a bit special. It's all down to clever use of the Displace filter, which enables us to apply ripple patterns to our water that are very hard for the eye to separate from the real thing. There's a fair amount of leg work involved to get things looking this good, though. It's not a simple matter of applying a filter and playing with the settings. We

actually have to create our displacement map from scratch before we can apply it. But fortunately there's no drawing or paths involved, just a clever combination of other filters and a bit of perspective tweaking to ensure our ripples subscribe to the laws of physics – you'll see them gradually merge in the distance as the eye would expect.

You'll need to be fairly rigorous in following the rather detailed settings listed in the steps: get one thing wrong (especially in creating the displacement map itself) and the technique can fall apart. If you forget to check the Lock Transparent Pixels button in Step 12, for example, the ripples can end up looking more like those you'd find in a pond.

BUILD THE FOUNDATIONS
Noise, Blur and Emboss are the basic ingredients

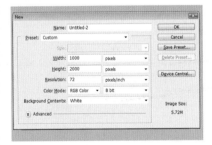

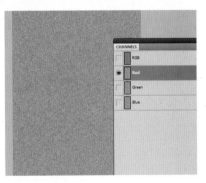

01 Create a new document Create a new document with the height roughly half as long as the width of your landscape scene. Make the new document width half that number again. For our example image, we set Height to 2000 pixels and Width to 1000 pixels. You should end up with a long, tall image.

02 Add some noise Next, go to Filter>Noise>Add Noise and add 400% of Gaussian, Monochromatic noise. Soften the noise with 2 pixels of Filter> Blur>Gaussian Blur. Now navigate to the Channels palette and select the Red channel.

PERFECTING THE MAP WITH TRANSFORM
Now to add perspective and alter the contrast with distance

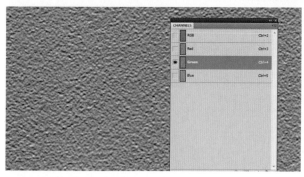

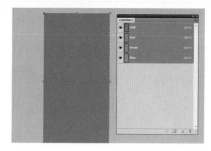

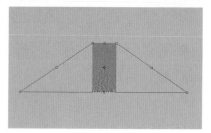

03 Emboss Go to Filter>Stylize>Emboss and choose Angle 180 degrees, Height 1 pixel and Amount 500%. OK this. This makes our noise three-dimensional. Repeat for the Green channel, this time using an Angle of 90 degrees rather than 180. This creates 3D texture in the other direction.

04 Emboss again Now select the RGB channel again. Note the texture has taken on a wavy, coloured effect. This is the beginning of our ripple displacement map. We need to alter the perspective, however. Use Cmd/Ctrl+A to Select All then go to Edit> Transform>Perspective.

05 Create perspective Drag the bottom left or right slider outwards and keep an eye on the Width figure in the Tool Options bar. Use Cmd/Ctrl and - to zoom out as you drag the handle outwards so you have enough space. Go to 800% if you captured your original scene with a wide-angle lens, or 600% for a standard lens. Press Enter twice.

Create a scene
The technique behind the art

Creating the reflection The top section of our scene provides the basis for our water reflection. We simply choose where the horizon should be, flip from there and move the flipped area down to match

Using layers The whole tutorial is completed with just three layers. The background layer contains the original scene, another layer for the reflection, and a third for the blue colouring

Catchlights This technique introduces white lines into the horizon area. These can actually look like the realistic catchlights you often get at the water's edge. Their strength is controlled in the latter steps

06 Crop unwanted info Now go to Image>Crop to get rid of information stored outside the canvas. Next, use Cmd/Ctrl+Shift+T to run the Transform again. Use Image>Crop once more to remove extraneous information and keep file size down. Use Cmd/Ctrl+D to deselect.

Rippled surface The ripples are added via the Displace filter. As we've run Transform Perspective on our displacement map, the ripples appear to get tighter with distance, as they would in reality

Deep blue The blue in the water is added for maximum realism. Only at the lowest angle is 100% of the surface reflected. At higher angles you start to see the blue of the water

07 Graduated selection Now select the Red channel. Press 'Q' to enter Quick Mask mode, D to reset the colour palette and 'G' to select the Gradient tool (Shift+G if Paintbucket is selected). Draw a line from the top of the canvas to the bottom. White should be the foreground colour.

APPLYING THE MAP TO OUR FLOODED LANDSCAPE
Create your water area and use the map to add realistic ripples

08 Reduce contrast
Press 'Q' to exit Quick Mask mode. We now have a gradient selection. Click the foreground colour swatch and change B (in H, S, B) to 50% to get a mid grey. Go to Edit>Fill, select Foreground Color and make the blend mode Normal. The graduated selection and grey fill reduce the contrast of the waves with distance.

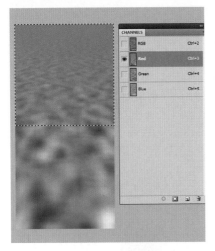

09 Crop and select Click the RGB channel. You'll see a small band at the very top of the image where the waves appear to get bigger again. Press 'C' to access the Crop tool and crop this out. Save the image as PSD file and open the landscape scene. Determine where the horizon is, and select everything above it with the Rectangular Marquee tool ('M').

Altering ripple size
You can alter the ripple size in two ways. By controlling the size of the document you use to build your displacement map, you can control the wave frequency. Double the suggested settings to create tighter, more frequent ripples. Halve them instead to create larger, more spread out ripples. The Displace filter settings control how pronounced the ripples appear. Double the suggested setting for more pronounced ripples, and halve it to create more subtle effects.

10 Add a blue tinge Use Cmd/Ctrl+J to float this selection to a new layer. Next, go to Edit>Transform>Flip Vertical. Use Shift and the down arrow key repeatedly to line the reflection up. Create a new layer and Cmd/Ctrl-click the reflection layer to load it as a selection. Click the foreground colour swatch and choose a deep blue.

11 Fade blue in Now go to Edit>Fill and select Foreground Color (blending mode Normal). Add a layer mask to the blue layer and select the Gradient tool ('G'). With white as the foreground and black as the background, drag a line from the bottom to a little above the horizon. Drop the layer opacity if the blue looks too strong.

12 Motion blur Select the reflection layer – we're going to add wind blur. Go to Filter>Blur>Motion Blur and set Angle to 90 degrees, Distance to around 10 pixels. We're now ready to apply the displacement map. Click the chequer board button near the top of the Layers palette to lock transparent pixels. Now go to Filter>Distort>Displace.

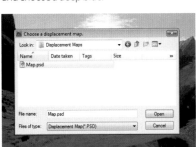

13 The Displace filter Make sure Stretch to Fit and Repeat Edge Pixels are checked. The Horizontal scale should be about half the setting of the Vertical scale, and the amount you enter for both determines the strength of the effect. We went for settings of 75 and 150. Select your saved displacement map from the dialog.

14 Tweak the horizon You may see a few white lines near the horizon. We can tone these down and blend the water edge a little by adding a layer mask to the reflection layer, selecting the Gradient tool and dragging from a little below the white lines to the horizon (using white and black colours), ensuring the line is perfectly straight.

15 Perfect to finish
If the water edge looks weak, select the layer mask on the reflection layer and go to Image> Adjustments> Levels. Drag the white Input slider leftwards. You can drag the white Output slider leftwards to reduce the depth of the water as a whole.

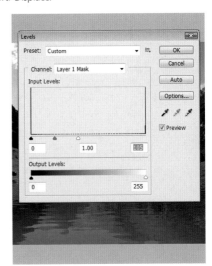

"Have fun with this tutorial, and don't forget to experiment with your own photographs"

Dramatic pet portraits

We all love our pet, so make their pictures better

W ouldn't it be great if we could use some of these pictures of our devoted doggy or pampered pussy in a Photoshop project? Well, your luck is in – in this tutorial we'll be using Photoshop's array of tools and adjustment layers to construct a portrait of a beloved pooch.

We start with a photo of a black Labrador, but you can use whatever photo you like. This tutorial will work as well on a dog as it will on a cat, bird, frog or giant land snail. We'll be utilising a number of Photoshop techniques and tools that you may or may not be familiar with. First we'll delve into one of Photoshop's best features,

namely the adjustment layers. These are very special because they're infinitely adjustable and can affect the whole picture or just a part of it due to their individual masks or if used as a clipping mask. We'll be using the Levels, Curves, Hue/Saturation and Exposure adjustment layers. These add contrast, change the brightness and modify the colour of the picture. We'll also be using the Dodge and Burn tools to affect shadows and highlights in order to bring some depth to the proceedings.

Have fun with this tutorial, and don't forget to experiment with your own photographs.

HOW MUCH IS THAT DOGGY...
...in the Photoshop windows

essentials

SKILL LEVEL
Beginner
Intermediate
Expert

TIME TAKEN
One hour

ON THE DISC
dog start.jpg
(courtesy
of www.sxc.hu/
photo/888364)
Pet curves
(Step 9).acv
Pet level (Step
10).alv
Final levels
(Step 14).alv

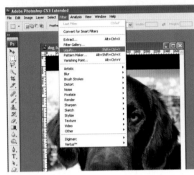

01 **Let's begin** We start by opening our source picture 'dog start.jpg' from the CD. We are using a black Labrador, but you can use whatever pet photo you want. First thing we notice is that the dog's nose is a bit overexposed, so we add an Exposure adjustment layer.

02 **Who nose?** Go to Layer>New Adjustment Layer>Exposure and change the Exposure to -3.00. The whole picture will now become a lot darker. But that's okay, because we're going to mask out everything except the dog's nose. Click the Exposure 1 layer mask, and with a large soft-edged brush paint with black over everything but the top of the nose.

03 **Mirrors of the soul** Let's go back to our dog layer. The eyes are going to be the key focus of the picture, so we're going to slightly increase the size of them. Go to Filter>Liquify and select the Bloat tool. Change the settings to Brush Size 440, Brush Density 100, Brush Pressure 60 and Brush Rate 60.

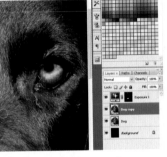

04 **Bloat** Move the brush over one of the eyes and click and hold until the eye is about twice the normal size – so it looks bigger but not silly. Repeat with the other eye. Hit OK to accept the changes.

05 **Bright eyes** Select the dog layer and make a copy by pressing Cmd/Ctrl+J (just in case you don't like your alterations and want to step back easily). Select the Dodge tool from the toolbox and set Range to Highlights and Exposure to 11%. Gently go around the irises of the eyes until they are brighter.

Tip

Using Levels and Curves
Making small adjustments to the levels and curves on a photo can have a dramatic effect – for example, improving colours or adding extra contrast. In this tutorial we used both Curves and Levels to bring out certain aspects of the picture. We've included two Levels (steps 10 and 14) and one Curves (step 9) preset with this project, which can be loaded into the picture using the appropriate adjustment layer. For instructions on how to use these, please go to **http://photo.net/digital-darkroom-forum/00Qp3c.**

06 **Colour fill** Once you're happy with the eyes, move on to the background. We need to add a Solid Color adjustment layer above the previously made Dog Copy layer. Go to Layer>New Fill Layer>Solid Color and change R to 0, G to 0 and B to 0. The colour will change to black. Now click OK.

07 **Reveal the face** Reduce Opacity of Color Fill 1 to about 50%, and on the layer mask paint with black and with a large soft-edged brush over the dog's face and ears. Once the face is visible, increase Opacity to 100%. Clean up any bits that are not needed by brushing over with white.

08 **Blue is the colour** Let's give the dog a nice blue tint. In Layer>New Adjustment Layer>Hue/Saturation, click the Colorize tickbox and change Hue to 209, Saturation to 25 and Lightness to -14. On the Adjustment layer mask use a black soft-edged brush and mask out the eyes and nose so they are the original colour.

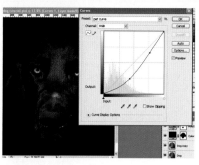

09 **Curves** Next, we're going to add some contrast by utilising a Curve adjustment layer above our Hue/Saturation layer (Layer>New Adjustment Layer>Curves). Change the curve so it curves downwards slightly (see example above).

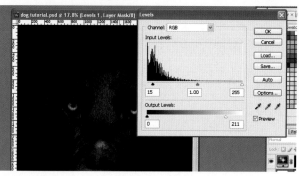

10 **Levels** Add a Levels adjustment layer above the Curves layer (Layer>New Adjustment Layer>Levels). Change the Input Levels to 15, 1.00, 255 and the Output Levels to 0, 211 (as in the example). Move to the top of your layer stack and hold Shift, Opt/Alt, Cmd/Ctrl+E to make a merged copy of all the current layers, then name it 'Merged'.

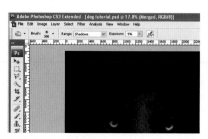

11 **Burn baby burn** Grab your Burn tool and set Range to Shadows and Exposure to 9%, then click the Airbrush button. Change your Brush Size so it's around 300 pixels and make sure Hardness is set to 0%. Select the Merged layer and gently (and repeatedly) brush under the eyes, ears and left-hand side of the face.

12 **Sharpen** Once you're happy with the burning, we want to sharpen our image. Go to Filter>Sharpen>Smart Sharpen. Set Amount to 100%, Radius to 2.0 pixels and Remove to Gaussian Blur. Alternatively, you could use Sharpen>Sharpen a couple of times.

::::: **Layer structure**
How we created our dramatic pooch

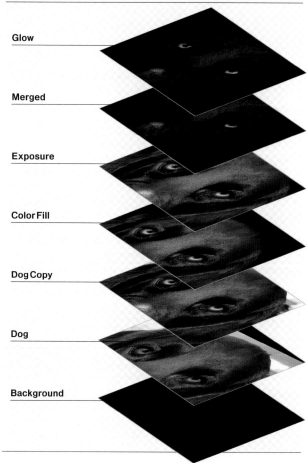

Glow

Merged

Exposure

Color Fill

Dog Copy

Dog

Background

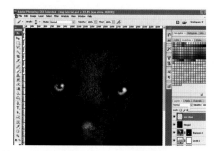

13 **Shine on** The eyes need a little work to bring them out of the picture. We add a shine to the left-hand side of both eyes. Make a new layer called 'Eye Shine' above the Merged layer, select the Brush tool and press 'D' followed by 'X' on the keyboard to set the foreground colour to white. Change Brush Size to 80 pixels.

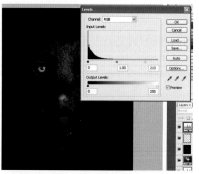

14 **Finishing touches** On the Eye Shine layer, click on each eye to give it a bit of shine, reduce the Layer Opacity to around 58%. Finally, add another Levels adjustment layer above the Eye Shine layer as in step 10, setting Input Levels to 0, 1.00, 210.

Add emphasis to eyes

Use Dodge and Burn to give the eyes a sparkle

5 minute fix

essentials

It's well known that a person's eyes are the windows to their soul. Here's a very quick way to draw more attention to them in a portrait image.

To add more punch to the eyes, we've used two tools for the job: Burn and Dodge. The first of these is great for deepening shadows, which in turn makes the highlights stand out. But to really create a polished effect, the Dodge tool is the perfect way to add that all-important sparkle.

Give it a go – it only takes five minutes!

KEY SKILLS COVERED
What you'll learn

DODGE TOOL
BURN TOOL

Before

After

Quick tip: For an extra boost, use the Burn tool and a small brush to darken the eyelashes along the top and bottom

USE THE DODGE AND BURN TOOLS
Add contrast to eyes in three quick steps

01 Non-destructive editing To edit non-destructively on your image, drag the image's layer onto the Create New Layer button in the Layers palette to duplicate. This way you can return to the original image at any point while editing.

02 Lighten Pick the Dodge tool and set its brush size so that the tip covers the coloured area of the iris. Set the tool's Hardness to 20%, and in the Options bar change Range to Midtones, Exposure to 30%, and tick the Protect Tones box. Softly paint over the iris to add contrast and brightness.

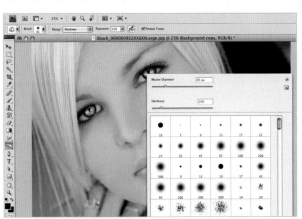

03 Darken the edges Select the Burn tool and set it to 15% Hardness with a brush size that fits over the outline of the iris. Set the Range to Shadows and Exposure to 15%. Apply the brush to the outside edge of the iris, making the area darker.

Start image

Tip

Painting fine hair strands

One of the trickiest tasks you'll face is colouring fine strands of hair. They'll often be semi-translucent so you'll need some background colour to shine through. Try to work over individual strands at 50%, or simply leave them black if too tricky. Where there's a big clump with some background showing through, it's best to use 50% background colour on the gaps, and 50% hair colour on the hair – you'll never get it exactly, so the reduced amount gives you a little extra leeway on the blending.

Add colour to your old photos

Hand colour the Curves way with precision colour control to transform old photos into full colour

here are countless recipes for hand colouring mono photographs floating around the internet, but this is probably the best.

Using Curves adjustment layers to produce our colours gives us the advantage of being able to go back in and tweak at any time to alter colour quickly and easily. Push the Red curve up a smidgen more to make the hair a little more auburn, or pull Blue down a touch with the skin curves to add a little more yellow.

When you add colour manually using the Color picker, you've got to go through the rigmarole of applying Hue/Saturation adjustments to change the colour hue or saturation. And if you want to darken or lighten the colour, you'll need a further Curves adjustment layer as is also required with the Solid Color adjustment layer method. A real hassle then – but there's none of that business here!

A big advantage of the Curves method is that not only can you tweak colour hue and saturation quickly and easily, but you

can also darken or lighten the underlying information to produce a darker or lighter shade – all with the same single adjustment layer. The RGB channel controls the lightness of the colour; the ratio of each of the colour channels determines its specific hue, and the amount each curve is pushed determines colour saturation. Go hard for strong effect and gentle for a weak look.

We have used a photo from iStockphoto to show you how the technique works, but the tutorial can be completed using your own old images.

essentials

SKILL LEVEL
Beginner
Intermediate
Expert

TIME TAKEN
1 hour

KEY SKILLS COVERED
What you'll learn

OPTIMISING CONTRAST WITH LEVELS

ADDING COLOUR TO MONOCHROME WITH CURVES

USING LAYER MASKS TO LOCALISE CURVES CHANGES

KNOCKING BACK BLOWN HIGHLIGHTS WITH LEVELS

 OPTIMISE TONAL RANGE AND CONTRAST TO START
We put Levels to use before setting up our skin colour

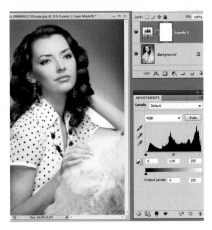

01 Levels for contrast We're going to start by ensuring our black and white image has a full range of tones and good contrast. Add a Levels adjustment layer using the button at the bottom of the Layers palette. Note the black and white Input sliders below the histogram.

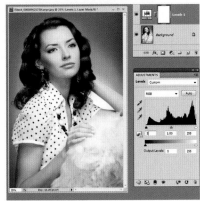

02 Set Levels endpoints Hold down Opt/Alt and move the black slider inwards until the white screen starts to show small areas of black. Move it back until the last spot of black disappears. Repeat for the white slider, albeit with the reverse of black and white. If spots already show without the slider moving inwards, just leave as is.

03 Build skin colour Now we're going to add our first colour for the skin. Add a Curves adjustment layer and select Red from the drop-down menu instead of RGB. This lets us add red or cyan to our black and white image – red up and cyan down. Push the curve up with one anchor point to add red as shown.

PAINT IN THE SKIN COLOUR AND START THE LIPS
We can use the layer mask to localise our colour adjustments

04 Finish off skin colour Now we select Blue from the drop-down menu and bring the curve down with a single point to subtract blue and add yellow. Move it downwards as shown in the screengrab above – about the same amount as the red curve was moved upwards.

05 Set up for skin paint With the Curves layer mask still active we invert with Cmd/Ctrl+I to turn it black. Now press 'D' to reset the Color palette to black and white, and use 'X' to toggle to white if necessary. Select the Brush tool ('B') and set to 0% Hardness and 100% Opacity.

06 Begin painting skin Zoom in to 100% using Cmd/Ctrl+Opt/Alt+0 and carefully paint into the skin area only. Use 'X' to toggle back to black if you make a mistake, and paint over the offending area to remove it. Toggle back to white and start painting again.

Colour concoction
How to build up the palette

Skin colouring Our skin colour is achieved with the Red channel pushed up with a single point on the curve, and the Blue channel pulled down a similar amount

Eyes The brown of the eyes is produced with the same colour mixture as for the hair, but we drop the RGB curve down as well to darken a little for maximum realism

Strong lips The lip red requires the Red channel curve pushed up a little, with both the Green and Blue channels pulled down quite hard to add magenta and yellow respectively

Hair colour The hair brown is made by pushing red up moderately far, green a touch, and blue downwards even less. Drop red down a little to take out the auburn tint

More red The fingernails can be coloured with the same lips recipe, but the underlying tone is lighter so we also need to darken by pulling down the RGB channel harder with a single curve point

07 Finish skin work Paint the whole skin area, avoiding eyes, lips, hair and clothes etc. Don't worry if the skin colour isn't quite right at this point. Use a large brush size around the hairline for a soft transition. Avoid fine hairs where possible.

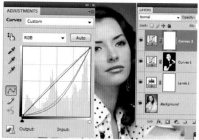

08 Add lip colour Now to add red to the lips. Add another Curves adjustment layer and start by selecting Green. Drag the green down quite hard with a single point to add magenta. Next, select Blue. Drag that down slightly further than the green to add yellow. Finally, push the red curve up just a touch.

TIME TO COLOUR ELSEWHERE
Lips, nails, eyes, eyebrows, hair and background

Layer structure
Bring the beauty to life

09 **Paint in lips** Next, invert the layer mask with Cmd/Ctrl+I and paint the colour into the lips only with a white soft brush, being carefully not to move into normal skin areas. We can darken the lips slightly by selecting the RGB curve, and then pulling it down just a little.

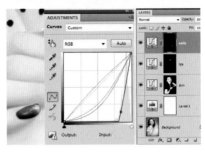

10 **Nail polish** We can use the same colour red for the fingernails. Add another Curves layer and move the Red, Green and Blue channels in the same way. Invert, paint into the fingernails only and this time pull the RGB curve down much further in order to match the lip colour. Name your layers now to prevent confusion later.

11 **Paint the hair** Now we're ready for the hair. Add another Curves layer and push red up a decent amount, green up a touch and blue down a tiny smidgen as shown. Leave the RGB channel. Invert and paint into the hair and eyebrows.

12 **Hair details** Where the hair and skin meet, you may need to blend by brushing in hair at 50% Opacity, and brushing skin out with black at 50% Opacity to avoid the colours mixing and producing a saturated result. Elsewhere, zoom in for individual strands, painting with a tiny brush at 50%.

13 **Eyes and background** Add another Curves layer with the same settings as the hair. Invert and paint into the eyes only. This time drop the RGB curve as well to darken the eyes. For the blue background add a further Curves adjustment layer, push blue up, green up a fraction and red down slightly less than blue. Invert and paint into the background only.

14 **Finishing touches** For the white area in the arm triangle that doesn't take the blue, add a Levels layer underneath the background Curves layer and set the White Output slider (bottom) to 200. Invert and paint into that area only. You'll now find the blue colour appears. Finish by tweaking the skin colour to suit – add a tan by dropping the RGB curve.

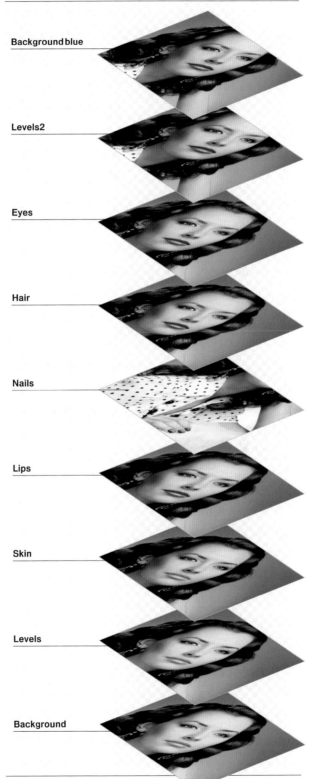

Background blue

Levels2

Eyes

Hair

Nails

Lips

Skin

Levels

Background

Start images

Finished composition

Super depth of field

Combine a number of exposures focused at different points to produce a pin-sharp image

robably the most talked about feature of Photoshop CS4 and beyond is the ability to combine images shot at different focal points to create one new image with huge depth of field – everything in focus from front to back.

It's not a new concept and has already been made possible with software such as Helicon Focus, but it's good to know that those investing in Photoshop's latest incarnation will have that luxury built in at no extra cost. The Depth Of Field feature is actually incorporated into Photoshop's existing Auto-Blend function which, up until CS3, had as its primary function correcting colour and exposure discrepancies for panoramas first stitched using the Auto Align feature. Fire up Auto-Blend, and you now get options for either Panoramic or Stacked images.

The most useful application will probably be macro/close-up photography, where even the narrowest of apertures (for

example, f/16-22) cannot prevent relatively shallow focus. Yet even with conventional lenses, sufficient depth of field isn't always possible where there's proximate foreground information that needs to remain pin sharp; the backdrop can start to fall off a tad if you guarantee close-up sharpness,

"The Depth Of Field feature is incorporated into Photoshop's existing Auto-Blend function"

even with precision focusing. You'll need to shoot a number of identical exposures in order to make this feature work, making sure that you move the focus barrel in relatively equal increments across the desired focal range, starting from the point you want in focus through to the furthest point in the image.

CREATING DEPTH OF FIELD IN CS4
Combine images with Stacks and Auto-Blend

essentials

SKILL LEVEL
Beginner
Intermediate
Expert

TIME TAKEN
30 mins

ON THE DISC
Depth of field source images

01 Open up files Shoot your frames, being careful to keep your tripod positioned in the same place as you alter the focus barrel. Process all your RAW files and open them all up in Photoshop.

02 Align source images Go to File>Scripts>Load Files Into Stacks. Click the Add Open Files button then check the box that says Attempt to Automatically Align Source Images. Photoshop will go to work performing the alignment process.

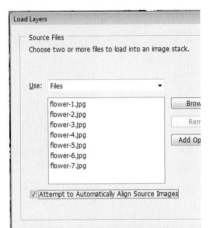

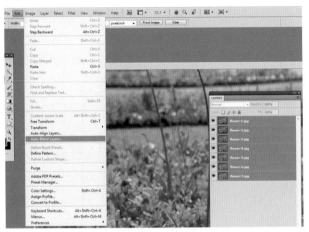

03 Auto-Blend Layers Now Shift-click the bottom layer and then the top layer in the stack to select all layers once the alignment process has finished. Next, go to Edit>Auto-Blend Layers.

04 Zoom to examine Ensure that the Stack Images option is selected rather than Panorama, and that the Seamless Tones and Colors box is checked. Zoom in to 100% with the shortcut Cmd/Ctrl+Opt/Alt+0.

Tip

How many exposures
Wider camera apertures (eg f/8.0) require more combined exposures than narrower ones. Seven frames proved to be a good ball park number for f/8.0 for a Canon EOS 28-70mm lens focused from near closest point to near infinity, on a camera with a full frame sensor. An f/11 scene worked well with six frames, and an f/16 scene seemed to show no gains after five. Better to use narrower apertures then to try to speed up the process in Photoshop!

05 Move around the image Move to the very top or bottom of your image by holding down the spacebar and dragging with the mouse, and then gradually move your way around the image to look for soft, blurry areas.

06 Locate the blur Blurry areas indicate that Photoshop has made a mistake in its calculations and needs a bit of manual help. Step one is to work out which layer our first chosen area of blurry info sits on.

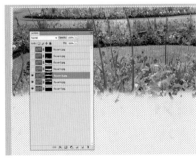

07 Select the blur layer Toggle the layer visibility by clicking the eyeball icon on the sides of each layer on and off to determine where the first piece of blurred information lies. Select the layer mask on the relevant layer.

IRON OUT ANY FOCUS PROBLEMS
Replace blurred areas with sharp info to perfect your image

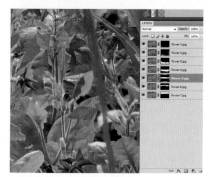

08 **Set up the Brush tool** Now press 'D' to reset the Color palette to black and white, and 'X' to toggle to black if white is your foreground colour. Select the Brush tool with 'B' and set Hardness to 0%.

09 **Estimate the sharp layer** Carefully brush out the blurred area on the image. Next, we need to work out which layer contains the information that will be sharpest in that exact place.

10 **Find the sharpest layer** We can do this by Shift-clicking each layer mask to temporarily disable it, and toggle visibility so that you can see the layers one at a time. Choose the layer where the area appears sharpest.

11 **Brush in sharpness** Shift-click the layer masks to turn them back on if necessary, and select the layer and layer mask where information is sharpest. Brush in the area using a white brush.

12 **Worth noting** Large blurry areas may need sharpness painted in from multiple layers – from one layer for the bottom half, for example, and from the layer above for the top half. It's best to keep toggling visibility to ensure you get the sharpest possible info.

Layer structure
How does your garden grow

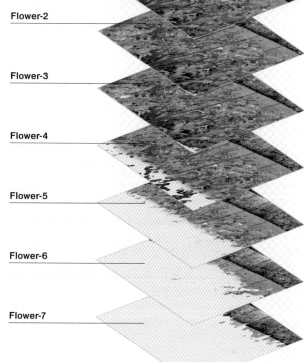

Flower-1

Flower-2

Flower-3

Flower-4

Flower-5

Flower-6

Flower-7

13 **Repeat the process** Now you need to repeat this process for the whole of your image, moving around and carefully brushing out blurred information and bringing in the sharper information.

14 **Crop to finish** Press 'C' in order to switch to the Crop tool, and then crop out any blank canvas produced in the alignment process, or soft edges that can't be fixed with the mask. Finally, press Enter to apply your crop.

Create a dreamy photo effect

Combine Blur and blending modes to produce a soft, dreamy effect

essentials

SKILL LEVEL

Beginner
Intermediate
Expert

TIME TAKEN

Five minutes

KEY SKILLS COVERED

What you'll learn

GAUSSIAN BLUR
BLENDING MODES
ADJUSTMENT LAYERS

I f you're looking for a quick way to give photographs a boost, then you can't get much quicker than this.

By adding a touch of blur along with a carefully chosen blending mode, you can produce soft, dreamy images in a flash.

Quick tip: Try and experiment with other blending modes to achieve other great effects

After

Before

5 minute fix

LOOKING DREAMY

A photo effect that can be created in minutes

01 Double up Open your image and go to Image>Mode>RGB. Now drag the background layer onto the Create New Layer tab at the bottom of the Layers palette. You can rename this layer by double-clicking on it.

02 Add some blur Head to Filter>Blur> Gaussian Blur, and a new window will appear. Enter 15px and watch how the image changes in the preview window. You can alter the amount as you wish – just ensure the basic facial outlines are visible. Now hit OK.

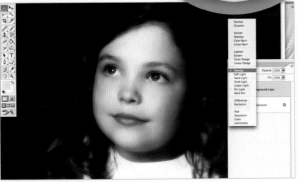

03 Finishing touch With the top layer still selected, set the blending mode to Overlay using the drop-down at the top of the Layers palette. Your photo will take on a whole new appearance. To reduce the redness, just click on the black and white circle at the bottom of the Layers palette, choose Hue/Saturation and set Hue to +3, Saturation to -2 and Lightness to 0. Click OK.

Before image

Improve your night-time images

Make your night shots stand out from the crowd with this glowing tutorial

N ight photography opens up a host of creative opportunities for interesting and dynamic imagery. Whether you're using light from the moon, street lights or painting with a torch, there are plenty of ways to illuminate your compositions.

A light source for night photography is just as important as the sun is for day photography. Without light we can't define shape, scale and depth. Light's contrast and colour help define subjects further.

We'll look at ways that Photoshop can enhance light, contrast and colour to create a more dramatic night image. Starting with Camera Raw, a plug-in included with PS, adjustments to the white balance, blacks and saturation will be made to enhance colour and detail.

We'll also look at the process of High Dynamic Range (HDR) photography by blending three exposures together. The merged image will then be tone mapped to produce a more dramatic finish.

The very nature of low light at night and the sensitivity in digital sensors often causes the problem of noise. We will look at a couple of ways to remedy this. One method will cover multiple exposures that are stacked together as a Smart Object. The Median blend mode will then be used to reduce noise. Another option we cover will look at the Noise Reduction settings in Camera Raw.

Panoramic stitching can provide a great way to cover a large expansive night-time scene. We'll show you how this works, then carry out a simple black and white conversion for a more traditional finish.

PREPARING YOUR NIGHT SHOTS IN PHOTOSHOP
Make adjustments using the Camera Raw plug-in

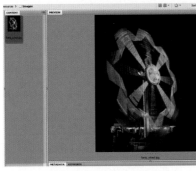

01 **Open the image in Camera Raw**
Open Photoshop and then go to File Browse to launch Bridge, the file browser. Click on the Folders tab and browse to the Tutorial folder on the CD. Select 'ferris_wheel.jpeg' and hit Cmd/Ctrl+R to open it in Camera Raw.

02 **Exposure adjustments** Move the Exposure slider to the right (+1.0) to make the lights look brighter. Move blacks to the right (+1.0). Move the Clarity slider to +60 to make the edges more defined. Increase Vibrance (+50) – this will increase colour in the undersaturated areas. Increase Saturation (this is a global adjustment) to +20 to make the colours stand out further.

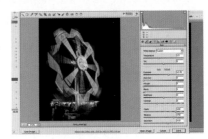

03 **Adjusting colour temperature** Move the Temperature slider to the left and right – the lights change colour. Depending on whether your image was shot at dusk or in the middle of the night and whether you have a mixture of artificial (eg street lights) or natural light sources (eg moonlight), you'll get different results. We've settled for -23 to bring out reds and greens.

REDUCE NOISE IN YOUR IMAGES
Layer stacking to reduce noise

04 **Opening images as a stack**
Excessive noise is a common problem when shooting night images on a digital camera. Here are a couple of options to improve this. In Photoshop open the File> Scripts menu and choose Load Files Into Stack. Browse for the images 'house_noise_01.jpeg' and 'house_noise_02.jpeg'. Hit Create Smart Object after Loading Layers and click OK.

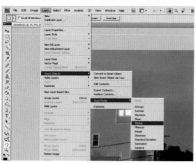

05 **Changing the blend mode** Once the image is loaded into Photoshop, choose Layers>Smart Objects>Stack Mode menu and choose Median. This will reduce the noise. Have a look at the images to see before and after.

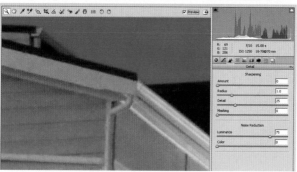

06 **Reducing noise in Camera Raw** Select 'house_noise_01.jpeg' in Bridge and hit Cmd/Ctrl+R to open it in Bridge. Click the Detail tab (two triangles icon), click and zoom in to 200%. Move the Luminance slider up to 75%. This reduces noise. If the image has coloured speckles, try moving the Color slider to the right to remove them.

07 **Experimenting with HDR** HDR stands for High Dynamic Range. A High Dynamic Range image has more recorded values from light to dark. This equates to smoother tones and greater image detail. Most digital camera sensors have a low dynamic range, so shooting multiple exposures of the same image and combining them increases tonal range. Here's how it's done…

08 **Merge To HDR** Open Bridge and browse for images 'skate_park_01' to '03' from the CD. Now go to Tools>Photoshop>Merge To HDR. This will load each image into a new dialog window. Make sure 32 bit is selected and the Response Curve is set to Automatic, then click OK.

HDR tone mapping
Produce a more dynamic finish

Dialog box Image>Mode>16 or 8 bit displays the Tone Mapping dialog box. Local Adaptation gives the best option, and displays a histogram that can be adjusted

Repeat photography The same subject is photographed multiple times with different exposures (shutter speeds) to give a range of exposures. Images are merged using the Merge To HDR option

Result To accept changes, hit OK. The image will be tone mapped to 16 or 8 bit, depending on what you chose. Once in these modes, further edits will be enabled

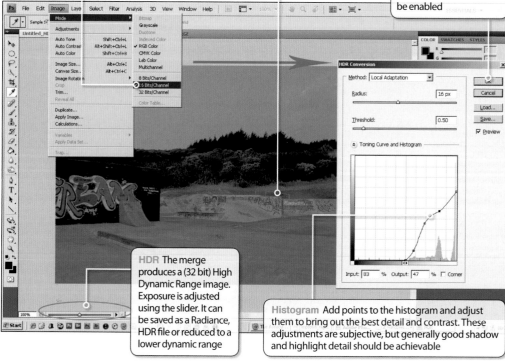

HDR The merge produces a (32 bit) High Dynamic Range image. Exposure is adjusted using the slider. It can be saved as a Radiance, HDR file or reduced to a lower dynamic range

Histogram Add points to the histogram and adjust them to bring out the best detail and contrast. These adjustments are subjective, but generally good shadow and highlight detail should be achievable

09
Converting to a lower bit depth In order to make further changes in Photoshop such as using filters, it is necessary to convert the merged image down to a lower bit depth –16 or 8 bit. Go to Image Mode> 16 bit.

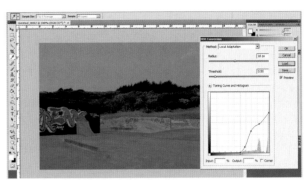

10
Local Adaptation During the conversion, a dialog box appears. Choose Local Adaptation from the drop-down menu. You can make manual adjustments by moving points on the histogram. These adjustments should allow you to bring out more detail in the shadow and highlight areas.

CREATIVE USE OF NIGHT SHOTS
Put your perfect low-light pics to creative use

Tip

Camera tips
Night shots need long exposures, so use a tripod to prevent camera shake. If your camera has manual overrides, play with ISO settings, shutter speed and aperture. A wide aperture (smaller F stop number) lets in more light, as do long exposures. Upping ISO increases light sensitivity, but also camera noise.

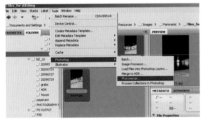

11
Go long Visit any print store and you will see loads of panoramic night shots. For some reason the format works well with the subject matter, so here's how to create one. When shooting for a panoramic image, try to use a tripod and overlap each image by 30-50%. If you have manual focus and exposure settings, switch these on. Open Bridge and go to Tools>Photoshop>Photomerge.

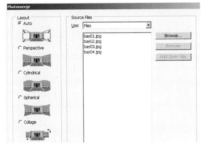

12
Merge settings Set the Merge options to Auto and make sure the Geometric Distortion box is unchecked. In this case it should help keep the horizon straight. It might be worth experimenting with and without for other images. It may take a minute or two to merge, depending on file sizes.

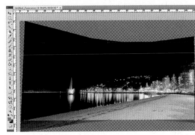

13
Removing excess Due to the nature of wide angle lenses, it's more than likely that you will need to crop out areas that don't fall within a rectangular ratio. With this in mind, it's important to allow for cropping and not to entirely fill the frame between shots. Shooting verticals will also give more room for cropping top and bottom.

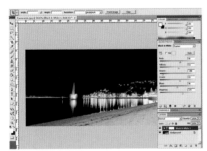

14
Black and white conversion If you want a more traditional feel, why not convert your night shots to black and white? Go to Layer>New Adjustment Layer and choose Black And White. Now experiment with the various sliders that relate to the original colours underneath.

Next time you are out photographing at night, make sure you take a few frames to turn into panoramas

Start image

KEY SKILLS COVERED
What you'll learn

DUOTONES
BLEND MODES
LAYER MASKS
CHANNEL MIXER
LEVELS ADJUSTMENT

Enhance contrast with duotones

Add punch to lacklustre images using these tricks

essentials

SKILL LEVEL
Beginner
Intermediate
Expert

TIME TAKEN
1 hour

ON THE DISC
Desert landscape.jpg

We get a strange buzz when a feature of Photoshop can be used for something that it wasn't necessarily intended for.

Take the Duotones function as the perfect example. This is an image mode that uses a number of 'inks' to transform your image. The two, three or four colours replace the existing colours in your image to create a particular effect, such as sepia. But duotones can also be used to enhance an image, using blend modes and layer masks. The technique involves creating a duplicate of your image in a separate window, and converting it to black and white. This allows you to then jump into Duotone mode and choose the desired inks. Turn the page for some interesting effects that can be made using different combination inks and blend modes.

For our main image we've used two duotones to enhance different areas of the image, each time changing the colour of the inks and finishing with a blending mode. You can mix up the colours of the inks for some interesting results and tonal variations.

This is a useful technique to keep whenever you see an image that is underexposed or faint due to being scanned. Sometimes it can be hard to restore the original definition and colour of an image if it's been scanned in, but using a duotone offers an alternative to Photoshop's range of Image Adjustments options.

SEPARATING THE BLUES FROM THE GREENS
Combine duotones and blend modes to boost contrast in the foreground

Tip

Boosting colours
If you get increased contrast and detail but it lacks punch in colours, add a Hue/Saturation adjustment layer (foot of Layers palette). Increase Saturation to +30 to boost colour in the entire image. The adjustment layer can be re-edited and is non-destructive.

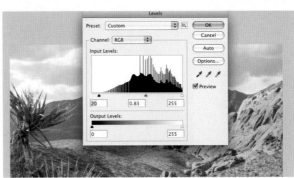

01 **Duplicate the image** Open the starting image 'Desert landscape.jpg' from your disc. To experiment with a duotone, go to Layer>Duplicate Layer. In the pop-up dialog box, set Document to New, and name it 'Green Grass'. Hit OK.

02 **Increase foreground contrast** The image should open in another window. Go to Image>Adjustments>Levels, and ignoring the sky, slide the far left and middle points of the histogram slightly to the right to boost contrast in the foreground.

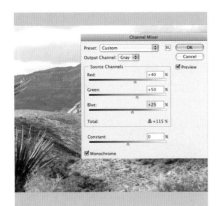

03 **Convert to monochrome** Go back to Image>Adjustments and select Channel Mixer. Tick the Monochrome box at the base of the window to turn your image black and white. Increase Green to 50% and Blue to 25%.

04 **Apply duotone** Change the image's mode to Grayscale (Image>Mode>Grayscale). The Duotone option is now available, found under Image>Mode>Duotone. In the Duotone dialog box, set Ink 1 to a dark brown tone and Ink 2 to a strong green. Hit OK.

05 **Duotone over original** Using the Move tool ('V'), drag the duotone image between windows onto the original image, holding Shift as you drag and drop to place the duotone directly over the top. The layer will be placed at the top of the Layers palette.

06 **Apply blend mode** Change the blending mode of the Duotone layer to Overlay from inside the Layers palette. Reduce the layer's Opacity setting to 80% to soften the effect. Select the background layer and go to Layer>Duplicate Layer. Select Document: New, and name it 'Blue Sky'.

07 **Convert to B&W** With the Blue Sky image open, go to Image> Adjustments>Levels and push the left and mid sliders to the right to make the sky more dramatic. Hit OK and select the Channel Mixer adjustment. Tick Monochrome, reduce the Blue slider to -10% and increase the Red slider to 70%.

OTHER EFFECTS

Duotones can be used to create a variety of image effects. Here are three examples to get your creative juices flowing…

Vintage
Create a vintage look by desaturating (Image>Adjustments>Desaturate) a copy of your image in a separate window. In Mode>Grayscale apply the Duotone mode using a dark brown ink and bright orange ink (Pantone 165 C). Drag the copy with the duotone effect onto the original. Screen blend mode will instantly date the image.

Sepia
For sepia, make a copy of the image (Layer> Duplicate Layer, set Document: New). Go Image>Adjustments>Levels and lighten slightly. Desaturate and go Image>Mode> Grayscale. Hit Duotone; apply a light brown ink with a mute brown (Pantone 875 C). Hit OK; drag onto the original. Apply the Color blend mode for sepia highlights/shadows.

High contrast
When working with an image in black and white, go to Image>Adjustments>Levels and boost contrast by moving the far right pointer to the centre of the Level's histogram. In the Duotone dialog apply a black ink and light cyan (ANPA 737-6 AdPro). Hit OK; drag to a copy of the original image. Apply Overlay blending for high contrast.

ADD DEPTH TO THE COMPOSITION
Use layer masks to separate the foreground and background

08 Duotone the sky Go to Image> Mode>Grayscale, then Image> Mode>Duotone. For the sky area, keep the same Ink 1 as before (dark brown) and set Ink 2 to an electric blue. Hit OK and, holding Shift, drag and drop this image onto the original composition.

10 Mask off the sky Use the Quick Selection tool to select the sky. Zoom in close, using Opt/Alt, to accurately add or remove areas of the selection. When this is complete, click the Add Layer Mask button inside the Layers palette.

11 Separate sky and grass Ctrl/Cmd-click on the layer mask's thumbnail to make the selection active. Click on the eye of the Green Grass layer and go to Select> Inverse. With this layer selected, click the Add Layer Mask button to complete the effect.

09 Blend sky into image The Blue Sky layer should be at the top of the stack. Click the eye next to the Green Grass layer to hide it. Change the Blue Sky layer's blend mode to Hard Light at 70% Opacity.

Layer structure
Creating our duotone image

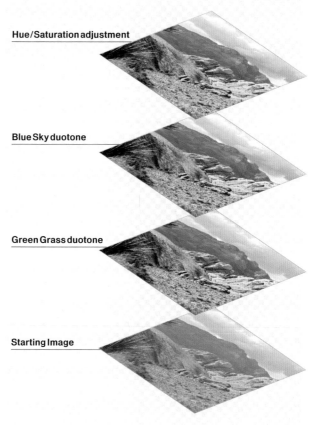

Hue/Saturation adjustment

Blue Sky duotone

Green Grass duotone

Starting Image

Add a faded vignette to photos

A quick and easy way to make portraits stand out

essentials

SKILL LEVEL

- Beginner
- Intermediate
- Expert

TIME TAKEN

- Five minutes

KEY SKILLS COVERED

What you'll learn

ELLIPTICAL MARQUEE

MASKS

GAUSSIAN BLUR

Sometimes you can capture the perfect expression of somebody in a photo, only to discover that the rest of the scene is ugly or distracting.

By adding a faded vignette to your subject, you will be able to eliminate all the background activity from your shot, while giving your portrait a lovely soft glow. It's easy to apply, and the results will make your images look professional.

This technique is also great if you want to blend a couple of images together on a page. Simply add another layer filled with colour or texture beneath your portrait and see your image blend smoothly.

Quick tip: Use a free texture image found online as a great background for your photo

Before

After

CREATE A BEAUTIFUL FADE ON PHOTOS

A simple technique to dramatically improve your portraits

01 Make a selection Open your photo and double-click the background layer to make it active. Now select the Elliptical Marquee tool from the toolbar and draw a shape around the area of the photo you want to keep. Anything outside the circle will not be visible.

02 Apply a mask Next, add a layer mask by clicking on the white circular icon at the foot of the Layers palette. There are two thumbnails on this layer – make sure that the layer mask thumbnail is active by clicking on it.

03 Create the fade In the menu bar go to Filter>Blur>Gaussian Blur. A dialog box will appear with a preview window. Ensure the Preview option is ticked and then alter the Radius setting to suit your image. Now you can add any background you wish to your image, by placing a new layer underneath and using the Fill tool to colour it.

Filter	View	Window	onOne	Help

Last Filter ⌘ F

Convert for Smart Filters

Filter Gallery...

Liquify... ⇧⌘X

Vanishing Point... ⌥⌘V

Artistic ▶

Blur ▶ — Average / Blur / Blur More / Box Blur... / **Gaussian Blur...** / Lens Blur... / Motion Blur... / Radial Blur... / Shape Blur... / Smart Blur... / Surface Blur...

Brush Strokes ▶

Distort ▶

Noise ▶

Pixelate ▶

Render ▶

Sharpen ▶

Sketch ▶

Stylize ▶

Texture ▶

Video ▶

Other ▶

Digimarc ▶

Browse Filters Online...

Before image

After

KEY SKILLS COVERED

What you'll learn

USING THE LASSO AND MAGNETIC LASSO TOOLS

MAKING SELECTIONS IN QUICK MASK MODE

ADDING ADJUSTMENT LAYERS

LAYER AND CLIPPING MASKS

EDITING PHOTOS WITH LEVELS AND HUE/SATURATION

ADJUSTING COLOURS USING SELECTIVE COLOR

Change the colour of your hair

The adjustment layers can give more natural-looking blonde hair than any bottle of dye can!

ne of the great things about Photoshop is its range of tools that make most photo-manipulations quick and easy. However, some transformations can only be achieved by bringing lots of Photoshop's techniques together.

For example, turning a blonde's hair darker in Photoshop can be fairly easily achieved, but turning a brunette into a blonde and getting a realistic and natural result is a little more tricky to achieve.

If you don't want your subject's hair to look fake, washed-out or an odd hue of yellowy-orange, there's no one-step technique. In this tutorial we're going to show you first how to make an accurate hair selection using a range of Selection tools (our favourites are listed in the side panel on the next page), and then how to use adjustment layers to change the colour.

Adjustment layers are great if you're going to be using a bit of trial and error with your photo-manipulation. They are fully editable too.

For this technique we'll be using a few different adjustment layers, because the most natural-looking results can only be achieved by building up the changes gradually.

If you want to use your own image alongside this tutorial, you'll find that your adjustments will need to be slightly different but the fundamentals will be the same; just remember that a little trial and error is the key to getting the result you want. If you would like to use our image, it's from iStockphoto.com, image no '9182427'.

essentials

SKILL LEVEL
Beginner
Intermediate
Expert

TIME TAKEN
2 hours approx

Tip

Save as Channel

When you've spent a lot of time creating a selection, the last thing you want is for something to go wrong and to lose all your hard work. To avoid this nightmare, go to the Channels tab in the Layers palette and click the Save Selection as Channel icon. Now, if you close the file or the computer crashes, just hold Ctrl and click the thumbnail of the new channel, and your selection will reappear. Save your updated selection periodically, and you'll be laughing!

⠿ START SELECTING
Make a selection of the hair

01 **A quick selection** Open the start image, then click and hold the Lasso tool and select the Magnetic Lasso tool from the fly-out menu. Use it to make a basic selection of the hair. Hold Shift+Opt/Alt while using the Lasso to add and subtract from the selection respectively.

02 **Seeing red** Use the normal Lasso tool to select any areas that the Magnetic tool is dodging around. Now press 'Q' to switch to Quick Mask mode. Use a small (around 9-pixel) airbrush and paint over the finer strands, for example on her neck/chest area. Use a white brush to add to the selection and black to subtract from it.

03 **Don't forget the eyebrows!** Refine the fringe area with the airbrush. You can reduce the opacity of the airbrush and build up the selection gradually if you're not as confident using the Brush tool. Reduce Opacity to around 40%, and with a larger brush size apply a single stroke over her right eyebrow.

SELECTION TOOL ROUND-UP

When it comes to making selections there are many options to choose from, and for elaborate selections a combination of methods will work best. Here are some of our favourites…

Magnetic Lasso The Magnetic Lasso tool will automatically snap to edges, so making simple selections is quick and easy.

Freehand Lasso A steady hand is needed for the Lasso tool, but using Opt/Alt and Shift to edit your selection makes things easier.

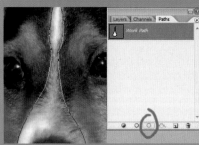

Pen tool The Pen tool is another option. Clicking the Load Path As a Selection icon in the Paths palette turns a path into a selection.

Brush tool Quick Mask mode allows you to use the Brush tool to make selections. Press 'Q' to toggle back and forth.

Color Range Select>Color Range makes selections of a certain colour a breeze. Adjust the fuzziness to get the right detail level.

⣿ | TIME TO ADJUST
We're nearly ready to start making colour changes

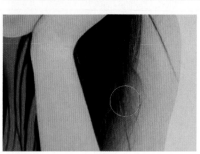  

04 Picking up strays Still at 40% Opacity, use sweeping brush strokes to make a semi-transparent selection of the hair over her ear. Repeat this over the area of stray hairs on her left arm. Check all the edges of your selection, and tidy and soften them with the airbrush.

05 Our first adjustment It's time to start adding our adjustment layers. Exit Quick Mask mode by pressing 'Q' again, and with your selection still active, click and hold the Add New Fill or Adjustment Layer icon in the Layers palette (the black/white circle). Choose Selective Color from the fly-out menu.

06 Colour change In the new window that's just popped up, choose Neutrals from the Color menu. Moving the sliders will drastically change the colour of the hair. Drag Cyan to -40, Magenta to -25, Yellow to -12 and click OK. Notice that this layer has a layer mask automatically applied to it, so it only affects our hair selection.

07 Level up Hold Alt while clicking on the New Adjustment Layer icon. Still holding Opt/Alt, select Levels in the pop-up menu then release the mouse button and Opt/Alt. A dialog box appears. Tick the Use Previous Layer to Create Clipping Mask box so that it's clipped to the layer below and is therefore also affected by the layer mask. Now click OK.

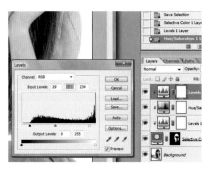 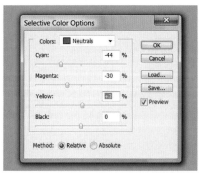

08 Adding layers Change the Input Levels to 0, 1.17 and 200. Add a Hue/Saturation adjustment layer, remembering to hold Opt/Alt and tick the Clipping Mask box again; move Saturation down to -34 and click OK. Hold Opt/Alt again and add another Levels adjustment layer; tick the Clipping Mask box then alter Input Levels to 29, 1.22 and 234.

09 Start tweaking Now we want to tweak the adjustment layers, so double-click the Selective Color adjustment layer's thumbnail in the Layers palette. In the Neutrals section move Cyan to -44, Magenta to -30 and Yellow to +3. In the Blacks section move Black to +3 and click OK.

FINISHING TOUCHES
Start to refine the image and get that polished finish

10 Levelling out After a bit of trial and error we changed the Levels 2 inputs to 21, 1.33 and 241, and Levels 1 inputs to 0, 1.24 and 205. Click on the layer mask attached to the Levels 2 layer, and use a black airbrush at 50% to fade out the impact it's had on her neck/chest slightly. Repeat this on the Levels 1 layer mask.

11 Going blurry On the Selective Color layer's layer mask, use this same brush to gradually reduce the lightened effect on her left arm. To soften the edges of the hair, still on the Selective Color layer's mask, go to Filter>Blur>Gaussian Blur. Enter a value of 30.8 pixels and click OK.

12 Tidying up Use a black airbrush on this mask to tidy any areas where our colour change edits have affected her skin, for example on her right arm. And use a small white airbrush (and a steady hand!) to refine any thin strands of hair, for example the two over her left arm.

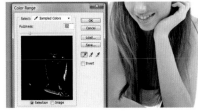

13 Remove the red The patch on her left arm looks too red, so go to Select>Color Range and click on the reddest area of her arm. Move Fuzziness to 35 and click OK. Double-click the Foreground Color palette and colour pick a grey shadow on her arm. Click further down and right for a darker shade (we chose R:183 G:152 B:126).

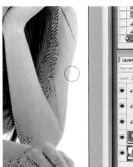
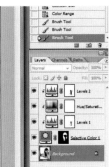

14 Paint over Change the Brush blend mode to Color, Opacity 50%, and paint over the red area on the background layer, then press Cmd/Ctrl+D to deselect. Double-check that there aren't any more areas you need to mask out on the Selective Color layer mask before applying the finishing touch.

15 Brighten up Once you're happy, go to the background layer and press Cmd/Ctrl+A to select the whole canvas, then Cmd/Ctrl+Shift+C to copy from every layer and Cmd/Ctrl+V to paste. Move this new layer to the very top in the Layers palette, change its blending mode to Soft Light and Opacity to 30%. And you're done!

Layer structure
Creating our model's new look

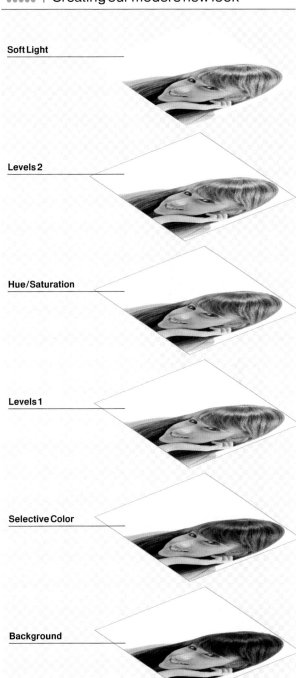

Soft Light

Levels 2

Hue/Saturation

Levels 1

Selective Color

Background

essentials

SKILL LEVEL

Beginner
Intermediate
Expert

TIME TAKEN

30 minutes

KEY SKILLS COVERED
What you'll learn

MAKING SELECTIONS

WORKING WITH ADJUSTMENT LAYERS

BLACK AND WHITE CONVERSIONS

TONING USING THE COLOR BALANCE AND CURVES TOOLS

Start image

Transform photos with split-toning effects

Replicate this traditional darkroom technique quickly

Tip

Elements users

The black and white conversion can also be done in Photoshop Elements 7. To do so, go to Enhance>Convert to Black and White. You can then use the colour sliders to convert the photo to black and white.

here are many ways to convert a digital colour image into black and white, and they all have one thing in common – a complete lack of colour.

A straight black and white conversion can leave photos looking a little bland. But what if there was a way of introducing colour into a black and white photo? It may sound like a contradiction in terms, but it's easy to add colour to a monochrome image. The process we're going to perform is called toning, and it's easy to do in Photoshop.

Photos are normally toned with single colours such as sepia – which has an antique feel and is especially suitable for portraiture because it gives flattering skin tones – or blue, which is used to give an image a cold feel, perhaps to a wintry landscape or still life.

In this tutorial we're going to go one step further and split tone an image. The photo is effectively toned twice – the shadows one colour, the highlights another, and the midtones taking on a blend

"The photo is effectively toned twice – the shadows one colour, the highlights another"

of both hues. It's easily achieved with Adjustment Layers, Color Balance and Curves. These techniques will work with any photos, so dig out your favourite. Alternatively, buy the image we've used by heading to **www.istockphoto.com**, image number '1772378'.

PREPARE YOUR IMAGE FIRST
Dim down any highlights in your photo

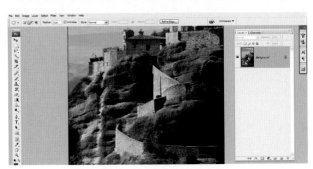

01 Getting started If your photo has a lot of bright highlights, these need to be dimmed down. For this we use the Elliptical Marquee tool ('M') to select the bright areas of the cliff and the stone walls. Click on the Add to Selection button in the Options toolbar and make your selection with a series of small circles.

02 Smooth the edges Now go to Select>Refine Edge, set Smooth to 10 and Feather to 150 pixels and hit OK. This smooths the edges of the selection so that the changes we make are applied gradually.

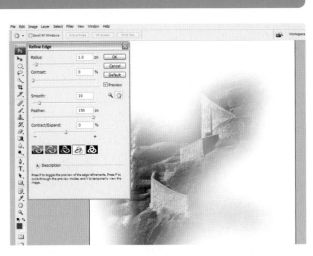

03 Darken highlights Click on the New Adjustment Layer icon at the bottom of the Layers palette (it's the half black, half white circle) and choose Brightness/Contrast. Set Brightness to around -150 and Contrast to around -50. Make sure the Preview box is checked so that you can see the effect of moving the sliders.

04 Select buildings Now use the Elliptical Marquee tool (M) again and select the buildings on top of the cliff, and the dark edges of the cliff to the right and at the bottom. The idea is to select the areas of the photo that we don't want to be affected by the next step.

05 Inverse the selection Go to Select>Inverse to reverse the selection. Now go to Select>Refine Edge again, and this time set Smooth to around 10 and Feather to around 250 pixels for a smoother graduation and hit OK.

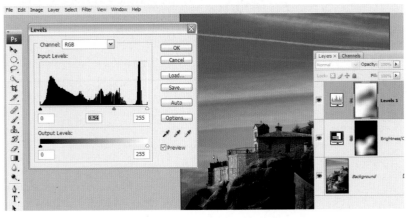

06 Darken the edges Click on the New Adjustment Layer icon at the bottom of the Layers palette again and this time select Levels. When the Levels window appears, move the slider to the right to darken the edges of the photo. Split toning works best with dramatic, high contrast images, so don't be afraid to overdarken.

::::: | **TIME TO GET TONING**
      | Begin to add your colours using Color Balance

07 **Convert to black and white** Now it's time for the black and white conversion. Click on the New Adjustment Layer icon again and select Black and White. Set blue to around -50. This dramatically darkens the sky.

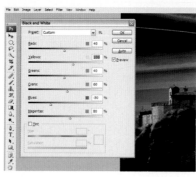

08 **Lighten the buildings** Now set yellow to around +100 to lighten the buildings on top of the hill and hit OK. This conversion has added contrast to the image in preparation for toning.

09 **Split tone** Now for the split toning. Click on the New Adjustment Layer icon at the bottom of the Layers palette again and select Color Balance. Select Shadows by checking the circle, and set the Cyan/Red slider to around -25 and the Yellow/Blue slider to around +25. This turns the image a deep blue.

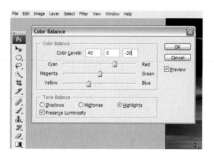

10 **Add copper** Now check the Highlights circle and set the Cyan/Red slider to around +40 and the Yellow/Blue slider to around -30. Feel free to experiment with the sliders to achieve an effect that you like, and click OK when you're done. You now have a split toned image with blue shadows and copper highlights.

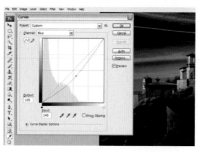

11 **Toning with curves** Click the eye icon next to the top layer to make it invisible. Create a new Curves adjustment layer and select Blue from the Channel menu. Grab the curve (it starts off as a straight line) and pull it downwards to turn the image a yellow colour. Try settings of around 105 for Output and 140 for Input.

::::: | **Layer structure**
      | Tone up your images

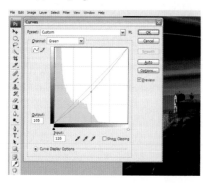

12 **Green channel** Now select the Green channel and pull the curve downwards again, with settings of around 105 for Output and 125 for Input. The photo takes on a rich brown sepia tone.

13 **Finishing off** Select the Red channel and pull the curve upwards to around 130 for Output and 120 for Input. You now have an image split toned with sepia and gold. The photo is a little flat, so create another Curves or Brightness/Contrast adjustment layer and increase the contrast just a pinch to bring the photo to life.

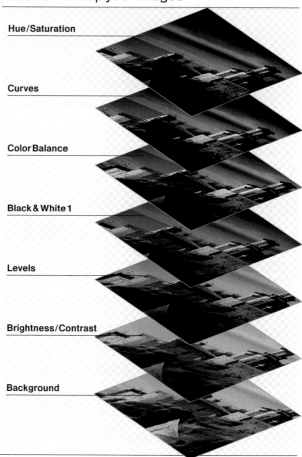

Hue/Saturation

Curves

Color Balance

Black & White 1

Levels

Brightness/Contrast

Background

Organise your layers

Three quick and easy ways to get your layers in order

essentials

L ayers are a fundamental part of Photoshop, which is why it's so vital to keep them organised and tidy.

In big projects, all those layers can soon mount up and leave you feeling bewildered and confused.

To keep things in order, we have three top steps you can implement to help control those layers. Discover how to colour your layers for instant recognition, tidy them away in a folder, or merge them together without losing any of your editing capabilities. So let's begin…

Quick tip: To move a selection of layers up or down the palette, hold Ctrl/Cmd and click the ones you wish to move. They'll link together so you can drag or delete

KEY SKILLS COVERED
What you'll learn

MERGE
COLOUR CODING
GROUPING

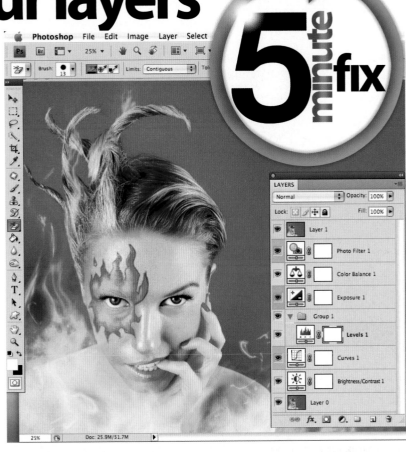

THE LAYERED LOOK
Three ways to get your layers organised

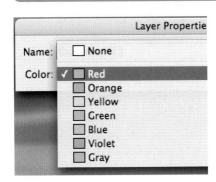

01 **Colour code them** If you like an at-a-glance way of arranging your layers, try this colour coding method. Choose any individual layer and Ctrl/right-click on the eye icon to the left of that layer. A colour list will pop up and you can select your desired hue with a simple click.

02 **Group them in folders** If your Layers palette is getting out of control, it's often a good idea to group similar layers in folders. Do this by simply clicking the folder icon at the bottom of the palette and dragging the desired layers into that folder. Don't forget to name each folder.

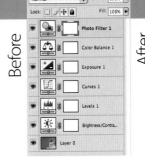
Before

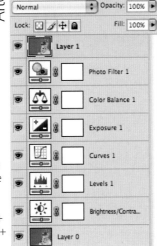
After

03 **Secret Merge technique** To merge all your layers together without losing the flexibility of being able to edit them individually, we have a nifty little trick called Stamp Visible. It's only available through this finger-twisting shortcut: Ctrl+ Alt+Shift+E for PC users and Cmd+ Opt+Shift+E for Mac users.

Start image

After

KEY SKILLS COVERED
What you'll learn

LIGHTEN TONAL INFORMATION WITH CURVES

FOCUS A CURVES ADJUSTMENT WITH THE BLENDING OPTIONS

LOCALISE AN ADJUSTMENT USING LAYER MASKS

USE SELECTIVE COLOR TO TARGET AREAS OF THE COLOUR RANGE

essentials

SKILL LEVEL

Beginner
Intermediate
Expert

TIME TAKEN

1 hour

ON THE DISC

Even skin before.jpg
Blotchy skin before.jpg
Olive skin before.jpg
Fair skin before.jpg
Coffee skin before.jpg

VIDEO TUTORIAL

Skin tones

Improving skin tone

Exciting new techniques to make skin tones glow

We've got three splendid techniques here for you, all focused on improving the skin tone of a portrait subject to perfection.

And we're not talking about those staple basics for removing spots, moles or wrinkles. No – we've got some exciting new techniques for improving the actual clarity and colour of skin.

First up is a method for evening out skin tone, which effectively balances shadows and highlights to produce a lovely creamy finish. It's pretty clever and works by using a combination of a Curves adjustment layer with the Blend If sliders in the Layer Blending options, giving far more precision over where our tonal adjustments are made.

Next up is a technique for removing blotchy reddish areas from Caucasian skin – sometimes natural, sometimes caused by forgetting to turn the heating on in winter, or perhaps by using the wrong kind of washing powder! You'll know it when you see it, and it's very difficult to remove without affecting the good areas. Our method knocks out the blotchy areas while leaving all the nice neutral skin areas fully intact.

Our final technique is all about improving the colour of skin tone. Skin colour is mostly made up of either reds or yellows with lesser amounts of complementary colours like cyan and magenta. By adding subtle hints of yellow, red, cyan, magenta or green to these areas, we can make skin look more appealing.

BALANCE OUT SHADOWS/HIGHLIGHTS FOR A CREAMY GLOW
Combine Curves with the Blending options to make this work

  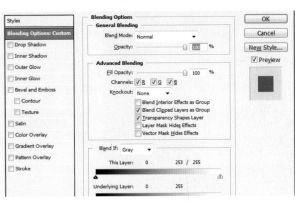

01 Lighten with Curves Open up 'evenskin before.jpg' from the CD. Start by adding a Curves adjustment layer using the button at the Layers palette base. Plot a single point on the curve midpoint, and click and drag the point upwards to lighten the tonal range as a whole.

02 Blend If slider Click FX at the bottom of the Layers palette and hit Blending options (or Ctrl/right-click the layer and pick Blending options). Locate the Blend If section of the dialog, hold Opt/Alt and click the white triangle on the right-hand side of the This Layer ramp.

Pro skin smoothing
This technique is a great professional alternative to the Gaussian Blur method of smoothing skin. Its advantage over blurring skin areas is that all the lovely natural skin detail (eg pores) is untouched, making for a far more naturalistic, authentic result. As it won't remove blemishes such as spots, it's best to get the worst out first with the Healing brush or Clone Stamp tool on a new layer above the background layer.

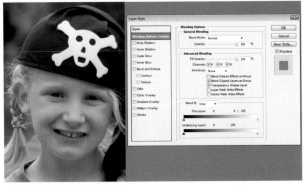

04 Paint into the skin OK the dialog and make sure the Curves layer mask is selected. Invert it with Cmd/Ctrl+I to Hide All. We're now going to paint the adjustment into the skin only. Take a soft white brush at 100% Opacity, zoom in a little and paint into the skin areas, avoiding the hair and the clothing.

03 Split the highlights The white triangle should split in two. Drag the left portion leftwards as far as it will go. It will sit on top of the black triangle. You'll notice the highlight areas suddenly dulling down. Click the Preview button on and off to see the difference.

Removing blemishes
You can remove blemishes before adding your Curves adjustment by adding a layer above the background layer using the button at the Layers palette base and selecting the Spot Healing brush. Set it to Sample All Layers in the Tool Options bar and click on any spots or blemishes. Switch to Clone Stamp if you're near edge detail, sourcing clean skin with Opt/Alt before clicking.

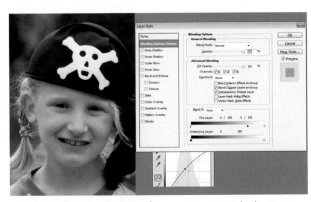 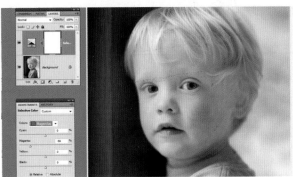

05 Protect the shadows If you want to protect shadow tones a little (not really necessary for this image), open the Blending options, split the black triangle and drag rightwards to suit. You may need to go the whole way if the shadow tones don't look smooth.

06 Fix blotches Open 'blotchy skin before.jpg' from the CD. Add a Selective Color adjustment layer using the button at the Layers palette base. Start by selecting Magenta from the drop-down Colors menu. Pull the Magenta slider leftwards and see if it has any effect on the blotchy areas.

SKIN RETOUCHING TOOLS

The following tools are all fundamental to improving the skin tone of any portrait subject, and unlike with other skin repair tools and filters such as the Healing brush tool or the Gaussian Blur filter, all the skin detail remains totally untouched.

Curves adjustment

The simple Curves adjustment can be used to make improvements by lightening skin and evening out shadows and highlights.

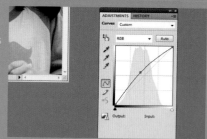

Blend If sliders

The Blend If sliders in the Blending options give you tonal control over any adjustment, protecting the brightest highlights here.

Selective Color adjustment

Selective Color is a powerful and surprisingly underused tool. It's perfect for subtle alterations in the colour make-up of skin.

Brush tool

A straightforward tool, but in combination with a layer mask, fundamental to ensuring your adjustments target desired areas only.

Layer mask

The layer mask ensures that we can localise our adjustments to specific parts of the image – the parts that need the adjustment the most.

REMOVE BLOTCHY AREAS
A Selective Color adjustment does the work here

07 Try magenta tones If it does have an effect, move the Yellow slider rightwards to add yellow to compensate for the increase in green. You probably won't need to increase by quite the same amount as you reduced magenta.

08 Try red tones If the Magenta slider has no impact, select Reds from the Colors drop-down menu instead. Start by dragging down the Magenta slider again and look carefully at the results. Next, experiment with the Yellow and the Black slider too.

09 Change the blending We removed the large blotches nicely by bringing down magenta and black and pushing yellow. You can prevent contrast being affected by changing the layer blending to Color. Our contrast effects worked well, lightening reddish patches a little, so we leave as is.

10 Remove from unwanted areas If surrounding skin tone shifts too much, which has happened here, invert the layer mask with Cmd/Ctrl+I and use a white brush at about 30% to build up the adjustment in the red areas only, working until those areas match the surrounding skin tone.

TWEAK SKIN COLOUR FOR YOUR CHOSEN COMPLEXION
Use Selective Color to target your skin type colour range

11 Enhance olive skin
We can create a bit more glow for olive skin by adding a bit of red to the yellow tones. Add a Selective Color adjustment layer and select Yellows from the Colors drop-down menu. Drag Cyan down to around -40% to add reds. Use the layer mask to focus on skin only if other areas are affected.

12 Knock back the olive To knock back olive or tanned skin a little, try selecting Yellows and dropping Yellow to about -20%, then do the same again after selecting Reds in the drop-down menu. It's a good idea to also drop Cyan to -10% in both, to throw a bit of red in. The reverse settings for yellow and cyan will produce a golden tan.

Compensating for digital
An excess of magenta is common with images shot digitally, as the technology is currently more sensitive to reddish areas of the colour spectrum. Quite often all you will need to do to make skin look a little more appealing is to add a Selective Color adjustment layer, select Reds, and drag Magenta down a touch to say -10. You can also push Yellows up a little by about +5. Turn layer visibility on and off to see the difference.

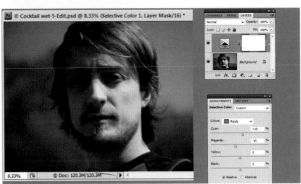

13 Reduce the rosy look For fair or rosy skin, start by adding a Selective Color adjustment layer. We can make a rosy complexion look a little less pronounced by selecting Reds and dropping Magenta to around -15% to add a touch of green. Around +10% Cyan can help neutralise things further.

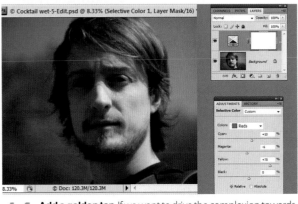

14 Add a golden tan If we want to drive the complexion towards a more golden yellow, in addition to the above corrections we can also push Yellow to as high as +70%. You may need to bring Magenta back up a bit to stop things looking a bit too green.

15 Warm up coffee skin For coffee coloured or black skin, add a Selective Color adjustment layer once again, and select Reds from the Colors drop-down menu. Try adding +30% Yellow to give a much more golden feel to the skin.

16 Neutralise coffee skin
For a more neutral colour, try adding +20% Cyan with Reds in the Colors menu selected, and -20% Yellow. Stronger settings are required in this step and the previous step for darker shades of skin.

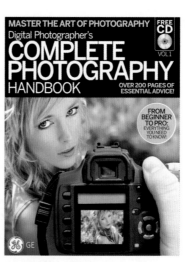

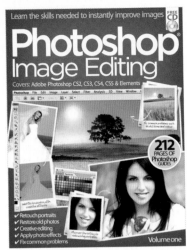

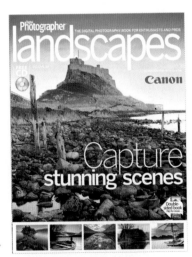

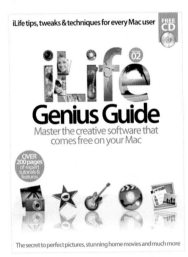

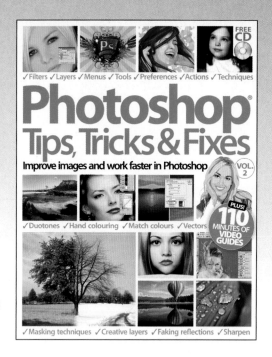